TRANSFORMING YOUNG ADULT SERVICES

Neil-Schuman purchases fund advocacy, awareness, and accreditation programs for library professionals worldwide.

TRANSFORMING YOUNG ADULT SERVICES

Edited by Anthony Bernier

Neal-Schuman
An imprint of the American Library Association

Chicago 2013

Printed in the United States of America

17 16 15 14 13   5 4 3 2 1

Extensive effort has gone into ensuring the reliability of the information in this book; however, the publisher makes no warranty, express or implied, with respect to the material contained herein.

ISBNs: 978-1-55570-907-5 (paper); 978-1-55570-958-7 (PDF); 978-1-55570-959-4 (ePub); 978-1-55570-960-0 (Kindle).

Library of Congress Cataloging-in-Publication Data
Transforming young adult services / edited by Anthony Bernier.
     pages cm
  Includes bibliographical references and index.
  ISBN 978-1-55570-907-5
  1. Young adults' libraries. 2. Young adults' libraries—United States. 3. Libraries and teenagers. 4. Libraries and teenagers—United States. I. Bernier, Anthony.
  Z718.5.T73 2013
  027.62'6—dc23
                              2013014651

Cover design by Kimberly Thornton. Images © Shutterstock, Inc.
Text design by Mayfly Design in the Sabon and Brandon Grotesque typefaces.

♾ This paper meets the requirements of ANSI/NISO Z39.48-1992 (Permanence of Paper).

CONTENTS

Part I: What's in an Age?

Part II: From White and Marginal to Civic Partners

Part III: Beyond Youth Development and Questions of Intellectual Freedom

FOREWORD

It is tempting to begin prefatory remarks by asking, What is a discipline? This of course is not a new question, although potential answers may have become even more elusive in recent years. As Anthony Bernier observes in the Introduction, the core audience for services, the focal points of the service dynamics, and the institutional context of study present questions that the essays in this volume attempt to address. If readers will allow me a digression, I would like to situate some initial thoughts within the locus of disciplinary inquiry. I ask for forbearance because any discussion of transdisciplinary inquiry (note that I do not use the more familiar, though nearly bereft of meaning, term *interdisciplinary*) depends on a definition of *discipline*. Also, the relevance of the inquiry presented here is founded on efforts to render the thought and research into young adult services as accessible as possible. That also relies on definitional beginnings. With some trepidation I invoke the name of Thomas Kuhn (1970: 175), who in *The Structure of Scientific Revolutions* argued that a discipline (or subdiscipline) is built around a paradigm, or "the entire constellation of beliefs, values, techniques, and so on shared by members of a given community," and "the concrete puzzle-solutions which, employed as models or examples, can replace explicit rules as a basis for the solution" of scientific questions. What happens when the constellation expands, when the boundaries of past inquiry no longer obtain?

Many formerly well-defined disciplines, even in the natural sciences, broke through those boundaries some time ago. In then rather nascent areas such as psychology, individuals like William James helped to create the kinds of questions that could be addressed. Psychology has changed markedly since James's day, but his groundbreaking thought should not be forgotten (and may find resonance in young adult services). At this point it may be useful to return to Kuhn (1970: 180): "A paradigm governs...not a subject matter but a group of practitioners." Up until this point one may think that I am denying the avowed purpose of this reader. The foregrounding must be clarified now. The transdisciplinary purpose of library and information science (LIS) is, specifically, to achieve the goals set out for and in this volume; that is, LIS cannot be constrained by the limitations of the past—limitations that too narrowly bound the scope of research and the envisioning of institution.

Bernier urges inquiry that emerges from LIS *as* a discipline. Fair enough. We return to the question of definition, this time with specificity, and ask, What is LIS? At the risk of being presumptuous, allow me to suggest some elements of a disciplinary framework within which young adult services can be examined and formulated. One element that many people dispute at the current time is the institutional locus of the services. Rather than irrelevant or peripheral, the institutional is essential. The institution itself is misunderstood and all too facilely dismissed by some who would deny that humans gravitate to places that embody meaning for them. Libraries are such a place; most importantly, they are places of human engagement and—dare I say it—construction. One need not be a social constructionist to accept that institutions are particularly human constructions, designed and created for purposes of interaction, exploration, and discovery. In other words, the library is a counterpoint to any naive solipsism that omits the interdependence that characterizes the human condition (if I can be permitted a bit of lofty language). There is no denying that "library as place" is a rather recent notion, but it does in some ways represent a return to ideas of the library as a learning environment. An excellent treatment of the library as place is the collection of essays edited by Buschman and Leckie (2007). Some of the essayists who contributed to that volume are also represented in this reader. The concept of the institution pervades all of the sections of the present volume and should be taken as something of a first principle for inquiry and practice in LIS. In fact, the institution is a locus for critical inquiry and practice.

Another and actually related idea is community. Institutions should not exist merely for self-perpetuation; their being has a foundation of connections among people. Institutions of specific types have specific kinds of connections as components of their essential natures. Communities look to institutions in some important ways as extensions of what they seek to be and do. Here a complex dynamic has to be introduced: Communities have multiple identities that should be recognized by the people who operate within institutions. Communities include embodied linguistic, cultural, and other groups that share one or many characteristics. To some extent the sharing is situational and can be recognized by physical and cultural environment. In other ways there are choices made by people, or what Michael Walzer (1983) calls "association." There is a serious challenge to institutions and those who work in them here; the positions many people make are based on skepticism and suspicion when it comes to official institutions, regardless of stated mission or services of the institutions. LIS as a discipline must have as a facet the understanding of the tensions that can exist between communities and institutions, and the research and praxis in the field must address the challenge directly. Services, including young adult services, are not abstractions; they are pragmatic, even as they should have sound frameworks.

Insofar as communities are individuals who share some binding ties, librarians (within the institutions of libraries) have to embrace the inevitable sharing and difference that will occur in all interactions. Librarians must learn to accept the community members as other selves who have qualities that are commonly human, that can be commonly occurring with themselves, and as unique individuals who have cognitive, linguistic, cultural, political, and other qualities that set them apart. The understanding librarians must aspire to is that difference: Young adults, for example, are not adults. African-American young adults are not Asian-American young adults. Those who live lives of affluence are not those who live in poverty. Acceptance of these ideas necessitates accepting a phenomenological foundation for LIS. That said, youth (while an essential but not totalizing characteristic) is a component of lifeworld. Services as phenomenological actions must embrace lifeworld as simultaneously a shared mode of being and a fact of individuality.

Thinkers who include Edmund Husserl, Maurice Merleau-Ponty, Emmanuel Levinas, and Paul Ricoeur have detailed precisely what these foundations entail. There is another essential characteristic of phenomenological intentionality (in addition to the acceptance of *I* and *Thou*): "Our consciousness—including of the mental acts that accompany many of our perceptions—is not merely a blank slate on which the phenomena write. Consciousness is intentional; it is directed; it has a purpose. Since consciousness is active, phenomenology must account for intentionality, for the realization that our perceptions are perceptions of something" (Budd, 2005: 46–47). Intentionality applies to the librarian and the community member equally; each has an active consciousness. An implication of intentionality is consciousness of one's own experiences. Young adults are subjects (in the sense of being reflective selves); they are not objects of professional service. It is appropriate to assume that the language of service should be able to embrace the selfhood and subjectivity of the patrons (see Zahavi, 2005). What the librarian can do, and young adult services demonstrates the point starkly, is help shape what that young adult is conscious *of*, what that person *perceives*.

A third principle, referred to by Bernier, is a particular species of ethical action. Communication and discourse are naturally components of young adult services. Communication carries an ethical necessity; freedom is one element of the necessity. This is customarily referred to as intellectual freedom in librarianship; in young adult services it can mean avoidance or negation of any paternalistic protection of individuals. The readers/information users are presumed to have sufficient agency that they are able to take responsibility for what they access, see, hear, and read. There has tended to be a sort of orthodoxy of official positions regarding intellectual freedom and freedom to read and view. Orthodoxy is not always bad, and is not always to be resisted; however, it should be examined critically. For example, some statements that may be taken as orthodox in particular settings could hold that gaming is deleterious to young adults. Such a claim has no merit on its face since it is not reasoned. The communicative ethics of young adult services should have a rational component, which includes the examination of what it is to be a young adult at this point in time and in the complex society. The ethical foundation in this context shares a goal with many ethical standpoints; the good life for young adults can be enhanced by services offered *in* libraries *by* librarians. The ethical responsibility of scholars and professionals is not to adopt a prescriptive model and apply it universally. The communicative ethics forms the third leg of the stool, along with the institution and phenomenology, to create the possibilities for a genuine LIS inquiry into young adult services.

I began with a question, and I attempted to answer it with some specificity. The question is well addressed by the authors who have contributed to this reader. The answer in this short Foreword is primarily my own, but it is derived not simply from solitary contemplation, but also through discussion with colleagues, including some of the authors here. Hence, it is intended to be at least somewhat reflective, showing what is in the best inquiry today as well as what can be in future study. There is little doubt that the work presented in these pages is a breakthrough; it is something unique in young adult services scholarship. It deserves a wide and critical audience.

John M. Budd

References

Budd, J. M. 2005. "Phenomenology and Information Studies." *Journal of Documentation* 61, no. 1: 44–59.

Buschman, J. E., and G. J. Leckie. 2007. *The Library as Place: History, Community, and Culture.* Westport, CT: Libraries Unlimited.

Kuhn, T. S. 1970. *The Structure of Scientific Revolutions.* 2nd ed. Chicago: University of Chicago Press.

Walzer, M. 1983. *Spheres of Justice: A Defense of Pluralism and Equality.* New York: Basic Books.

Zahavi, D. 2005. *Subjectivity and Selfhood: Investigating the First-Person Perspective.* Cambridge, MA: MIT Press.

PREFACE

The study and practice of young adult (YA) services within the context of library and information science (LIS) appears to be quickly approaching a crossroads. While increasingly a productive and dynamic subfield among practitioners over the past 10 to 15 years, especially with regard to rapid technological change, LIS scholarship on YA services has largely been overlooked—particularly with respect to how the profession defines or envisions its target population.

Researchers and practitioners alike have become lulled into a borrowed and false consensus on the vision of young people generally deployed in LIS. The essays appearing in *Transforming Young Adult Services* attempt to anticipate the coming debate, articulate some of its defining features, and help inaugurate a long-needed professional deliberation about how best to face the decisions that lie not too distantly in the future of LIS YA services in particular and youth studies more generally. As critical youth studies sociologist Greg Dimitriadis (2008: 105) has noted, "We have an imperative to reimagine our object of study—one that forces us to reengage with the lives of youth on fresh terrain."

Since its inception, and for many historical and professional reasons, the LIS field has failed to sufficiently or clearly define its core audience of YAs. A constructive criticism inaugurated in this collection is that LIS has relied on other professions and disciplines to identify who young adults are and what they need. Justified largely by a feint to interdisciplinarity, LIS has simply borrowed and applied variously and uncritically from these visions of young people. The field of education, for instance, imagines youth as "students" and "pupils." The fields of psychology and social work construct youth as "clients" or objects of study. The field of criminal justice constructs youth as "suspects," "criminals," and "perpetrators." And sports envisions them as "athletes."

The essays contained in this collection call attention to the implications of this circumstance. Together they intend to instigate a debate among LIS researchers, practitioners, and students to articulate a vision of youth that will transform research on and practice of professional YA librarianship.

One consequence of this long-established pattern of deriving an LIS vision of YAs from other fields has been the production of an imported, intellectually static, and moribund consensus about who young people are as well as the institution's relationship to them. If LIS has, for instance, relied on psychology for its vision of youth, then our LIS training and preparation, reader advising and reference, collection development, management, programming, outreach, and YA spaces will necessarily manifest youth-as-trouble, troubled, and at risk. In books, articles, and essays at conferences, in training workshops, on websites and blogs, and in our LIS classrooms, there is ample evidence demonstrating that this is precisely what we do.

Informed by today's stronger emphasis on working directly with young people as "participants" and "partners," these essays attempt to inaugurate the incorporation of that growing influence into a transformative, more focused *LIS-specific* vision of youth and our institutional relations with the millions of teenaged youth we serve as well as the adults who support them. This collection includes a more critical, evidence-based, and theoretically rich engagement with YA librarianship than previously ventured. Much of the reason LIS finds itself now in these intellectual doldrums results from a long-standing aversion to engaging critical social theory. This collection begins to address the yawning gap in our work.

In *Transforming Young Adult Services* readers will discover research articles and essays that augment and enrich the many up-to-date and sufficiently detailed lists of resources that currently inform LIS and professional YA practice (e.g., resource guides, manuals, collection building references, sample forms and documents, program and outreach models, and tips for using technology). *Transforming Young Adult Services* does, however, more conceptually and historically examine our conventional categories of service and how they both produce and manifest an inadequate and derived institutional imagination of today's youth. These essays ask hard and even uncomfortable questions about what we have come to define as "best practice" as opposed to what we can actually prove as being best practice. And the book inaugurates what will hopefully become a new debate about how LIS constructs and conceives of YAs as well as how we might proceed in creating a more LIS-specific vision.

With over 40 million YAs ages 12 to 18 in the nation today, any conversation about constructing a single vision will necessarily occur at a high level of abstraction and contain broad generalizations. And yet, the nature of our status as professionals, in either research or practice, obliges us to articulate some notion of who we serve, how, and why. If YA librarianship is to improve and advance professional impact, influence, and profile within LIS, as these essays implicitly and collectively argue, it must identify this important population *for itself* rather than continuing to rely on visions of youth articulated by other disciplines and developed for their own respective purposes.

LIS has a unique mission. And while we often do serve in various teaching modes, we are not by definition psychologists or social workers or police officers or athletic coaches. This collection argues that it is high time we rise to define our users ourselves. LIS needs to do this to enhance our own disciplinary and institutional needs, to improve our relationships with the nation's young people, and to more precisely focus on how these components combine.

In order to achieve these aspirations, *Transforming Young Adult Services* called upon some of our best YA researchers and evidence-based practitioners to write from their specializations and strengths. Collectively, these contributors demonstrate facility with the most recent scholarship and writing on youth studies and YA librarianship. Their work has culled, sifted, and synthesized our LIS literature to produce a resource identifying several essential topics for YA practice. The topics addressed in this collection include youth identity and formation, YA materials and collections, youth development, race, youth participation and intergenerational connections, critical perspectives on youth studies, intellectual freedom, and professional ethics.

While many of the essays build on interdisciplinary insights to inform analysis, they do so *within* our LIS context and are directed at our particular LIS circumstances. It is one thing to draw from different fields of inquiry; it is another to recline on them to define core features of our own work. However, irrespective of the disciplinary, research, or practice tradition from which these authors write, each of the contributors responds to a single question: How should LIS imagine today's young adults?

The collection is organized into three sections meaningful to LIS scholars and students as well as to professional librarians. While all of these essays challenge prevailing LIS approaches, the sections are arrayed in order of the degree to which they do.

The first section opens with a topically conventional yet provocative collection of essays titled "What's in an Age?" This section examines visions of youth based on categories of age/chronology and youth identity. While these and other topics may at first appear familiar, a closer reading yields their more critical insights and engagement with nominally conventional concerns.

The second section, "From White and Marginal to Civic Partners," introduces topics on broader and more critical themes such as the social constructions of race, collection development, and youth participation.

The third and final section, "Beyond Youth Development and Questions of Intellectual Freedom," broadens the topic theoretically and offers radical insights—including visions of YAs as active agents in their own right capable of rolling back adultist "tribalism" within and beyond the library environment. These essays challenge the long-standing youth-as-object developmentalist agenda, and conclude with an examination of the ethical implications of imagining an LIS youth vision for the ever-challenging notion of intellectual freedom.

The concluding essay, "Historical Contexts and Consequences of the LIS Youth Consensus," furthers the analysis in this collection by synthesizing the potential benefits and consequences for a YA services profile willing to engage critical social theory and critical youth studies. The essay explores a variety of potential paths for LIS to deliberate on and debate in our future attempts to reconcile a new vision of today's young people. Here readers will find provocative new frames in which to evaluate and consider the work of LIS researchers and practitioners alike. It contextualizes a notion of citizenship applied to young people, our interventions in collection management and youth literacies, YAs as intergenerational agents, and how a new vision of young people impacts the physical spaces of libraries.

While no one collection can legitimately claim to address all relevant topics, or even the most important topics to the same degree, *Transforming*

Young Adult Services attempts to apply a critical analysis to the broadest, most compelling, and most practical aspects of YA librarianship.

As mentioned previously, however, this collection does not attempt to offer readers another resource guide. The profession is already very good at producing those. Nor does it claim to finally answer all of the vexing questions it raises. Rather, this book helps articulate some of the conceptual features that inform, underlie, and frame how we currently perceive, position, and value our work; how we define our young adult users; and how our institution binds these perceptions to research and practice.

In addressing such fundamental aspects of YA librarianship, this collection offers the potential to enrich the experiences of LIS students as well as those conducting research or practicing in the field. LIS students will gain a firmer grasp of the historical assumptions and contemporary challenges they face as they prepare to enter the profession, and thus will be better able to understand the potential for dynamic innovation, debate, and creativity it offers.

LIS faculty will likewise find this a rich collection of concepts and arguments to spark lively, productive discussion and assignments to prepare students as more reflective practitioners.

For professionals, paraprofessionals, and administrators currently responsible for YA services, this collection connects and contextualizes larger concerns that have colored and informed the legacy practices they inherit, as well as helps them better evaluate the choices before them that may otherwise have gone unrecognized. And while much of this material relates most directly to public library environments, school library and media specialists will find a great deal of this material relevant as well.

Certain aspects of YA librarianship have changed rapidly in the recent past. LIS has valiantly attempted, for instance, to reconceive our institutional identity with respect to the daily application of technology. However, technology represents a delivery system; it does not articulate a professional service vision.

Many LIS approaches conceptually lag. This is especially observable in LIS's continued reliance on other disciplines to underwrite a key component of our professional obligation—to define our user. But for our work to progress and gain broader legitimacy and influence, the mere deployment of our institutional resources and professional skills is not sufficient.

LIS requires its own institutional imagination of young people to successfully serve and contribute to the well-being of our communities. This collection attempts to inaugurate such a discussion and help transform YA librarianship so that LIS not only keeps pace with a rapidly changing social environment but also contributes to leading that discussion. No doubt debate and deliberation will follow. Indeed, perceptive readers will detect disagreement among and between many of the authors in this collection. The authors, however, welcome that as a sign of a healthy profession.

Authors and Topics

The first section of this collection, "What's in an Age?," addresses the core question of how LIS should envision YAs from seemingly conventional trajectories. These contributions explore the center of YA services: youth identity formation and the relationship of chronological age to notions of "young adult." In Chapter 1, LIS scholar Denise E. Agosto, associate professor at Drexel University, conducts a content analysis of three years of LIS research and practitioner writing about YA services to uncover a pattern of professional discourse that, despite the past decade's intense policy-level discussion about youth involvement, continues to project itself as an "adult-centered" practice. Agosto's essay, "Envisaging Young Adult Librarianship from a Teen-Centered Perspective," rather than explicitly answering the question about what our LIS vision of youth should be, inaugurates our discussion by urging LIS to become better aligned with a deeper and systematic concentration on youth experience.

In Chapter 2, "Dialogism, Development, and Destination: Young Adults in Contemporary Culture," Karen Coats, professor of English at Illinois State University, extends Agosto's investigation by reaching deep into contemporary YA fiction to better root out an LIS vision of today's youth through the experience of youth users. Coats filters the question of identity through literary criticism and a theoretically sophisticated analysis to argue the importance of understanding how youth identity is "dialogically engaged" in a project of individual "self-fashioning." Mobilizing the postmodern category of analysis of the self as a fluid and complex process,

Coats suggests, would serve LIS research and practice better than a traditional modernist approach to the self as more static and solid.

Well-known YA literature critic and columnist Michael Cart, past president of the Young Adult Library Services Association (YALSA) and the first recipient of the YALSA/Greenwood Publishing Group Service to Young Adults Achievement Award, revisits youth identity in yet another provocative way in Chapter 3, "Crossing Over: The Advent of the Adultescent." Cart examines historical and contemporary texts in youth psychology as well as current sociological and economic exigencies to reevaluate concretized age-based notions of how LIS has categorized young library users. In Cart's analysis, current social conditions suggest that the prevailing LIS category of "youth" itself now requires redefinition based not on a "teen" notion of youth but on an "emerging," more prolonged process to adulthood. Cart explores the institutional implications of this insight through the LIS practices of book reviews and collection development procedures.

While each of these contributions ostensibly addresses conventional and fundamental categories of LIS research and practice, they more importantly interrogate cardinal and legacy practices from different perspectives. After many years of lectures, workshops, conference presentations, books, and articles about the need for LIS to more deeply engage "youth participation," what emerges is that the notion has failed to gain broad or sufficient institutional penetration into daily practice. It is also clear that what constitutes LIS's current demographic definition of youth also at least partly obstructs the emergence of a less concrete or flexible notion—one more contested or negotiated despite the long-standing impulse for LIS to lock it down into arguably simplistic, digestible age-based categories. We need to confront this dilemma head-on and further explore its potential for imagining an LIS-specific vision of young people.

Emerging from a critical stance on static notions of youth are other probing questions. The contributors to the collection's second section, "From White and Marginal to Civic Partners," address many of them. In Chapter 4, Kafi D. Kumasi, assistant professor and youth scholar at Wayne State University's School of Library and Information Science, employs critical race theory in "'The Library Is Like Her House': Reimagining Youth of Color in LIS Discourses" to provoke implications of white racial privilege in defining today's YA library-using population. However, unlike previous authors who argue that we must concentrate greater resources on youth experience, Kumasi argues that because the current construction of YA library users in the LIS imagination is coded racially as white, the first order of business requires greater reflection on the white privilege of LIS professionals. In an insightful and provocative article, Kumasi challenges the intellectual and conceptual efficacy of the escapist "color blind" cliché.

Like Coats and Cart who argue for the inclusion of YA literature itself as a meaningful factor in how LIS should envision today's YA library users, LIS doctoral candidate Lucia Cedeira Serantes of the University of Western Ontario's Faculty of Information and Media Studies extends the question in Chapter 5, "Misfits, Loners, Immature Students, and Reluctant Readers: Librarianship in the Construction of Teen Readers of Comics." This historical analysis reflects on how the field manifests its visions of library users through its reception of particular literary genres. In an engaging content analysis of historical LIS reactions to comics since their introduction in the 1930s, Cedeira Serantes documents the institutional marginalization of both the literary form and its enthusiastic young readers. The materials sitting on our library shelves tell an unfortunate and lingering tale.

In Chapter 6, Executive Director of the Youth Activism Project (YAP) Wendy Schaetzel Lesko even more dramatically opens the question of how LIS should envision today's youth in "Beyond Coaching: Copiloting with Young Adults," an analysis of where a genuine and broad youth participation aesthetic might lead. Where LIS conversations of the past few decades have energetically promoted rudimentary "youth partnerships" and "collaborations" through Teen Advisory Groups and collection development focus groups, Lesko introduces a more radical turn in imagining youth as full partners with libraries in *intergenerational* efforts across the institution's larger civic arena. Lesko demonstrates what American history has taught us for generations: young people not only possess an abiding and material interest in current civic issues but also have responded well above expectations time and again, either when they mobilize themselves or are called forward to do so. Youth in large numbers, LIS should remember, were productive farmers of urban victory gardens during the 1940s, activists in the 1960s civil rights and antiwar movements, gainful protestors against harsh anti-immigration policies in the mid-2000s, and today constitute a large portion of participants in the Occupy movement. Lesko points out how YAP's intergenerational School Girls Unite effort serves as yet another demonstration (this time on the international stage) of the impact youth can make not just for the future but today as well.

Thus, in this second section we see the emergence of a broader and deeper critique of recent and past LIS YA research and practice as insufficiently engaged with many significant contemporary issues and debates, due in part to its inadequate and derived vision of youth. While the critique of an underacknowledged racial privilege in LIS is not new, it is certainly a new question to raise when assessing YA services specifically. Few observers have so clearly drawn connections between the collections on library shelves and the ways in which LIS deploys its vision of youth as Cedeira Serantes does here. And while the rhetoric promoting youth participation is not new either, few researchers and institutions have mined the intergenerational partnership model illustrated by Lesko.

The third and final section, "Beyond Youth Development and Questions of Intellectual Freedom," further deepens and expands the critique of the current state of LIS research and practice as it pertains to envisioning YAs. By introducing and exploring more explicit theoretically informed questions, the contributions in this section boldly begin to separate from the prevailing and popular LIS modernist framework (one rather preoccupied with experience as the major mode of analysis), and instead pursues questions more associated with postmodernism (analytical modes concentrating more on meanings and power). Currently, LIS concentrates nearly exclusively on determining, measuring, and deriving understanding from questions regarding the experience of YAs in libraries as users of institutional resources. The contributions in this final section, on the other hand, seek to understand how LIS should envision or imagine YAs by questioning not their experience but the *meanings* they derive from and through their experience with the public value libraries offer and sometimes even withhold.

Sociologist and former University of California faculty Mike Males, senior researcher with the Center for Juvenile and Criminal Justice, addresses how LIS should envision today's YAs in Chapter 7, "Tribalism versus Citizenship: Are Youth Increasingly Unwelcome in Libraries?" Males accomplishes this largely by reintroducing LIS to the work of classical anthropologist Margaret Mead. Unlike for Coats and other pro-youth development authors in this collection, Males's investigations into today's youth demographics and patterns of technological adoption are part of a critical youth studies scholarship that is growing increasingly skeptical of the explanatory power of the dominant youth development paradigm. In arguing against the youth/adult bifurcation at the core of youth development, Males contends that youth and adult relationships are "synergetic" and relational, not inherently or biologically oppositional. The consequence of ignoring this counteranalysis, he asserts, risks concretizing "adult tribalism" and further hardening social institutions like libraries against the possibility of age-integrated or intergenerational futures.

In Chapter 8, Paulette Rothbauer, associate professor at the University of Western Ontario's Faculty of Information and Media Studies, also grapples with the question of how LIS should envision today's YAs in "Imagining Today's Young Adults in LIS: Moving Forward with Critical Youth Studies." By extending concerns opened here by Males, Rothbauer more deeply probes the historical assumptions of youth as an "essential stage" in human development rooted in the field of psychology since the late nineteenth century. In arguably the collection's most radical and frontal engagement with the long-dominant paradigm of YAs in LIS research and practice, Rothbauer examines many of the stereotypes that LIS has long taken for granted and through which YA services have largely been defined. Rothbauer resolves that "our heavy reliance on theories of human development is, perhaps, unwarranted." In Males and in Rothbauer in particular, we begin to see a rising tide of critical youth studies scholars no longer willing to abide a strict and sturdy developmentalist apparatus in LIS's derivative envisioning of YAs. Thus it is here that we begin to first glimpse the coming "crossroads" suggested earlier.

The author of Chapter 9, "Intellectual Freedom or Protection? Conflicting Young Adults' Rights in Libraries," is attorney-at-law, LIS scholar, and instructor at San Jose State University School of Library and Information Science Cherie Givens. In light of the preceding chapters, Givens's approach to the question of how LIS should envision today's youth further prefigures the crossroads LIS is quickly approaching. Specifically, Givens asks how LIS should align itself ethically in addressing contemporary youth's rights and intellectual freedom. Here the conflicting paradigms of modernism's universal notions of static age and maturity "development" chafe against postmodernism's increasingly urgent questions regarding the socially constructed meaning of chronological age itself. Her thesis is that LIS must constantly weigh the legal status of youth (with all its inconsistencies, ironies, contradictions, and complexities) against our professional virtues and ethical commitments.

The Challenge Ahead

If Givens's answer to the question about how LIS should align itself ethically to maximize YA intellectual freedom appears a bit unsatisfying, it is only because the challenges ahead remain so unclear, conceptually indeterminate, and increasingly contested. While among the most contentious continuing issues in YA librarianship, the topics of intellectual freedom and what we might now call youth's "right to the library" have never confronted us so directly. Instant and ever-broader access to information and communication, for example, arrives in lockstep with technological surveillance. Yet, choices and policies must be made. These issues number among our professional obligations.

Thus, if LIS remains as uncritical, unclear, and derivative about its notion of young people as a user category as it has in the past, we will never arrive at satisfying or just solutions to the vexing issues of censorship and security versus youth access to information in a democratic culture. And if we elect to remain unclear about our own LIS vision of youth, neither will our institutional pronouncements, ethical guidelines, or other aspirational documents help; no ritualistic incantations about intellectual freedom, references to the American Library Association's Library Bill of Rights, or even the Constitution itself will resolve these questions. They do, however, require the critical interventions of LIS scholars and practitioners.

Of course, the necessity of better articulating an LIS-specific vision of today's youth extends well beyond the complexities of intellectual freedom and access. Without recognizing the need for a clear LIS-specific notion of the population YA librarianship serves, all of the key areas discussed in these essays would be denied the intellectual and conceptual resources required to enliven, inform, or advance research and practice. And additional topics such as management, research methods, staff development,

YA services history, and volunteerism (to name just a few)—while not explicitly addressed in this collection but are no less essential to quality practice—will continue to suffer as well.

In perhaps still the most seminal observation made to date on LIS research on YA services, Christine A. Jenkins (2000: 119) noted: "If the history of library programs and services for children is insufficiently studied, the history of programs and services for young adults is nearly nonexistent." At long last, we need to reconcile why this statement remains true. The authors in this collection might well have begun to address this deficiency, and they would add that at least part of LIS's historic reluctance (or avoidance) to engage YA services more fitfully has resulted in the discipline's addiction to answers about YAs furnished by other fields of inquiry. The authors hope these essays spark a debate to help LIS define young adults for itself. Of course, there are many reasons why LIS research on YA services remains in this debilitating state, but a more comprehensive assessment exceeds the scope of this book and in fact remains unaddressed at this writing.

Anthony Bernier
Oakland, May 2013

References

Dimitriadis, G. 2008. *Studying Urban Youth Culture*. New York: Peter Lang.
Jenkins, C. A. 2000. "The History of Youth Services Librarianship: A Review of the Research Literature." *Libraries and Culture 35*, no. 1: 103–140.

ACKNOWLEDGMENTS

The editor and authors would like to thank the following colleagues for their generous and constructive comments on earlier drafts of this collection: Marilyn Irwin, PhD, associate professor, School of Library and Information Science, Indiana University, Indianapolis; Melanie A. Kimball, PhD, assistant professor, Graduate School of Library and Information Science, Simmons College; Ed Kurdyla, E. L. Kurdyla Publishing, *Voice of Youth Advocates* (*VOYA*) and *Teacher Librarian*; and Joy Rodriguez, MLIS, JD.

Thanks are due as well to one of LIS's unsung national treasures, Charles Harmon, formerly of Neal-Schuman Publishers, whose steady faith in the project from the start ensured it would succeed, and to Christopher Rhodes, Rachel Chance, Jenni Fry, and the staff of ALA Editions, for their patience and equanimity.

My personal thanks to manuscript readers Joy Rodriguez, Zemirah Gonzales Lee, Carmen Martinez, Douglas Smith, and to my youth studies students at San Jose State University who all inspire me to continue reaching for the legitimacy this work deserves.

This project was aided by support from the Institute of Museum and Library Services and the School of Library and Information Science at San Jose State University.

Introduction

Anthony Bernier

Each generation of American professional experts sends up its own "clear-cut" answers, its own doctrinal certainties and Olympian universalisms, about *youth*. In stepping back to examine this history for library and information science (LIS), two broad discursive constructions of young adults (adolescents) have swung pendulously back and forth under various names since the invention of the "child sciences" in the late nineteenth century. One expert discourse articulates the degree to which society should exercise *power and control* over the young. Another, in contrast, favors concepts of *freedom and intimacy*. Each doctrine advances its own governing vision of youth rooted in assumptions and truth claims tethered to particular contemporary cultural preoccupations, procedures, techniques, policies, methods, and strategies. In introducing this collection of essays concerned with how LIS should envision today's young adults (hereafter YAs), this introduction argues that while there certainly are distinctions to be drawn between late nineteenth century and contemporary visions of youth, today's LIS vision, borrowed from these early expert discourses, is actually more similar than different. Stated another way, today's LIS vision of YAs reflects the influence of developmental psychology's models advanced originally over a century ago rather than its own vision rooted in more contemporary thinking or its own institutional needs.

The essays collected in *Transforming Young Adult Services* examine some of the historical traces of this legacy and inquire after the implications and consequences these assumptions have visited on the strategic and institutional delivery of YA services. This analysis grows from an assessment that LIS has primarily pursued its connection to youth through the life of the library rather than by examining how the library can matter in the life of YAs. Together these essays and their collective analysis attempt to prefigure future LIS research, practice, and debate.

A core argument advanced here is that one consequence of perpetuating and uncritically reproducing dated and derived views of youth constitutes an intellectual failure of LIS to incorporate more recent theoretical and conceptual models.[1] In avoiding engagement with critical social theory, LIS in general and YA librarianship in particular have thus defaulted into borrowing essentially unchallenged century-old visions of youth from other disciplines rather than constituting a vision more suited to its own singular and distinct mission. Thus, this collection will apply the recent observation by Gloria Leckie, Lisa Given, and John Buschman (2010: xi), directly to YA services: "there is a tendency in LIS to adapt theoretical perspectives from other disciplines, often doing so without a critical or complete understanding." This debilitating avoidance has delayed and deflected LIS's relevance for the institution, the development of professional capacities; has visited decades of dated approaches on the nation's young people; and has contributed to LIS's lagging far behind today's best thinking on youth.

The Nineteenth Century and the Wallpaper Threat

Why, I have seen wallpaper which must lead a boy brought up under its influence to a career of crime; you should not have such incentives to sin lying about your drawing-room.

—OSCAR WILDE, 1882

In the late nineteenth century our culture increasingly ascribed to the powerful claims of "scientific" certitude. Science rendered its claims through empirical or positivist inquiry (today we might call it "modernist"), and tried through this approach to become "professional" about raising the young. It was during this period that two giants of modernist child-rearing philosophy made their names as experts—psychologist G. Stanley Hall and the less well-known Emmett L. Holt (see Hulbert, 2003). Separately and together they successfully influenced generations of mothers, nurses, caregivers, social workers, journalists, criminologists, educators, and policymakers. Together they sought in particular to steel mother and child against the unnerving influences of industrialized urban life. And together they reflect the nascent discourse on youth that continues to echo in today's LIS research and practice.

On the one hand, Hall represents the more famous "freedom and intimacy" child-rearing and "child-saving" discourse of the late nineteenth century. The notion of freedom and intimacy was founded on scientific claims—that is to say on positivist claims—to "expert knowledge" and to the exercise of the cultural power flowing from it. Considered more a "romantic" than a rationalist, Hall combined something of a post-Darwinian biology (nature adapts, changes, and evolves) with a proto-Freudian psychology (powerful emotional energies of the unconscious mind). He defined adolescence in particular as a "developmental turning point, a larval stage" (Hall, 1904).[2] Hall, it should be noted, included strong doses of those particularly Freudian preoccupations with sex and gender.

G. Stanley Hall's Universal Claims about the Needs of Youth

"Freedom and intimacy" according to Hall were based on the following:
- Autonomy
- Nature
- Love and bonding
- Liberty and experimentation
- Child-centeredness
- Progressive/evolutionary development

In Hall's view youthful passions required channeling. In one of his several appearances before national audiences of librarians, for instance, he warned attendees at the 1919 American Library Association conference that girls' books must be "calculated to fit them for domestic life or womanly vocations." Teens in general, he wrote, "are emotionally unstable, and must have excitement" or the consequence would be that youth would seek excitement on their own in "sex or drink" (Hall, 1905, 1908).

Here it can clearly be observed was the beginning of what I have termed today's "youth development industrial complex" (hereafter YDIC). This ostensibly inevitable, naturalized, seemingly imperative, normative, and ever-burgeoning institutional agenda constitutes an elaborate and sprawling apparatus of career interests, pedantic ideology, and age-segregated diversionary procedures intended to deflect the biological *instability* hard-wired, Hall argued, into all youth.

In keeping with other soaring and imperialist tropes of the nineteenth century, Hall also inaugurated the term *adolescent race*, which conflated pseudo-Darwinian notions of racial and adolescent inferiority (compared only to an implicitly idealized "adulthood") to argue that society needed to civilize youth in ways not too dissimilar from the way in which other "childlike and savage races" were thought to have been "civilized." This nineteenth-century age-race synthesis echoes endlessly in today's views of presumed antisocial youth behaviors with "youth violence," "teen pregnancy," "teen substance abuse," "the teen brain," and a seamlessly endless list of moral panics, including today's hot panic about so-called youth cyberbullying. According to Hall's science, without constant adult surveillance through civilizing programming efforts, such as those promulgated by today's YDIC, society would suffer the consequences of innate youthful savagery run amuck.

On the other hand and in contrast to Hall, the "power and control" approach was launched and advocated by Emmett L. Holt. As with Hall, Holt advanced a rubric of child-rearing strategies rooted in scientific management. But unlike Hall's "softer" approach, Holt advocated a strict and didactic catechism of control that included routines, regulations, and rules. This "harder" approach deployed a rhetoric revaluing women's domestic roles—effectively promoting bourgeois motherhood from the familiar domestic manager into a more powerful paraprofessional child-rearing specialist. It was mothers the young required, according to Holt, for the "steadiness to fortify them against a disorderly—and ever more materialistic, distracting—world" (Hulbert, 2003). "In these days," wrote Holt, "of factory and locomotive whistles, trolley cars and automobiles, music boxes and the numberless mechanical toys in the nursery, door-bells and telephones in the house," sensory bombardment was already inflicting youth. A strong, consistent, rational, and regular regimen of control was

Emmett L. Holt's Universal Claims about the Needs of Youth

Holt's "power and control" approach included the following characteristics:
- Conformity
- Nurture
- Hierarchy of authority
- Prevention
- Parent-centeredness
- Traditional/conventional development

required to ensure that youth yielded up "compliance without conflict" in the face of modern society. If achieved, Holt promised, youth would mature into sturdy and independent middle-class adults.[3]

Holt's harder approach can easily be recognized as the early predecessor to today's zero tolerance attitudes and policies. Where Hall wished to nurture youth into compliance with Victorian middle-class propriety, Holt meant to extract compliance and conformity through the raw assertion of adult authority.

A century later, their similarities should be easier to detect. While Holt's views clearly differed in the definition, nature, and degree of control adults were urged to apply to youth, his greater resonance with Hall is apparent. Both built their theoretical houses on the foundations of nineteenth-century positivism. They shared confidence in the capacity of empirical science to identify universal and biological patterns. And Holt and Hall also viewed youth as inherently flawed. For them, youth were dangerously susceptible to behaviors closely associated with the great unwashed masses of laborers and immigrants then teaming in American cities, as well as the problems posed, they felt, by the "darker" races. Indeed, both viewed youth as an "inferior" race similar to dark-skinned people and women. Both viewed young people necessarily as a breed apart, as inherently compromised, as damaged and deficient.

Holt and Hall differed only in how they proposed to fix or "solve" the youth problem. Ultimately, the innovation they advanced in the late

The Nineteenth-Century Origins of Scientific Youth

Hall's freedom and intimacy meets Holt's power and control:

- Theories are based on nineteenth-century positivism and empirical modernist science.
- Both identified universal and biologically determined patterns.
- Visions of youth are consistent with similar visions of marginalized populations (women, immigrants, Native Americans, and African-Americans).
- Focus is on differences compared to idealized white middle-class adult males.

nineteenth century was that they respectively felt that they had discovered how the problem *could* be fixed.

It is easy to detect these century-old similarities and their relationships to contemporary practice, of course, if they are examined in light of more recent and burgeoning critical scholarship on the history of youth (Fass and Grossberg, 2012; Kasinitz et al., 2008; Klapper, 2007; Sanchez-Eppler, 2005; Soland, 2000). LIS, however, has traditionally exhibited little curiosity on this matter.

The Twentieth Century:
A Continuing Consensus of Deficit and Difference

The "success" or "failure" of either of these efforts to dilute or deflect the presumptive bestial instincts lurking within all youth remains a debatable proposition among historians, policymakers, and youth studies scholars to this day. But what has not been debated is the consensus of vision that impugned such natural impulses to youth in the first place or the way in which institutions like libraries were committed to dealing with them (Lukenbill, 2006). The exercise of institutional authority and adult power was and continues to be viewed as a necessary, proportional, and scientific response to exorcising the Manchurian demons liable to erupt at a moment's notice in any youth. In connecting this earlier nineteenth-century vision of youth to today, historian Stephen Mintz (2004: 383) observed:

> *We may cling to the idea in the abstract [that youth is valuable in and of itself], but in practice American culture—oriented toward mastery and control—views childhood as a "project," in which the young must develop the skills, knowledge, and character traits necessary for adulthood success.... Those who cannot adjust are cast adrift....*

For much of the twentieth century youth professionals closely adhered to this foundational youth-as-breed-apart construction. Early in the twentieth century, clergy representing the "soft" approach, as it were, advocated training and competitive boxing programs to divert the otherwise presumptive wayward drift of urban boys. Teachers dispensed, perhaps ironically, the "hard" approach through corporal punishment. Other "solutions" to deflect the inherent savage tendencies in youth included the inventions of the Boy Scouts, Girl Scouts, Woodcraft Rangers, and a wide variety of extracurricular programs (Baxter, 2008; Boyle, 2004).

While the specific history of an LIS response to YA service throughout the period between the late nineteenth century and the first half of the twentieth remains largely unstudied, libraries did certainly provide service to young people. And while the notion of what constituted service varies a great deal, the scant scholarship on historical LIS youth services largely recalls the experiences of children's librarians as they, chiefly middle-class white women, sought to gain professional status within the institution. But for historical treatments of library services specifically to YAs we possess even less scholarly analysis (Jenkins, 2000; Braverman, 1979).

What evidence we do have about services for youth in general points to how it was not until late in the twentieth century before LIS began to institutionally question the unchanging nature of youth embedded in the universal and ahistorical assumptions of Hall and Holt. Indeed, youth practitioners from various occupations began to see a more varied landscape in which *some* youth were better able to adjust to adult society than others.

Professionals continuing in the soft tradition began to develop an arsenal of programmatic responses to assist those youth they felt would benefit from their help. Those continuing in the hard tradition began inventing their own lexicon of age-based municipal injunctions, codes, curfews, among other statutory measures, to punish the wayward. Neither approach, however, questioned the core assumption that youth were inherently flawed social beings. Some simply required less supervision, while others required more punishment.

As in many domains of direct youth services (social work, psychology, education, and criminology, among others), libraries adopted the "youth-at-risk" and "prevention" discourse to manifest their concern for youth variously defined as walking that razor's edge between middle-class propriety and the uncivilized abyss.[4] LIS adopted the soft approach and engineered their service techniques, skills, methods, and practices on that programmatic model. Libraries would contribute to the civilization of youth by deploying the weapons at their disposal: an arsenal of moral suasion delivered through the cultural superiority afforded them through literacy and reading. Indeed, as William Lukenbill (2006) has pointed out, "Understanding this to be a *primary social responsibility*, librarians easily condemned as harmful to youth certain types of literature and other forms of mass entertainment...while at the same time supporting only literature judged by them to be of higher cultural value" (emphasis added).[5]

More recently, and particularly since the late 1960s, YA librarians have set out to provide their own brand of at-risk program offerings and collection management practices. Here the basic model recruited youth largely to serve as polite audiences for enlightened or rogue adults (including librarians) to receive curricular content often reminiscent of classroom instruction. These programs sought, among other things, to help youth stay in school, stay off drugs, get better test scores, eschew violence and gangs, avoid teen pregnancy and smoking, among other fixatives.[6]

Despite the continual assumptions and claims that these antisocial behaviors were grounded in empirical science, evidence-based research actually revealed how seldom youth engaged in them. Kids were not behaving badly. Indeed, as critical youth scholar Mike Males (2010, 11) observes, "It does not seem to matter that the wild scares and save-the-kids remedies do not turn out to be justified by a reasonable examination of information available."

Nevertheless, and evidence to the contrary, that was of little moment in the unfolding of the youth-at-risk juggernaut. Further, LIS exhibited little evidence that it knew very much about producing such programs, even less about how to evaluate or research them, and in fact has never been able to causally link particular library programming with specific behavior outcomes—good or bad. All this goes largely unremarked upon to this day.

Subsequent innovations and changes since the late 1980s have witnessed library YA service professionals pledged to another wave of borrowed discourse—a slightly different discourse but the same assumptions.

During this period, rather than continuing to view youth as at-risk recipients of professional attentions and aspirations, LIS institutionally began to adopt an intervention paradigm widely known as the "youth development" model wherein community "assets" are carefully cultivated, arrayed, and deployed so that youth access to these "building blocks" would guide them into maturing as "healthy adults" (Flowers and YALSA, 2011; Meyers, 2010; IMLS, 2009; Gorman and Suellentrop, 2009; Walter and Meyers, 2003; Jones and YALSA, 2002). Under this approach, more progressive LIS practitioners pursued a strategy wherein selected youth would play more "participatory" roles in their libraries and communities (Spielberger et al., 2005). This turn toward the youth development paradigm in libraries mirrors the adoption of this approach earlier and much more broadly across other direct youth service occupations.

For LIS this represented a rather radical paradigm shift. No longer would progressive institutions imagine all youth as being at-risk but rather as valuable community "partners" and resources—resources nevertheless requiring training in and the acquisition of discrete, predetermined, prescriptive priorities, opportunities, and "skills." Libraries consequently instigated various schema in which some young people's participation and involvement were, to various degrees, actively solicited. This is the era of burgeoning Teen Advisory Groups, Teen Leadership Councils, and other configurations in which small clusters of selected youth directly engage library staff in various discussions about the delivery of YA services.[7]

Nevertheless, while progressive institutions have moved more swiftly to adopt the youth development model, the transition across the field in general has been slow and uneven. More generally, libraries may well be among the last major institution to systematically eschew the at-risk approach to youth services. Further, confusion, conflation, and ignorance about this transition remain widespread. And one is as likely to encounter libraries deploying the at-risk approach as the youth development model. Some use both simultaneously without recognizing the differences.

Regardless, the innovation introduced by LIS's growing adoption of the youth development model ostensibly inverts the youth-at-risk paradigm's previous concentrations exclusively on avoiding and preventing negative youth behaviors and deficits. Instead, informed by the YDIC agenda, libraries attempt to fortify youth with positive attributes within their communities (see for example Brautigam, 2008; Alessio and Patton, 2007; Pierce, 2007; Weinberger, Ilvevag, and Giedd, 2005; Lerch and Welch, 2004; Vaillancourt, 2002). Here libraries, as other youth services, began to infuse discrete and parsed skills in their programming models that would better ensure the transition of youth into "thriving" middle-class adults.

Critically Engaging the Youth Consensus

The key term in LIS's still gradual turn from viewing all youth as at-risk to the youth development model is, however, *ostensible*. Because in addition to the ideological patterns cited above, the century-old positivist master narrative governing the LIS youth consensus is the overarching conceptualization of youth as irreducibly and biologically other, essentially different from a normative vision of adults, and forever plagued by real or potential crisis and turmoil.

Be they all biologically different, damaged, and unchangeable (views preceding Hall and Holt); be they all damaged yet changeable (Hall and Holt); be they partially or even sporadically damaged (youth at risk); or be they just lacking the requisite tools and skills to thrive as adults (youth development model), youth are nevertheless viewed as living a fundamentally different and marginal experience—one presumably always less than and ever at odds with the normative adult community. And "difference" has been interpreted nearly universally in opposition and conflict, or at best with a latent and always at hand conflict between youth and adults (see for example Rockefeller and Welch, 2012).

It was, after all, Hall whose studies of youth in the late nineteenth century characterized youth itself as a phase of "storm and stress" (from the German *Sturm und Drang*) to fuse development biologically with the social experience of young people. The operative features of this continuing view assume that conflict between youth and parents, youth and adults, and youth and authority; radical mood swings; and risk-taking behavior (including latent predilections toward violence and disruptive behaviors) are normal.

As detailed previously, more recent interpretations of the youth consensus envisions all youth, during this storm-and-stress conflict mode, in one of either two ways: sentimentally as biological innocents (it's not their fault, they were born that way) or as consciously imbued with super volition, power, and agency (they're dangerous and they make poor choices). One week it's panic about homicidal bullying; the next it's assertions rationalizing risk taking due to biological differences, such as the "teen brain" discourse (see Payne, 2012; Kelly, 2011; Sercombe, 2010).

After being subjected to over a century of these unquestioned assumptions of youth deficiency, or a less-than status, there is little evidence that LIS even notices the naturalized and essentialized characterizations of youth experience in today's popular media, culture, and scholarship (Bernier, 2011). Yet this youth consensus is incorporated seamlessly into policy, practice, and research. Thus, as if hopping from one foot to the other, we continue to marginalize and relegate youth within this bifurcated world of false binary opposites. In either case, the consistent focus on inherent deficiencies of youth remains unquestioned.

What other field of social science claims to have been entirely correct and remains unchallenged about its foundational and universal assumptions for over a century? And what are the consequences for an entire profession continually reproducing and applying those assumptions systematically in practice and research?

Taken together, the youth consensus remains alive and well in LIS. Indeed, while there have been slight changes in tactics over time, it has uncritically enjoined over a century of child science grounded in dated modernist approaches.

Contemporary Language Describing Century-Old Assumptions about Youth

The following table illustrates some of the ways in which this pedestrian discourse plays out in current language.

Features of the Youth Consensus	
Sentimental View of Youth	*Youth as Superagents*
Innocent	Dangerous
Dutiful	Entitled
Passive	Aggressive
Precious	Frenetic
Victim	Perpetrator
Needy	Headstrong
At-risk	Privileged
Asset	Liability
Creative	Unimaginative
Individual	Peer predators
Private/secretive	Exhibitionist
Self-conscious	Calculating
Rudderless	Plotting and cunning
Gifted	Underperforming

More important still, rather than developing its own vision of youth grounded in its own research for its own legitimate institutional purposes, LIS has unquestioningly and nearly exclusively relied on the influence of only one field of scholarly inquiry instead. The reliance on developmental psychology has led to a systematic pathologizing, objectifying, and problematizing of nearly every nook and cranny of youth experience. The consequence has led LIS to adopt and reproduce universal, ahistorical, biologically determined, and socially inept assumptions about its putative youth user. And these assumptions labor on in both research and practice. Literary critic and scholar Kent Baxter (2008: 7) connected these conceptual and historical dots well when he observed, "These commonplace beliefs about the developmental stage construct adolescence as a significant threat unless the energies and desires associated with it are correctly funneled into a productive, and morally acceptable, activity." And since the *Ragged Dick* series of the nineteenth century, libraries have positioned reading and library use as among these funneling strategies.

Engaging these concerns with the aid of critical social theory might help us better understand why so many young people tell us decade after decade how little libraries matter to them (see for example Howard, 2011; Abbas et al., 2007, 2008; Cook, Parker, and Pettijohn, 2005; Chelton, 2002; Fisher, 2003; Hill and Pain, 1988). Benefitting from the growing theoretical influences and insights of critical youth studies, however, is not the same as reclining on the dated assumptions in developmental psychology. But through this present investigation it will also become clear why the rest of youth studies scholarship tends to ignore LIS interventions and why LIS contributes so little to youth studies scholarship (see Macleod, 2011).

Cracks in the Consensus: An Emerging Critical Approach to LIS's Youth Consensus

Innovations in the youth sciences since the late nineteenth century are not negligible. While Hall and Holt viewed all youth as instinctually damaged goods, they both shared optimistic views for saving youth from their inherent flaws and for protecting them from dangerous influences. Youth-at-risk frequently viewed only selected youth as damaged. And the more contemporary youth development model assesses youth as assets or partners to be carefully cultivated as preprofessional resources for the competitive job and global marketplace.

Thus, the historical youth discourse has indeed come to understand that biology does not *necessarily* foreclose on the future of all youth to grow, learn, mature, and develop. These innovations certainly rolled back views of youth prior to the late nineteenth century envisioning youth as unchanging creatures with little differentiation between the teenaged years and adulthood.

LIS and other youth service professions therefore owe these influences a great debt. Where LIS, for instance, formerly sought to justify YA services resource allocation by identifying and quantifying particular skills through output measures, progressive institutions now look to *outcome* measures to defend and advance these programmatic offerings and advocate for increased resource allocations (Dresang, Gross, and Holt, 2006; Walter, 1995). Of course, this is not to denigrate the collection of data about YA services per se, only to contextualize the assumptions undergirding them. In either instance, however, the current regime of measured empirical evidence valued by the institution is rooted only in envisioning and identifying user skill deficits and the teaching of clinically predetermined and largely curricular applied skills. LIS refers to these skills as "bibliographic," "information seeking," "information behaviors," "information literacy," or similar terms reflecting the acquisition of library-determined procedures or habits of mind.

What LIS has not done, however, is take full and critical measure of what we might call this prevailing youth consensus and examine it for the vision of youth it borrowed from the YDIC paradigm. Even the more recent rendition, "*positive* youth development," manifests this youth consensus and in so doing continues to ignore a variety of unexamined assumptions about youth across these many decades (Lerner et al., 2005; Damon, 2004). The YDIC hegemony can only ever see youth as half-empty. And it is a consensus baked deeply into LIS approaches, research, training, and practice as well.

While the LIS youth consensus is strong, nevertheless, as is evident in the essays contained in this volume, it is becoming increasingly clear that LIS is rapidly approaching a conceptual crossroads about the inadequate and derived nature of this vision of today's youth. Thus, it is incumbent on the profession, particularly those engaged in YA services, to recognize that despite the not unimportant changes wrought by the historical assumptions since Hall and Holt, there is much more cohering these seemingly different approaches than separating them.

The section that follows offers a substantial list of questions and concerns about the YDIC informed by recent critical social theory, and its more specific application to critical youth studies, to help focus reflection on some of the major liabilities LIS has incurred as a consequence of its youth consensus and its reliance on other disciplines to articulate a vision of today's young people.[8] These concerns help equip the reader to enter and engage the coming debate over how LIS should envision today's young people.

Ahistorical and Grand Truths Examined

One such concern is that LIS might consider revising the current and simplistic ahistorical and acultural constructions of all youth embedded in the YDIC. Young people are as variegated, complex, and dynamic as any broad demographic population. Few transhistorical or pancultural generalizations hold up under universal models or criteria, and LIS currently possesses no evidence to the contrary. The sweeping generalizations LIS uses to describe youth or young adults, and the discrete skills LIS may feel they need, thus must be contingent on and highly qualified by the individual, time, and local social circumstances (see Chapter 1).

Not all YAs need skills or care about identifying "neighborhood boundaries" as called for in the highly regarded Search Institute study (2007) "40 Developmental Assets for Adolescents" (see also Benson, 2010). Nor do all youth need or desire the experiences it prescribes. Yet LIS's youth consensus legacy, particularly in its close relationship to developmental psychology and its participation in the YDIC, inherently purports to hold true these assumptions for all youth in all cultures, all communities, under all material circumstances.

Further to the matter addressed in this collection, given that LIS does not as a rule conduct actual primary or evidence-based research on the psychological, biological, neurobiological, anthropological, sociological, or historical experiences of young people, LIS has good reason to be cautious and measured with the language, concepts, models, and generalizations it mobilizes and advances in envisioning them.

Another concern defining this century-old ideological consensus about youth is, of course, that young people continue to be envisioned as inherently deficient—a "problem" population—by the larger society, qualifying as a group that sociologists refer to as "othered."[9] Where Hall and Holt viewed all youth as biologically flawed specimens, the more contemporary discourse of youth service experts and professionals largely view youth as inherently lacking the "skills" and knowledge necessary to succeed in the competitive adult world. Viewed from this perspective, the LIS vision also effectively constructs youth as inherently, and especially informationally, flawed (Bernier, 2007).

Another concern with the youth consensus is obsession with an idealized future in which all behavioral, cognitive, and skill development, indeed all youth experience, is evaluated, parsed, and measured through an established sequence. All experience is filtered through and directed toward some distant and imagined adulthood. Such skills include developing responsibility, planning and decision making, resistance skills, and, among other criteria, something called restraint.

As with other components of developmentalist assumptions, the focus on the future contains little concern for or recognition of the actual present moment that youth actually and fleetingly inhabit. And it is in this particular criticism that the notion of youth development is revealed not to be concerned with the lived experience or meanings of youth at all—but only the future of an idealized and self-actualized *adulthood*. As Sandy Fraser (2005: 16) from England's School of Health and Social Welfare has put it, youth "have been valued and understood in term of being 'a work in progress' towards adulthood, concerning what they might become and not who they presently are."

Education critic Jonathan Kozol (2005: 95) expresses skepticism of this assumption more poetically when he writes, "Childhood...[should not be] merely basic training for utilitarian adulthood. It should have some claims upon our mercy, not for its future value to the economic interests of competitive societies but for its present value as a perishable piece of life itself."

Another concern defining this ideological consensus of youth serving only as a training ground for the future emanates from the undue and nearly unchallenged dominance of youth services and youth studies research by the field of developmental psychology (Waterman, 2005). Both Hall and Holt were renowned psychologists (as were their mentors). And little of the power that psychology wields over today's youth studies research and practice agendas has diminished since their original interventions.

The manifestations and consequences of this particular circumstance are many. One component of psychology's dominance is observable in how it is tethered to nearly an exclusive focus on pathological youth behavior as measured only against a mythical norm of idealized values, such as complete and literal abstinence from drinking, violence, smoking, drugs, sex, and impure thoughts. Any cursory examination of practitioner or scholarly publications going back decades reveals an unbroken literary legacy focusing nearly exclusively on instances of destructive, antisocial, and counterproductive behaviors—in other words, behaviors subversive of or counter to idealized middle-class adult society. In the meanwhile, the daily prosocial behaviors, achievements, experiences, and meanings of the vast majority of youth go nearly unremarked upon.

LIS research has largely nestled itself under psychology's disciplinary wing. Its own version concentrates nearly exclusively on the informational deficits youth presumably need fulfilled for some future self-actualization (Bernier, 2007). But LIS has not been content to limit its vision of youth as objects in need of information. It has also promoted this view of pathology to its patrons as well. Adult and YA shelves both bulge with these psychology-influenced titles, and there is little evidence that libraries are even aware of this seemingly ever-present collection bias. It may at along last prove useful to ask if imagining YAs as *subjects* in their own rights and on their own terms will not be more beneficial for LIS than forever viewing them merely as objects of clinical diagnoses.

Another dimension of psychology's dominance in shaping the LIS youth consensus discourse is the near unbroken concentration on youth as individuated beings. For all its recent gestures toward advancing a more positive vision of young people, the YDIC paradigm does not seek, for instance, to develop critical consciousness about young peoples' own *collective* or shared roles, experiences, opportunities, or meanings in society (see for comparison Ginwright, Noguera, and Cammarota, 2006). Rather it parses youth into individual experiences connected to seemingly neutral and normative assumptions of private achievement, behavior, and experience. LIS research and practice continue to envision young users largely as singular individuals seeking discrete access to information such as in summer reading or skills-based programs like after-school tutoring and examination preparation (see Farrugia, 2011; Armaline, 2005).

This is a discourse currently on nodding terms with a rapidly spreading neoconservative political agenda fetishizing individual effort and private experience to the exclusion of social or collective contexts, varying material circumstances, history, and cultural pluralism. Consequently, YDIC ideology is layered thick with requirements for proving how specific and evermore discrete activities and programs are necessary to impart particular utilitarian goals, objectives, and most especially measurable skills to "improve" or "prepare" individual youth—and the YDIC exhibits finding little value in the ways in which youth collectively contribute to the broader culture.[10]

Indeed, libraries have with few arguable exceptions—such as Teen Advisory Groups—effectively resisted youth culture and its own demonstrated preferences for collective experience, group identity, building social capital through peer or family associations, or even community or social identity formation. This can be seen even in the ways in which libraries manifest their view of youth in public space. The most vivid illustration can be seen in the near universal library policy forbidding the sharing of a computer screen: the infamous one-butt-to-a-chair commandment. This policy, enforced by libraries across the nation, runs directly counter to the ways in which youth on a daily basis demonstrate how they prefer to use library resources and occupy public space (Taffel, 2001).

Neither is this concentration on LIS's individuating the service vision unique to the current youth consensus environment. Historian Miriam Braverman (1979: 244) noted this propensity explicitly as reaching back to the very beginning of young adult services, "young people's librarians saw the book as a force contributing to individuality and to the making of better human beings through books."[11]

Another concern of the youth consensus, one growing from the YDIC's blinkered view on individuation, is that it is no accident that youth services professionals deploy this developmentalist discourse freighted with the ultimate aim of imparting particularly instrumental skills connected to a middle-class orientation. Child rearing for conscription or assimilation into the settled middle class has been the driving vision of the child sciences since their inception. And the current paradigm, no matter its name, is no different. The YDIC vision, dispensed either from the public library or other local agencies, attempts to reproduce and enforce idealized middle-class values, practices, behavior, and worldview. This consensus, for instance, privileges middle-class views about the state, family, education, work, and strict obedience to adult authority for setting and monitoring youth behavior. LIS largely shares this avoidance of social class awareness,

awareness of its own identity as a middle-class-oriented institution and the service implications issuing from these assumptions (Pateman and Vincent, 2010). Developing, experimenting with, or valuing alternatives is not highly valued, such as might be observed in the institutional avoidance of service to foster youth, for instance, or promoting occupations not requiring higher education.

Further, the lack of social class analysis or the service implications of material conditions highlights how the YDIC paradigm ignores critical systemic, social, or environmental links to assessing what youth need or why they need it. Consequently, there is no critical literature in LIS youth services analytically or systematically grappling with the complexities of (increasing) structural economic inequalities or the material circumstances challenging youth—this despite historically high rates of child poverty and youth unemployment (BLS, 2011).

Beyond the already too narrow "digital divide" concept, worn increasingly threadbare with the arrival of ubiquitous portable digital communication devices, there is little direct LIS response to growing neoconservatism, massive deindustrialization, intergenerational poverty or unemployment, or even grotesque income disparities (Harvey, 2012; see also White and Wyn, 2004). For large portions of LIS inquiry, social class remains largely invisible to those coming from greater privilege (see Belton, 2010).

Not unrelated to the YDIC's hesitancy to deal directly with the impacts on youth of social class and material circumstance is its additional and inexplicable avoidance of the role the state plays (for good or ill) in the experience of youth. Government figures enormously in how youth experience their culture. Starting with the schools they attend from kindergarten through high school and beyond, to the programs in which they participate, to the parks and other amusements sponsored in part or in whole by government, and to the very libraries in their communities, the state must be viewed as a component of how we assess youth experience and meaning. Further still, without recognizing this essential institutional component of modern life, the YDIC therefore cannot enter into a critical engagement of the ways in which the state increasingly withdraws or even fails to support youth.

In relying so thoroughly and uncritically on hegemonic YDIC assumptions, the YA component of LIS has thus also sidestepped its share of analysis regarding the responsibility of the library as a component of state authority. Libraries are funded variously, it should be noted, by local, city, county, and federal government. This, of course, makes librarians and support staff government workers.

As such, there may well be implications worth investigating for YA practice we have yet to systematically examine. What proportion of the library's publicly supported resources, for instance, constitutes an equitable share devoted specifically to young people? How would that be determined? What are our roles in determining this calculation? In the context of professionals as government workers, what are practitioner and researcher roles and obligations in perpetuating, reproducing, complying with, or resisting inequitable resource allocation?

Another concern regarding LIS's youth consensus connection to the YDIC is that this middle-class vision remains rather silent on racial and gender constructions. Despite decades of critical youth scholarship documenting both the vagaries of sexism and racism, as well as social and political activism particularly of young feminists and nonwhite youth to improve social equity, oftentimes even leading these campaigns, the YDIC is silent on such topics (Boyle and Lutton, 2005).

Unless we are willing to assume that gender, racial, and class oppression do not impact youth at all, we must question the omission at long last of these social realities and their enduring institutional impacts on the ways in which they reverberate in the daily experience of young people. And this concern, of course, does not even take into account the many abuses of adult power on daily display in the media.

Inasmuch as the youth consensus freezes a universal vision of all youth as static and unchanging across all time and space, according to the YDIC, it must also be noted that it necessarily does the same for youth's binary opposite: adulthood. Not only does this youth consensus lock in a static deficit position with respect to culture and history, it also simplistically freezes the notion of adulthood in infallibility. The YDIC's exclusive concentration on youth avoids any consideration of adult influence (either individually or collectively) on youth other than as objective and benign facilitators for dispensing and supporting skill acquisition. More careful attention to headline news might counsel how not all adults deploy their age-based privilege and power with wisdom and equanimity.

Taken together, the YDIC's enthusiastic commitment to addressing the disproportionately sunny side of youth experience, and in identifying youth as always only ever a project in progress, ignores the direct implications of institutional, historical, material, and cultural realities that also daily impact the lives of youth. LIS's near ecumenical adoption of this paradigm through its youth consensus does little to advance the institution's value to youth studies, to real and complex communities, or with the large majorities of youth who disregard libraries as contributing meaningfully to their current lives.

A Word about This Collection

The essays in this collection attempt both to analyze LIS's youth consensus default vision of today's young adult and to inaugurate new questions, approaches, and ideas to fuel a long-needed debate. Readers will encounter authors with differing opinions. Some continue to mine and exploit the youth development model for what it contributes to work with young people. Some demonstrate ambiguous or conflicted opinions about this prevailing paradigm. And readers will also encounter authors beginning to call into question what I call the YDIC increasingly from a more distant and critical perspective.

This is as it should be in any robust and professional debate. While it is the chief intention of this collection to provoke debate, readers may not find it entirely satisfying or definitive. They will hopefully, however, find validity and be persuaded about the importance of this debate to the health and advance of LIS work, the institution, and its connections with young people and their communities. Thus, the central point of this work is not to endorse one particular view or to replace one hegemonic paradigm with another but to open up important questions from all of the positions and concerns advanced here and to propel the debate forward.

At base, however, beyond posing questions and proposing responses to the core concern about how LIS should envision today's young people, this collection lodges a profound concern that the profession, in near derelict avoidance and incuriosity about its own legacies, contributions, and impacts, has failed to reach for or address the larger continuities and contradictions in our work. LIS has, especially with respect to the social theory challenges swirling around academic and professional circles in the past quarter-century, nearly ignored critical engagement about service to young adults.

Mature and powerful disciplines produce the visions of youth they need to remain productive and viable. Psychology produces youth as patients, clients, and research subjects. Education envisions youth as students and pupils. Criminal justice imagines youth as suspects and perpetrators. Communities of faith envision congregants. Even the physical education department envisions youth as athletes. Yet, uninformed by more recent critical social theory, LIS allows others to perform our intellectual labor and define our users.

As a profession, we have come to believe too fully in the models furnished us by these disciplines, disciplines with vested intellectual and ideological interests in their own institutional agendas. Much of this manifested in LIS viewing young people against a backdrop of perpetual sentimentality or exaggerated threat. Why has LIS reclined so long in the shadow of other disciplines? Why have other youth studies fields ignored LIS scholarship (Heath, 1983, 2001; McLaughlin, Irby, and Langman, 1994)? Why has LIS exhibited such an historic consensus about envisioning youth in these ways?

This misguided institutional legacy has obscured and deflected the emergence and advance of our own knowledge and vision of young people at the expense of serving a much wider array and deeper scope of youth than might otherwise have been the case. It has prevented us from being viewed more seriously as contributors to knowledge about youth by other scholarly and service traditions. And it has no doubt contributed to why YA services is not even taken seriously by our own larger LIS conceptualizations (Pateman and Vincent, 2010; McCook, 2004; Rubin, 2004).

Why cannot LIS entertain and fitfully engage earnest debates about different ways to envision the young people we serve? Why has LIS failed to articulate its own vision of what libraries should be in the life of YAs, rather than perpetually defining them as needy youth in the life of the institution? Should the nature of our professional and ethical obligations to LIS and to the communities we serve be limited to uncritically deploying derived visions? Or do our obligations extend to and include fitful intellectual engagement with the larger social and historical streams of our age? Youth historian Philip Graham (2005: 1) characterized part of the problem this way:

> *Now that women have been liberated, the grey power of the elderly has been asserted, racism is publicly ostracized, and facilities for the disabled are legally required in all public places, the teens have become the last group whose disempowerment is invisible because it is so much taken for granted.*

We ought not be among the professions that take youth for granted. And are we not capable of or entitled to a fitful deliberation over our own vision of youth? The authors appearing in this collection welcome you to this discussion and to the coming debate.

Notes

1. Indeed, it is not only librarianship that has failed to theorize the category of age. "But unlike race and gender, age has been a largely undertheorized and unchallenged category" (Baxter, 2008: 17).
2. Others may more easily recognize this vision of youth in the work of psychologist Erik Erikson (1968).
3. Of course, libraries were not immune from the class-based agenda promoted by late nineteenth-century social reformers. "This felt cultural superiority of librarians led them to a concept of the library as a sort of benevolent school of social ethics. The library, 'while not expressly a school of manners and morals,' was 'much and closely concerned in maintaining a high standard in both'" (Perkings, 1885: 40).
4. The Drug Abuse Resistance Education (D.A.R.E.) program—originating in the Los Angeles Police Department—has become the internationally emblematic model for this approach. In this vision, all youth require massive programmatic intervention because all youth are variously susceptible to drug abuse without it. Despite consistent and independent research finding that no-use programs such as D.A.R.E. are likely ineffective, they continue to thrive in schools paid for by federal dollars (Brown, 2001).
5. For a much more thorough and critical historical treatment of the connection between reading and moral agenda of libraries and librarians, see Honeyman (2005).
6. Although virtually all YA service manuals engage in this approach to one degree or another, here is a sampling: Gorman and Suellentrop (2009); Brehm-Heeger

(2008); Alessio and Patton (2007); Mediavilla (2001); Anderson (2004); Mc-Grath (2004); Mondowney (2001); and Vaillancourt (2000). For a more historical treatment of YA programming since the 1960s, see Craver (1988).

7. It is instructive to note here that for all the guidelines, best practices, and advice literature promoting such participatory and partnership-oriented practices, there has been precious little LIS research produced demonstrating the value of these activities to libraries or even to youth themselves. This is not to diminish the importance of such materials in developing a professional dialog. But these works must be differentiated from systematic, methodologically sound, primary scholarly research capable of providing supportable evidence and generalizable conclusions. See Gillespie (2004) and Tuccillo (2005).

8. For a recent international perspective critical of modernist youth developmentalism, see Macleod (2011). From among many newer critical youth studies treatments, see Gilchrist et al. (2009); Jones (2009); Rothbauer (2009); Baxter (2008); Best (2007, 2008); Côté and Allahar (2006); Honeyman (2005); Heywood (2001); Lesko (2001); and James and Prout (1997).

9. "Youth researchers spend their lives researching and writing about inequality, exclusion, non-participation, disadvantage and disengagement, in other words treating youth research as research on youth related problems" (Holm and Helve, 2005: xi). "Othering" is defined as the "process by which a group...is marked as fundamentally different from what is perceived to be normal or mainstream" (Dimitriadis, 2008: 1). See also Chelton (1997).

10. The YDIC is very good at pointing out such things as "boundaries" and detailing "social competencies" but never acknowledges that youth might find benefit in building experience or meaning with and among each other. "Peer" is predictably followed by the word *pressure*.

11. While one can perceive some daylight between the library's compulsion to individuate young adult users and youth as active agents in the larger culture in the 1969 LIS classic *The Fair Garden and the Swarm of Beasts* by Margaret Alexander Edwards (1994), a clear response to the era's famous student activism, the larger thrust of her work does not break stride with the LIS legacy of individualization and deficit views of youth and what they need to become successful middle-class adults.

References

Abbas, J., M. Kimball, K. Bishop, and G. D'Elia. 2008. "Youth, Public Libraries, and the Internet, Part Four: Why Youth Do Not Use the Public Library." *Public Libraries* 47, no. 1: 80–85.

Alessio, A. J., and K. A. Patton. 2007. *A Year of Programs for Teens*. Chicago: American Library Association.

Anderson, S. B., ed. 2004. *Serving Older Teens*. Westport, CT: Libraries Unlimited.

Armaline, W. T. 2005. "Kids Need Structure": Negotiating Rules, Power, and Social Control in an Emergency Youth Shelter. *American Behavioral Scientist* 48, no. 8: 1124–1149.

Belton, B. 2010. *Radical Youth Work*. Lyme Regis, Dorset, England: Russell House.

Benson, P. L. 2010. *Parent, Teacher, Mentor, Friend: How Every Adult Can Change Kids' Lives*. Minneapolis: Search Institute Press.

Bernier, A. 2007. "Not Broken by Someone Else's Schedule: On Joy and Young Adult Information-Seeking." In *Youth Information-Seeking Behavior: Theories, Models, and Issues*, edited by M. K. Chelton and C. Cool, xiii–xxvii. Lanham, MD: Scarecrow Press.

———. 2011. "Representations of Youth in Local Media: Implications for Library Service." *Library and Information Science Research* 33, no. 2: 158–167.

Best, A., ed. 2007. *Representing Youth: Methodological Issues in Critical Youth Studies*. New York: New York University Press.

———. 2008. "Teen Driving as Public Drama: Statistics, Risk, and the Social Construction of Youth as a Public Problem." *Journal of Youth Studies* 11, no. 6: 651–669.

BLS (Bureau of Labor Statistics). 2011. "Employment and Unemployment Among Youth—Summer 2011." News release, August 24. http://www.bls.gov/news/.release/archives/youth_08242011.pdf.

Boyle, P. 2004. "How FDR's New Deal for Youth Got Decked." *Youth Today* 13, no. 1: 1–40.

Boyle, P., and L. Lutton. 2005. "Youth Development's Racial Challenge." *Youth Today* 14, no. 8: 1–31.

Brautigam, P. 2008. "Developmental Assets and Libraries: Helping to Construct the Successful Teen." *Voice of Youth Advocates* 31, no. 2: 124–125.

Braverman, M. 1979. *Youth, Society, and the Public Library*. Chicago: American Library Association.

Brehm-Heeger, P. 2008. *Serving Urban Teens*. Westport, CT: Libraries Unlimited.

Brown, J. H. 2001. "Youth, Drugs, and Resilience Education." *Journal of Drug Education* 31, no. 1: 83–122.

Chelton, M. K. 1997. "The 'Overdue Kid': A Face-to-Face Library Service Encounter as Ritual Interaction." *Library and Information Science Research* 19, no. 4: 387–399.

———. 2002. "The 'Problem Patron' Public Libraries Created." *The Reference Librarian* 36, no. 75–76: 23–32.

Cook, S. J., S. Parker, and C. E. Pettijohn. 2005. "The Public Library: An Early Teen's Perspective." *Public Libraries* 44, no. 3: 157–161.

Côté, J. E., and A. L. Allahar. 2006. *Critical Youth Studies: A Canadian Focus*. Toronto, ON: Pearson Prentice Hall.

Craver, K. W. 1988. "Social Trends in American Young Adult Library Service, 1960–1969." *Libraries and Culture* 23, no 1: 18–38.

Damon, W. 2004. "What Is Positive Youth Development?" *Annals of the American Academy of Political and Social Science* 591, no. 1: 13–24.

Dimitriadis, G. 2008. *Studying Urban Youth Culture*. New York: Peter Lang.

Dresang, E. T., M. Gross, and L. E. Holt. 2006. *Dynamic Youth Services through Outcome-Based Planning and Evaluation*. Chicago: American Library Association.

Edwards, M. A. 1994. *The Fair Garden and the Swarm of Beasts: The Library and the Young Adult*. Chicago: American Library Association.

Erikson, E. 1968. *Identity, Youth, and Crisis*. New York: Norton.

Farrugia, D. 2011. "Homeless Youth Managing Relationships: Reflexive Intersubjectivity and Inequality." *Young* 19, no. 4: 357–373.

Fass, P. S., and M. Grossberg, eds. 2012. *Reinventing Childhood after World War II*. Philadelphia: University of Pennsylvania Press.

Fisher, H. 2003. "A Teenage View of the Public Library: What Are the Students Saying?" *Australasian Public Libraries and Information Services* 16, no. 1: 4–16.

Flowers, S., and YALSA (Young Adult Library Services Association). 2011. *Young Adults Deserve the Best: YALSA's Competencies in Action*. Chicago: American Library Association.

Fraser, S. 2005. "Situating Empirical Research." Chapter 2 in *Doing Research with Children and Young People*, edited by S. Fraser et al. London: Sage.

Gilchrist, R., T. Jeffs, J. Spence, and J. Walker. 2009. *Essays in the History of Youth and Community Work: Discovering the Past*. Lyme Regis, Dorset, England: Russell House.

Gillespie, K. M. 2004. *Teen Volunteer Services in Libraries*. Lanham, MD: Scarecrow.

Ginwright, S., P. Noguera, and J. Cammarota, eds. 2006. *Beyond Resistance! Youth Activism and Community Change*. New York: Routledge.

Gorman, M., and T. Suellentrop. 2009. *Connecting Young Adults and Libraries: A How-To-Do-It Manual*. 4th ed. New York: Neal-Schuman.

Graham, P. J. 2005. *The End of Adolescence*. New York: Oxford University Press.

Hall, G. S. 1904. *Adolescence: Its Relation to Physiology, Anthropology, Sociology, Sex, Crime, Religion and Education*. New York: Appleton.

———. 1905. "What Children Do Read and What They Ought to Read." *Public Libraries* 10: 391–392. Cited in *Apostles of Culture: The Public Library and American Society, 1876–1920*. Madison, WI: University of Wisconsin Press, 1979.

———. 1908. "Children's Reading as a Factor in Their Education." *Library Journal* 33: 123–128. Cited in *Apostles of Culture: The Public Library and American Society, 1876–1920*. Madison, WI: University of Wisconsin Press, 1979.

Harvey, D. 2012. *Rebel Cities: From the Right to the City to the Urban Revolution*. London: Verso.

Heath, S. B. 1983. *Ways with Words: Language, Life, and Work in Communities and Classrooms*. Cambridge, England: Cambridge University Press.

———. 2001. "Three's Not a Crowd: Plans, Roles, and Focus in the Arts." *Educational Researcher* 30, no. 7: 10–17.

Heywood. C. M. 2001. *A History of Childhood: Children and Childhood in the West from Medieval to Modern Times.* Cambridge, UK: Polity Press.

Hill, L, and H Pain. 1988. "Young People and Public Libraries: Use, Attitudes, and Reading Habits: A Survey of 13–16 Year-Olds in Nottinghamshire." *International Review of Children's Literature and Librarianship* 3, no. 1: 26–40.

Holm, G., and H. Helve. 2005. Introduction to *Contemporary Youth Research: Local Expressions and Global Connections.* Burlington, VT: Ashgate.

Honeyman, S. 2005. *Elusive Childhood: Impossible Representations in Modern Fiction.* Columbus, OH: Ohio State University Press, 113–114.

Howard, V. 2011. "What Do Young Teens Think About the Public Library?" *Library Quarterly* 81, no. 3: 321–344.

Hulbert, A. 2003. *Raising America: Experts, Parents, and a Century of Advice about Children.* New York: Knopf.

IMLS (Institute of Museum and Library Services). 2009. *Libraries and Museums and 21st Century Skills.* Accessed April 2012. http://www.imls.gov/pdf/21stCenturySkills.pdf.

James, A., and A. Prout. 1997. *Constructing and Reconstructing Childhood: Contemporary Issues in the Sociological Study of Childhood.* Washington, DC: Falmer Press.

Jenkins, C.A. 2000. "The History of Youth Services Librarianship: A Review of the Research Literature." *Libraries and Culture* 35, no. 1: 103–140.

Jones, G. 2009. *Youth.* Cambridge, UK: Polity Press.

Jones, P., and YALSA (Young Adult Library Services Association). 2002. *New Directions for Library Service to Young Adults.* Chicago: American Library Association.

Kasinitz, P., J. H. Mollenkopf, M. C. Waters, and J. Holdaway. 2008. *Inheriting the City: The Children of Immigrants Come of Age.* Cambridge, MA: Harvard University Press.

Kelly, P. 2011. "An Untimely Future for Youth Studies." *Youth Studies Australia* 30, no 3: 47–53.

Klapper, M. R. 2007. *Small Strangers: The Experiences of Immigrant Children in America, 1880–1925.* Chicago: Ivan R. Dee.

Kozol, J. 2005. *The Shame of the Nation: The Restoration of Apartheid Schooling in America.* New York: Crown Publishing.

Leckie, G. J., L. M. Given, and J. E. Buschman, eds. 2010. *Critical Theory for Library and Information Science: Exploring the Social from Across the Disciplines.* Santa Barbara, CA: Libraries Unlimited.

Lerch, M. T., and J. Welch, J. 2004. *Serving Homeschooled Teens and Their Parents.* Westport, CT: Libraries Unlimited.

Lerner, R. M., J. B. Almerigi, C. Theokas, and J. V. Lerner. 2005. "Positive Youth Development: A View of the Issues." *Journal of Early Adolescence* 25, no. 1: 10–16.

Lesko, N. 2001. *Act Your Age! A Cultural Construction of Adolescence.* New York: Routledge.

Lukenbill, W. B. 2006. "Helping Youth at Risk: An Overview of Reformist Movements in American Public Library Services to Youth." *New Review of Children's Literature and Librarianship* 12, no. 2: 197–213.

Macleod, C. 2011. *"Adolescence," Pregnancy and Abortion: Constructing a Threat of Degeneration.* New York: Routledge.

Males, M. A. 1999. *Framing Youth: Ten Myths about the Next Generation.* Monroe, ME: Common Courage.

———. 2010. *Teenage Sex and Pregnancy: Modern Myths, Unsexy Realities.* Santa Barbara, CA: Praeger.

McCook, K. 2004. *Introduction to Public Librarianship.* New York: Neal-Schuman.

McGrath, R. V., ed. 2004. *Excellence in Library Services to Young Adults.* 4th ed. Chicago: American Library Association.

McLaughlin, M., M. Irby, and J. Langman. 1994. *Urban Sanctuaries: Neighborhood Organizations in the Lives and Futures of Inner-City Youth.* San Francisco: Jossey-Bass.

Mediavilla, C. 2001. *Creating the Full-Service Homework Center in Your Library.* Chicago: American Library Association.

Meyers, E. 2010. "Youth Development and Evaluation: Lessons from 'Public Libraries as Partners in Youth Development.'" Chapter 10 in *Urban Teens in the Library: Research and Practice,* edited by D. E. Agosto and S. Hughes-Hassell. Chicago: American Library Association.

Mintz, S. 2004. *Huck's Aft: A History of American Childhood.* Cambridge, MA: Belknap Press.

Mondowney, J. G. 2001. *Hold Them in Your Heart: Successful Strategies for Library Service to At-Risk Teens.* New York: Neal-Schuman.

Nichols, S. L., and T. L. Good. 2004. *America's Teenager—Myths and Realities: Media Images, Schooling, and the Social Costs of Careless Indifference.* Mahwah, NJ: Lawrence Erlbaum Associates.

Pateman, J., and J. Vincent. 2010. *Public Libraries and Social Justice.* Surrey, England: Ashgate.

Payne, M. A. 2012. "'All Gas and No Brakes!' Helpful Metaphor or Harmful Stereotype?" *Journal of Adolescent Research* 27, no. 1: 3–17.

Perkings, F. 1885. "Public Libraries and the Public with Special Reference to the San Francisco Free Public Library." *Library Journal* 10. Cited in *Apostles of Culture: The Public Library and American Society, 1876–1920.* Madison, WI: University of Wisconsin Press, 1979.

Pierce, J. B. 2007. *Sex, Brains and Video Games: The Librarian's Guide to Teens in the Twenty-First Century.* Chicago: ALA Editions.

Rockefeller, E., and R. Welch. 2012. "Seven Nasty Things Guys May Bring to the Library: Rude Language, Challenging Authority, Physical Violence." *Voice of Youth Advocates* 34, no. 6: 574–575.

Rothbauer, P. 2009. "Exploring the Placelessness of Reading among Older Teens in a Canadian Rural Municipality." *Library Quarterly* 79, no. 4: 465–483.

Rubin, R. E. 2004. *Foundations of Library and Information Science.* 2nd ed. New York: Neal-Schuman.

Sanchez-Eppler, K. 2005. *Dependent States: The Child's Part in Nineteenth-Century American Culture.* Chicago: University of Chicago Press.

Search Institute. 2007. "40 Developmental Assets for Adolescents." Accessed April 2012. http://www.search-institute.org/content/40-developmental-assets -adolescents-ages-12-18/.

Sercombe, H. 2010. "The Gift and the Trap: Working the "Teen Brain" into Our Concept of Youth." *Journal of Adolescent Research* 25, no. 1: 31–47.

Soland, B. 2000. *Becoming Modern: Young Women and the Reconstruction of Womanhood in the 1920s.* Princeton, NJ: Princeton University Press.

Spielberger, J., C. Horton, L. Michels, and R. Halpern. 2005. *New on the Shelf: Teens in the Library.* Chicago: Chapin Hall at the University of Chicago.

Sternheimer, K. 2006. *Kids These Days: Facts and Fictions about Today's Youth.* Lanham, MD: Rowman and Littlefield.

Taffel, R. 2001. *The Second Family: How Adolescent Power Is Challenging the American Family.* New York: St. Martin's Griffin.

Tuccillo, D. P. 2005. *Library Teen Advisory Groups.* Lanham, MD: Scarecrow.

Vaillancourt, R. J. 2000. *Bare Bones Young Adult Services: Tips for Public Library Generalists.* Chicago: American Library Association.

———. 2002. *Managing Young Adult Services: A Self-Help Manual.* New York: Neal-Schuman.

Walter, V. 1995. *Output Measures and More: Planning and Evaluating Public Library Services for Young Adults.* Chicago: American Library Association.

Walter, V. A., and E. Meyers. 2003. *Teen and Libraries: Getting It Right.* Chicago: American Library Association.

Waterman, A. S. 2005. "Reflections on Changes in Research on Adolescence from the Perspective of 15 Years of Editorial Experiences." *Journal of Adolescence* 28, no. 6: 681–685.

Weinberger, D., B. Elvevag, and J. N. Giedd. 2005. *The Adolescent Brain: A Work in Progress.* Washington, DC: National Campaign to Prevent Teen Pregnancy.

White, R., and J. Wyn. 2004. *Youth and Society: Exploring the Social Dynamics of Youth Experience.* Oxford, England: Oxford University Press.

PART I

What's in an Age?

1

Envisaging Young Adult Librarianship from a Teen-Centered Perspective

Denise E. Agosto

Young adult library services were founded on the idea of meeting teens' needs and interests, yet an adult-centered perspective dominates both the research and practice in this area. This chapter presents a small-scale content analysis of recent professional literature as proof of the prevailing adult-centered perspective. It is then suggested that a teen-centered perspective for public library research and practice is a better approach in terms of benefits to the target population. A truly teen-centered perspective means that we must change our thinking to (1) conceptualize adolescents as "teens" instead of "young adults"; (2) focus on teen development; (3) focus on teens as individuals first and foremost, and as members of their age and other demographic groups second; and (4) make teens—not information resources—the center of our work.

Library services for teens were founded on the idea of providing information resources to meet teens' needs and interests, yet since their inception much of the related research and practice has been conducted from an adult-centered perspective. For example, a great deal of the scholarly and professional writing relating to teens and libraries has taken the form of theoretical or thematic analyses of young adult literature, with the goal of enabling librarians to encourage youth to read the highest quality books.

Certainly, there is value in encouraging teens to read (or watch or listen to or play) high-quality materials, but this approach is an adult-centered approach, with adult scholars and adult librarians assuming that they know what kinds of resources teens need and want and that they can identify the best books (or websites or video games) to meet teens' needs and interests.

This concept of adults determining what is "best" for teens has also led to an emphasis on collecting and recommending award-winning materials, with adults serving as the driving forces behind award designations. There are literally hundreds of youth literature awards, many of which are for young adult (YA) materials (Hilbun and Claes, 2010). Even in the case of youth choice awards, librarians still typically select the short lists, and adults still determine what is best for teens.

"Teen-centered" refers to (1) direct youth participation in program and service design, (2) research that uses teens as research subjects or participants, and (3) library programs and services based on research that uses teens as research subjects or participants. In a more teen-centered approach to library research, teen behaviors, thoughts, and preferences would serve as the main sources for research data, as opposed to information resources serving as the most common data for analysis. In a more teen-centered approach to library practice, teens themselves would serve as the experts of their own thoughts, behaviors, needs, and preferences, and teens themselves would determine what resources and services are the best fits to their needs and interests. This is not to suggest that current library research and services for teens are exclusively adult-centered. There is an element of the teen-centered approach in both practice and research, with a growing number of public libraries setting up teen advisory boards and other mechanisms for enabling teens to provide input on program and service design (Tuccillo, 2010), and with a small but significant body of teen-centered library and information science (LIS) research being disseminated via academic outlets each year (see, for example, some of the entries on the Young Adult Library Services Association Research Committee [YALSA, 2009] research bibliography).

The concept of a teen-centered approach to public library services is not new. Librarians have been encouraging teens to participate in library services on a limited basis for decades. Tuccillo traced teen participation in both public and school libraries back as far as the early twentieth century, and she argued that librarians have placed importance on fostering teen participation ever since. What is new is the *level* of teen participation that is required to achieve the vision of a truly teen-centered approach.

The question that drives this chapter is, What should be the central focus of today's library research and services for teens? I will argue that the teen-centered focus is the best approach for creating the public library research and services that can best benefit teens. With this goal in mind, I will show how we must change our thinking in order to lead the field toward a truly teen-centered approach. My intention is not to suggest the elimination of the adult-centered approach but to nudge us further into teen-centered thinking, with the goal of making the teen-centered approach the guiding perspective of library research and services for teens. In this vision, the adult-centered approach does not disappear, but it does become less of a focus, falling beneath the broader teen-centered umbrella guiding library services and research for teens.

An Analysis of Representative Current Literature in Library Services for Teens

Before I can outline necessary changes for making the teen-centered vision a reality, I need to provide some proof of my contention that the adult-centered perspective is dominant. One way to determine the prevailing perspective of a field is to analyze its professional literature. Looking at the current LIS professional literature for teen librarians, many of the articles focus on analyzing information resources, programs, and services from the adult authors' perspectives, without gathering data or input directly from teens. As an example of how the adult-centered perspective dominates the current teen librarianship professional literature, I will analyze the most recent three complete years of articles published in *Young Adult Library Services*.

Young Adult Library Services is, of course, the member journal for YALSA. It is edited and run by active YALSA members, most of whom are teen librarians working in public libraries. Its writers' guidelines explain: "*Young Adult Library Services* is a vehicle for continuing education of librarians working with young adults (ages 12–18) that showcases current research and practice relating to teen services and spotlights significant activities and programs of the division" (YALSA, 2011). Thus, the target audience of the journal is teen librarians, and the intent is to provide them with the most relevant and significant research, lessons from practice, and YALSA news and activities. It is not intended to be a research journal read by academics, but a continuing education resource for practitioners. For many teen librarians, it is their main external connection to the field of youth librarianship after completing graduate school.

I used the *Library Literature and Information Science Full Text* database to gather all of the articles published in *Young Adult Library Services* for the period 2008–2010, a total of 220 articles. I hypothesized that authors of research articles were more likely to include direct input from teens in the form of data than authors of practice-based articles. To calculate the percentage of research-focused and practice-based articles within the dataset, I defined *research* very broadly as any article that (1) included analysis of some form of data, defining data in the broad sense of any text, such as a book or website; any information collected via a survey, interview, experiment, or other data-gathering means; any information collected systematically about a library program or service, such as attendance or circulation figures, or any use of a theoretical or conceptual framework; and (2) included at least one scholarly reference. All other articles, such as descriptions and announcements of information resource awards, program reports that described programs but did not analyze program success or impacts, editorials, and so on, were considered practice articles.

I used standard qualitative content analysis techniques to analyze the main topics of the articles in the dataset, coding each article for one main topic, iteratively collapsing the emerging list of topics into broader categories until there were eight distinct topic categories for the practice-based articles and five topic categories for the research articles. In some cases, an article could have fit into two or more categories. I chose just one main category per article to simplify analysis and reporting. I used simple descriptive statistics to calculate the quantitative findings.

Practice-Based and Research-Based Articles

Table 1.1 shows the percentages of practice and research articles in the dataset. Of the 220 articles published during the three-year period, 21 (9.5 percent) could be considered research using the very broad definition of *research* on page 36. The remaining 90.5 percent were practice-based articles. As a journal aimed at practitioners and intended partly as a vehicle for dissemination of professional association news, it makes sense that the majority of the articles were nonresearch pieces. However, this analysis indicated that teen librarians who keep up with the field only through professional journals such as this one were exposed to only a small body of the relevant research, just five to ten items per year for this particular journal during the period of analysis.

TABLE 1.1

Practice/Research Breakdown of Articles Published in *Young Adult Library Services*, 2008–2010

Category	2008	2009	2010	Total
Practice (nonresearch)	64 (91.4%**)	53 (84.1%**)	82 (94.3%**)	199 (90.5%)
Research	6 (8.6%**)	10 (15.9%**)	5 (5.7%**)	21 (9.5%)
TOTAL	70 (100%**)	63 (100%**)	87 (100%**)	220 (100%)

**Percent of total articles published for that year.*

Main Topics of Articles

Data analysis of the practice articles yielded eight main topics, as shown in Table 1.2. The most frequent main topic was "teen book/resource awards," accounting for 43 of the 199 total practice articles, or 21.6 percent. Articles falling into this category were announcements of award winners, discussions (as opposed to scholarly analyses, which were considered research) of award-winning books and other information resources, texts of teen resource award acceptance speeches, and descriptions of teen information resource awards.

TABLE 1.2

Categories of Main Topics for Practice Articles Published in *Young Adult Library Services*, 2008–2010

Topic	2008	2009	2010	Total
Teen book/resource awards	18 (28.1%)	14 (26.4%)	11 (13.4%)	43 (21.6%)
Other awards/grants	3 (4.7%)	4 (7.5%)	3 (3.7%)	10 (5.0%)
Programs (e.g., book clubs) and services (e.g., reference)	9 (14.1%)	9 (17.0%)	15 (18.3%)	33 (16.6%)
Editorials/columns/ professional advice	10 (15.6%)	9 (17.0%)	8 (9.8%)	27 (13.6%)
Books and other resources for teens	7 (10.9%)	4 (7.5%)	7 (8.5%)	18 (9.0%)
Professional books/other professional resources	10 (15.6%)	2 (3.8%)	15 (18.3%)	27 (13.6%)
Conferences and professional associations	3 (4.7%)	5 (9.4%)	18 (22.0%)	26 (13.1%)
Administration/budgeting/ advocacy/marketing/ collaboration	4 (6.2%)	6 (11.3%)	5 (6.1%)	15 (7.5%)
TOTAL	**65 (100%*)**	**53 (100%*)**	**82 (100%*)**	**199 (100%)**

*Column does not add up to 100% due to rounding.

An additional 18 (9.0 percent) practice articles discussed "books and other resources for teens," such as bibliographic essays of recommended teen books about a particular topic or representing a particular genre. Combining the information resource awards category with the other information resources category, a total of 61 (30.7 percent) of the practice articles were discussions relating to teen information resources, most commonly fiction books. This means that nearly one-third of the practice articles focused on teen resources.

The other most common practice topics included "programs and services" (33 articles, or 16.6 percent), "editorials/columns/professional advice" (27 articles, or 13.6 percent), "professional books/other professional resources" (27 articles, or 13.6 percent), and "conferences and professional associations" (26 articles, or 13.1 percent).

Table 1.3 shows the five categories of main topics found in the research articles. Again, articles relating to teen books and other information resources accounted for the largest combined category. Together, "analyses of books and other resources for teens" (nine articles, or 42.9 percent) plus "analyses of teen book/resource awards" (two articles, or 9.5 percent) total 11 articles, or 54.4 percent of the research articles. This means that more than half of the research articles were analyses of information resources for teens. "Analyses of programs and services" was the only other research category representing more than 10 percent of the research articles.

TABLE 1.3

Categories of Main Topics for Research Articles Published in *Young Adult Library Services*, 2008–2010

Topic	2008	2009	2010	Total
Analyses of teen book/ resource awards	1 (16.7%)	0 (0.0%)	1 (20.0%)	2 (9.5%)
Analyses of programs (e.g., book clubs) and services (e.g., reference)	2 (33.3%)	1 (10.0%)	0 (0.0%)	3 (14.3%)
Analyses of books and other resources for teens	2 (33.3%)	6 (60.0%)	1 (20.0%)	9 (42.9%)
Analyses of professional books/other professional resources	0 (0.0%)	1 (10.0%)	(0.0%)	1 (4.8%)
Analyses of teen behaviors/ health/development	1 (16.7%)	2 (20.0%)	3 (60.0%)	6 (28.6%)
TOTAL	**6 (100%)**	**10 (100%*)**	**5 (100%*)**	**21 (100%*)**

Column does not add up to 100% due to rounding.

Teen Input Represented in Articles

Table 1.4 shows the number and percentage of practice and research articles that included some form of direct input from teens. I defined "input" as *any* mention of teens' words, thoughts, or behaviors, such as quotes from verbal conversations or e-mails, anecdotal tales of direct observation of teen behaviors, or more formal data collected via surveys, interviews, and so on. Of the 199 practice-based articles, just four (2.0 percent) included teen input. Of the 21 research articles, just four (19.0 percent) included any data or input from teens. The hypothesis that a greater percentage of research articles than practice articles would include direct input from teens was correct, but the numbers were still very low overall. Just eight (3.6 percent) of the 220 articles in the entire dataset included any input whatsoever from teens, and again the definition of teen participation was very liberal.

TABLE 1.4

Articles Including Teen Input Published in *Young Adult Library Services*, 2008–2010

Category	Number	Percent
Practice articles with teen input	4	2.0% (of 199 practice articles)
Research articles with teen input	4	19.0% (of 21 research articles)
TOTAL ARTICLES WITH TEEN INPUT	**8**	**3.6% (of 220 total articles)**

Analysis of the Teen-Centered Perspective in Articles

The goal of this analysis was to examine whether a youth-centered or adult-centered perspective dominated in the recent teen librarianship professional literature, based on content analysis of one representative journal. The analysis showed that the most common article topic in *Young Adult Library Services* between 2008 and 2010 was a discussion or analysis of teen information resources, most often books. Only a small percentage of practice or research articles included any direct input from teens, even casual mention of one single e-mail or conversation excerpt. Again, of the 220 total articles published during this three-year period, just eight articles (3.6 percent) included any direct input from teens in the form of quotes, survey responses, interviews, e-mail communications, casual observational data, conversations, anecdotes, and so on. The remainder of the articles (96.4 percent) were written from the adult perspective, such as bibliographic essays or reports of library programs presenting the authors' assessments of literary quality or program success. Some of these authors might have taken into account teens' opinions and viewpoints, but if so it was not discussed and readers would be unable to determine any teen input.

Thus, based on this small-scale analysis, it seems that little teen-centered work is making its way into the journal. For many teen librarians, professional journals such as this one are their main source of information about developments in the field of teen librarianship. To move to a more teen-centered approach across the field as a whole, one important step is increasing teen input in the professional writing.

I want to stress here that my purpose is *not* to criticize this journal. It reflects the prevailing perspective of its field and can only publish youth-centered work if potential authors—mainly librarians and library school faculty—write and submit youth-centered work. My point is that based on analysis of the items published in the field's member journal, very few librarians, university faculty, and others are submitting work based on teen input or research data collected from teens. Change needs to take place within the field before the professional literature can reflect it. I should note here that YALSA has recently begun a new journal devoted to publishing research, *Journal of Research on Libraries and Young Adults*. It remains to be seen the extent to which the journal will publish a higher percentage of teen-centered research. Regardless, *Young Adult Library Services* stands as a good example of the kinds of research and professional writing that teen librarians and teen LIS researchers publish in the professional literature, and this body of work has been shown to be overwhelmingly adult-centered.

Changing Our Thinking to a Teen-Centered Perspective

Focus on "Teens," Not "Young Adults"

The purpose of this book is to start a conversation about how students, practitioners, and scholars should conceptualize young adults, as well as to shape the future of library services for this population. The analysis presented above leads me to conclude that we must change our thinking to make teens the central focus of our practice and research. To move toward a truly teen-centered approach, we need to include teens in the conversation, to include teens as much as possible in the process of designing and delivering teen library programs and services, and to make teens themselves our most frequent sources of research data.

Related to the question of what should be the central focus of today's library research and services for teens is what we should we call this population. The answer to that question comes easily for me: *teens*. A truly teen-centered approach to library research and services means replacing the term *young adult* with a term that teens understand and appreciate. We should call this population *teens* because this is a term that they understand and use. For our work to be truly user-centered, we must use, as much as possible, the language that our population identifies with and uses to describe itself.

I learned the importance of using language that teens can understand and appreciate as I have learned virtually every important lesson about teens—from a teen. Years ago I was the head of the children's and young adult departments of a medium-sized public library. A few weeks before I began my new job, the library where I worked had created a new young adult fiction section, a long wall lined with YA paperbacks perched on painted metal shelves. A neon sign above the shelves read, "Young Adult Paperbacks." One day not long after I had begun working I noticed a teenage girl staring at the sign. "What do you think of this new section?" I asked her.

She answered my question with a question: "Who are these books for? I might read some of these books, but I can't figure out who they're for."

"They're for people your age," I explained.

"Then I think you should do this," she said, removing her coat and holding it up to the sign to cover up the words "Young Adult." Now the sign read simply "Paperbacks." "It's confusing. We're not adults yet, you know," she added, shaking her head as she walked away empty-handed.

She was right, of course. *Young adult* is a term known only to librarians (and publishers) to mean "adolescents." As Aronson (2002: 82) explained: "The term YA is an odd one; it refers to no clear developmental age group. If anything, it seems to apply to people in their 20's who are just leaving college, beginning careers, and starting families."

Cart (2010: 3) pointed out, "The amorphous part [of the term *young adult literature*] is the target audience for the literature: the young adults themselves. For it's anybody's guess who—or what—they are!" He cited YALSA's "Two Hundred Years of Young Adult Library Services History" bibliography (Bernier et al., 2010), which traced the use of the term in the professional library literature back as far as 1944.

In my many years of research with teens I have found them to voice consistent objections to the term. So why then do librarians, library researchers, and publishers use this term to refer to teens and sometimes to preteens? Pulliam (2010: 2) suggested that publishers adopted the term *young adult* in the 1960s since "the term 'adolescent' was perceived by teens as condescending and necessarily denoting immaturity." The term had to have been in use in the library field earlier, as the American Library Association's (ALA) Young Adult Services Division began in 1957 (Cart, 2010). Regardless of the specific date it entered usage in library research and practice, the intent behind adopting the term seems to have been to give teens respect as full-fledged human beings by calling them adults who just happen to be young. But teens *are* full-fledged human beings, just as babies, children, adults, and senior citizens are all full-fledged human beings, regardless of their ages. We don't have to call teens adults to lend them human legitimacy.

I choose to use the terms *teens* and *teenagers* because they are widely used and understood by both teens and adults. The teens I conduct research with also often call themselves "kids." I do use the term *kids* when speaking with teens, but I don't use the term in academic and professional writing because it is not as specific as teens or teenagers.

The point here is not the specific term that we use. It's not the actual words that matter; it's the thinking behind the use of the words that matters. In a few years or decades, the terms *teens* and *teenagers* might fall out of fashion with the target population, and they might start calling themselves something else. If that happens, I hope I'll be astute enough to pick up on the change and to adopt the new term. If we want to serve teens' best interests, we need to place them at the center of our work and to communicate with them as partners in designing and delivering library research and services. We need to use language that they understand, and language that other adults outside of the field of librarianship understand. We must think of teens as the experts of their thoughts, behaviors, and lives, and we must use their language as much as possible to give authentic voice to this population.

Making teens the central focus in our work also means broadcasting our lessons and messages about what we have learned from teens to a wider audience than just other librarians and LIS researchers. We need to broaden the target audience for our academic and professional writing and presenting to other adults outside of the library field—to adults with influence over teens' lives and livelihoods, such as parents, guardians, teachers, informal educators (such as museum professionals and religious group leaders), government officials, program funders, and so on. We can teach these other adults about the importance of listening to teens and about the importance of respecting teen cultures.

Focus on Teen Development

Since most developmental theories and concepts were developed based on data collected from teens as research subjects, they offer us a teen-centered basis for designing library research and services by enabling us to mold our work in ways likely to optimize developmental benefits for teens. I have argued for a number of years that public and school library services can, and should, promote teens' healthy development. Based on my research with Sandra Hughes-Hassell, I have argued that public and school libraries can and should promote teen development in seven areas: the social self, the emotional self, the reflective self, the physical self, the creative self, the cognitive self, and the sexual self (Agosto and Hughes-Hassell, 2006a). I have further argued that we need to broaden our view of the developmental benefits of public library services beyond the traditional focus on homework and leisure reading to support a much fuller range of developmental areas (Agosto, 2007, 2010).

Moving from the research literature to the professional literature, longtime teen services librarian Tuccillo (2010: 14) listed a number of benefits of greater teen participation in program and service design and delivery, including promoting positive youth development at the community level:

> *Some essential rationales for offering youth participation opportunities include the fact that they provide a catalyst for teenagers to enter adulthood as readers, learners, and library supporters; they promote reading and the library by teen participants to their adolescent peers, who in turn will hopefully also partake in what the library has to offer; they proliferate library usage by helping teens to eventually pass on their love of books and libraries to their offspring; they uphold the concept of positive youth development in our communities; and they affirm the prospect of librarianship as a career option for young people.*

These are important benefits to teens, but they are not the only benefits. We need to think of potential benefits on a much broader scale than just turning teens into more avid readers, library users, and possibly future librarians. We need to talk to teens about their goals for using library resources and services and make these our goals as well. As seen in this quote, in teen library practice the philosophy behind encouraging teen participation has been grounded in the belief that library use is inherently good, and that increased library use is the goal in itself. We need to move away from this library-centered focus to the teen-centered focus in which the goals of library services are not increased use of library services and resources but increased social, intellectual, creative, and entertainment opportunities, especially for teens with economic, educational, physical, social, cognitive, and other disadvantages.

As my past work has shown, teens turn to public libraries for much more than just information-related purposes. Public libraries commonly play three roles in teens' lives: (1) the library as information gateway, (2) the library as social interaction/entertainment space, and (3) the library as beneficial physical environment (Agosto, 2007, 2010). Moving beyond just focusing on the library as information provider to focusing on these three categories of benefits enables us to serve a much wider range of needs.

Still, the question of whether theories and concepts of youth development should drive teen library research and practice cannot be answered by simply saying "yes." Developmental theories must be viewed as general guidelines—general patterns of growth and development. They should not be viewed as exact rules outlining all teens' behaviors, nor should they be seen as immutable laws for planning library programs and services.

We must remember that a theory is a lens for looking at something, be it library services, human behaviors, or anything else. In the social sciences, theory is rarely an absolute law or an absolute truth. With respect to teens and developmental theories and concepts, we must always remember that humans are first and foremost individuals and secondly products of their environments. Teens live and grow in many environments, including cultural, socioeconomic, age-related, racial, ethnic, linguistic, and other contexts. These environments, as well as teens' individual personalities, physicalities, intellects, and life experiences, make them individuals—individuals who in some cases might not represent general developmental patterns. As helpful as developmental theories and concepts can be, they can be dangerously misleading if we accept them to the point of forgetting about basic human differences (as in the digital native discourse described below).

Thinking of developmental theories as rough guidelines, not immutable rules, means remembering that each teen, each person, is unique. Teens' needs and interests vary radically from one person to the next, and as a result, each library needs to turn to its own teen population to discover its unique needs and interests as the basis for designing library services.

As researchers, librarians, and students we stand outside as concerned—deeply concerned—adult observers, but we adults are merely interpreters of teens' thoughts, behaviors, preferences, and needs, as well as designers and promoters of the research and services that can identify and fulfill them. This means that we must constantly talk to teens via formal and informal avenues to follow changes in how they think, behave, and interact—not how adults *expect* them to think, behave, and interact.

Indeed, Kunzel and Hardesty (2006: 5) explained that in the public library teen-centered approach to practice, program and service design should begin with asking teens for ideas:

Teen-centered means that the first point of reference for every decision and plan and action is teens' longings and desires and interests, stated and unstated. Teen-centered means going to the source—asking teens questions and listening—*and then putting the answers to work.*

Now a cautionary note: We stand as adult outsiders looking into the teen world, but as librarians and researchers who work with teens, we must be careful not to create an "us versus them" narrative, a "teens are different than we are" attitude. Sure, teens are members of distinct youth cultures, but teens are people first and youth second. Perhaps nowhere is this dangerous "us versus them" narrative more prevalent than in the digital natives (Prensky, 2001) discourse. This discourse is not the sole purview of the library field, but it has taken a strong hold in library research and practice (see Biladeau, 2009; Gilmore-See, 2007; Harris, 2009; Ojala, 2008). Yes, those with more experience online tend to be more advanced, more comfortable technology users. However, these advanced digital skills are largely results of the effects not of *age* but of the *information age*. We must be careful to challenge the widely accepted digital natives view of all teens as technology experts and enthusiasts because it simply doesn't hold true for all teens (Agosto and Abbas, 2010). Similarly, media portrayals often lump teens into one big group—often one big troublesome group (Bernier, 2011). These portrayals are dangerous stereotypes that we must challenge while promoting awareness that teens are individuals first and members of their age group second.

Focus on Teens over Information Resources

The monolithic digital natives view of all teens as technology enthusiasts and digital whizzes is largely a resource-centered view: it defines teens by the resources that they use. In the field of library services much of the scholarly and professional writing has taken a similar resource-centered view, most commonly a YA literature-centered view. In the professional literature analysis presented at the beginning of this chapter, for example, by far the most common article topic was teen information resources, particularly books. Certainly it is legitimate and important for LIS students and librarians to be familiar with the wide range of books and other information resources available to today's teens, but it's not enough as a human-centered field for us to focus on literary quality, or on analyzing information resources to identify the "best" ones. Focusing on teens and their information needs first, and on the kinds of resources that can fulfill those needs second, arms librarians, LIS students, and researchers with longer-lasting knowledge that they can apply for decades to come as they work with teens.

From an educational standpoint, LIS educators should focus first on teaching students about teen information needs and behaviors. After students understand the kinds of needs that information resources can fulfill for teens, we can then use specific information resources (everything from print novels to social network sites to online newspapers to video games) to show how these resources can fulfill teens' needs. We need to remember that books and other information resources are not just creative works to be appreciated for their literary and artistic qualities, but tools for meeting teens' varying needs and interests. Popular titles will come and go, but teens' needs and interests are more static. Thinking about information resources from the teen-centered perspective equips us to better serve teens and to serve them for the longer term.

Conclusion

Going back to the question of what should be the central focus of today's library research and services for teens, I want to repeat the major themes that I have discussed in this chapter. First, moving toward a truly teen-centered perspective means respecting teens as the experts of their own thoughts, behaviors, preferences, and needs. This means including teens as research participants, as partners in library services design, and basing teen library services on research that gathers data directly from teens. Second, developmental concepts and theories continue to be useful for providing general lenses and explanations of teen behaviors, but they must be seen as general guidelines within which there is wide individual variance. Teens are individuals first and members of their age groups second. We must recognize, respect, and honor individual differences and avoid stereotypes. Third, we need to approach our study of information resources for teens not with the goal of determining the "best" resources from a literary and artistic standpoint but with the goal of learning how resources can best fulfill teens' needs and interests.

Based on the small-scale analysis discussed above, it seems the adult-centered perspective dominates the current professional writing, as just 3.6 percent of the articles analyzed included any type of teen input, from direct teen input in the form of casual verbal feedback on library programs and services to service design based on teen-centered research. Placing teens more squarely at the center of research and practice can be fairly simple, such as incorporating teen input into analyses of YA literature via focus groups, online literature circles, and other conversations with teens, or designing library programs based on research into teens' information needs, uses, and behaviors. Of course, more teen-centered research is needed in the first place to enable librarians to build programs around it, and teen services librarians need more exposure to the teen-centered research that is being conducted. This is one way that professional journal editors can help to move the field more toward the teen-centered perspective—by publishing brief reports and discussions of the practical applications of this research.

Again, it is important to point out the limitations of the small-scale study presented in this chapter. I examined only one of several journals that publish professional literature relating to library services for teens. Much of this work is also disseminated via books, blogs, and other venues, none of which were included in the analysis. Further, the analysis covered just three years and therefore did not afford historical analysis or examination of trends over time. Future investigations could examine a wider range of publication venues and longer time periods. Even more useful would be the examination of library school curricula to determine the extent to which the teen-centered approach is presented in course topics and readings. The examination could consider questions such as the following:

- To what extent do courses across institutions address library services and research from a teen-centered focus?
- To what extent do they present a literature-centered approach?
- How many institutions offer courses in teen information needs and behaviors? In youth development?

An understanding of prevailing educational approaches could lead to additional suggestions for moving the field more toward the teen-centered approach advocated throughout this chapter.

The good news is that, based on the most recent version of "YALSA's Competencies for Librarians Serving Youth," YALSA (2010) at least is advocating a more teen-centered focus. Six of the seven areas of competencies mention at least briefly the importance of including teens in designing library services. As Flowers (2011: 14) interpreted the competencies: "Youth participation in library decision-making is important as a means of achieving more responsive and effective library and information services for this age group." If we keep in mind the important underlying concepts of individuality, teens as the experts of teen cultures and needs, and an emphasis on teens over information resources as the central focus of the field, we can follow this important movement toward more teen-centered library services for teens and take fuller advantage of our potential for improving teens' lives.

References

Agosto, Denise E. 2007. "Why Do Teens Use Libraries? Results of a Public Library Use Survey." *Public Libraries* 46, no. 3: 55–62.

———. 2010. "Urban Teens and Their Use of Public Libraries." In *Urban Teens in the Library: Research and Practice,* edited by Denise E. Agosto and Sandra Hughes-Hassell, 83–100. Chicago: American Library Association.

Agosto, Denise E., and June Abbas. 2010. "High School Seniors' Social Network and Other ICT Preferences and Concerns." In *Proceedings of the 2010 American Society for Information Science and Technology Annual Meeting (ASIST),* in Pittsburgh, PA, October 22–27, 2010. https://www.asis.org/asist2010/proceedings/proceedings/ASIST_AM10/submissions/25_Final_Submission.pdf.

Agosto, Denise E., and Sandra Hughes-Hassell. 2006a. "Toward a Model of the Everyday Life Information Needs of Urban Teenagers: Part 1, Theoretical Model." *Journal of the American Society for Information Science and Technology* 57, no. 10: 1394–1403.

———. 2006b. "Toward a Model of the Everyday Life Information Needs of Urban Teenagers: Part 2, Empirical Model." *Journal of the American Society for Information Science and Technology* 57, no. 11: 1418–1426.

———. 2010. "Revamping Library Services to Meet Urban Teens' Everyday Life Information Needs and Preferences." In *Urban Teens in the Library: Research and Practice,* edited by Denise E. Agosto and Sandra Hughes-Hassell, 23–40. Chicago: American Library Association.

Aronson, Marc. 2002. "Coming of Age: One Editor's View of How Young Adult Publishing Developed in America." *Publishers Weekly* 249, no. 6: 82–86.

Bernier, Anthony. 2011. "Representations of Youth in Local Media: Implications for Library Service." *Library and Information Science Research* 33, no. 2: 158–167.

Bernier, Anthony, Mary K. Chelton, Christine A. Jenkins, and Jennifer Burek Pierce. 2010. "Two Hundred Years of Young Adult Library Services History." *VOYA.* http://www.voya.com/2010/03/30/chronology/.

Biladeau, Shirley. 2009. "Technology and Diversity: Perceptions of Idaho's 'Digital Natives.'" *Teacher Librarian* 36, no. 3: 20–21.

Cart, Michael. 2010. *Young Adult Literature: From Romance to Realism.* Chicago: American Library Association.

Flowers, Sarah. 2011. "Leadership and Professionalism: Competencies for Serving Youth." *Young Adult Library Services* 9, no. 2: 10–15.

Gilmore-See, Janice. 2007. "Kids 2.0." *School Library Media Activities* 24, no. 3: 55–58.

Harris, Christopher. 2009. "Excuse Me. Do You Speak Digital?" (Interview with J. Palfrey). *School Library Journal* 55, no. 9: 30–33.

Hilbun, Janet W., and Jane Claes. 2010. *Coast to Coast: Exploring State Book Awards.* Westport, CT: Libraries Unlimited.

Kunzel, Bonnie, and Constance Hardesty. 2006. *The Teen-Centered Book Club: Readers into Leaders.* Westport, CT: Libraries Unlimited.

Ojala, Marydee. 2008. "Social Media, Information Seeking, and Generational Differences." *Online* 32, no. 2: 5.

Prensky, Marc. 2001. "Digital Natives, Digital Immigrants." *On the Horizon* 9, no. 5: 1–5.

Pulliam, June. 2010. "Monstrous Bodies: Femininity and Agency in Young Adult Horror Fiction." Unpublished doctoral dissertation, Louisiana State University, Baton Rouge, LA.

Tuccillo, Diane P. 2010. *Teen-Centered Library Service: Putting Youth Participation into Practice.* Santa Barbara, CA: Libraries Unlimited.

YALSA (Young Adult Library Services Association). 2009. "Current Research Related to Young Adult Services, 2006–2009: A Supplement Compiled by the YALSA Research Committee." http://www.ala.org/yalsa/sites/ala.org.yalsa/files/content/guidelines/research/09researchbibliography_rev.pdf.

———. 2010. "YALSA's Competencies for Librarians Serving Youth: Young Adults Deserve the Best." http://www.ala.org/yalsa/guidelines/yacompetencies2010/.

———. 2011. "Young Adult Library Services Author Guidelines." http://www.ala.org/yalsa/products&publications/yalsapubs/yals/authorguidelines/.

2

Dialogism, Development, and Destination

Young Adults in Contemporary Culture

Karen Coats

Young adults fashion their identities from the images and discourses that culture makes available to them. This chapter closely examines the literature written for young adults and argues that such literature can serve as a means to interpret how young adults imagine themselves. In addition, this chapter argues that library professionals should stay abreast of current brain research, which demonstrates that young adults' brain development drives them to process information differently from children or adults. Furthermore, by applying this theoretical knowledge to programming, librarians can encourage healthy experimentation and support diversity among young adults.

In the quest of library science professionals to imagine or perhaps reimagine today's young adults, we could do much worse than looking closely at the literature written for the age group. Although in some ways it is certainly an imperfect mirror, teen literature must speak to its audience with both realistic depictions and metaphors that resonate with their experience of themselves; hence, if a book, film, TV series, or song has uptake with young adults, we can assume that it speaks to them and thus tells us something about who they imagine themselves to be. But perhaps more importantly, the way we live now, that is, how we negotiate our identities in postmodern culture as both adults and teens, is through dynamic interaction with visual and textual models and the discourses they produce, enable, sustain, and challenge.

This is nothing new, of course. As nineteenth-century writer Israel Zangwill put it: "There is a drop of ink in the blood of the most natural of us; we are all hybrids, crossed with literature, and Shakespeare is as much the author of our being as either of our parents" (Zangwill, 1896: 297). Perhaps not Shakespeare these days, but certainly the products of popular culture are key players in the feedback loop that teens use to fashion their identities. I use the term *fashion* advisedly here because, forward thinkers from past centuries like Zangwill aside, there has been a significant shift in the way academics think about the self, at least in theory, that is pertinent to the central concern of this volume: How should library and information science (LIS) imagine today's young adults? In the contemporary academy, we no longer think of identity as something that emerges organically from inborn potentialities that develop progressively in fairly standard and predictable ways unless something happens to inhibit that development. Instead based on current research on brain development, I suggest that we conceive of identity as the outcome of a series of identifications and interactions with culture that produce multiple trajectories toward multiple endpoints; that is, rather than growing toward some authentic, core self that is somehow innate, we self-consciously fashion our identities from the images and discourses that culture makes available to us. This interaction is dialogic and dynamic, which is to say that we work out our identities not once and for all but in a continual process of testing, reflection, and social feedback with the goal of achieving a sense of inner coherence and external recognition.

Teenagers are actively engaged in the project of self-fashioning; indeed, it is during the teen years that they are most heavily invested in seeking out possibilities for identification in order to craft an identity that has uptake in contemporary life. In this essay, then, I will explore some of the theoretical shifts that make a difference in the way scholars construct an idea of who contemporary teens are and what their central existential project consists of, using examples and trends in young adult literature to illustrate and ground the theory. It is my contention that understanding the theoretical contexts of how identity is shaped can offer some practical insights into what the LIS vision of today's teens can and perhaps should look like so that we might serve them better by encouraging healthy experimentation and supporting diversity.

Ideological Contexts for Imagining Teens

Most scholars who study youth culture agree that adolescence is a relatively recent category, although they disagree on when it actually began or what factors enabled it to come into existence. In *From Romance to Realism: 50 Years of Growth and Change in Young Adult Literature*, Michael Cart (1996) outlines the debate, asserting that the category of young adult emerged as part of American culture. He notes that some scholars like Alleen Pace Nilsen and Kenneth L. Donelson (1993) believe that the category of adolescence bloomed following and as a result of the American Civil War. Betty Carter (1994: 9), however, argues that the demand for specialized job training that required prolonged education set the stage for the "birth of adolescence." Nilsen and Donelson's claim to an earlier recognition of this special stage of life is bolstered by the 1904 appearance of G. Stanley Hall's two-volume work, *Adolescence: Its Psychology*; after all, the psychological mapping of a specific life stage requires, at least to some degree, the prior discovery or acknowledgment of the territory to be mapped. The mapping of this particular territory could be seen as traversing a wasteland of sorts, a journey across a more or less vacant expanse between childhood and adulthood where nothing very important or salutary happens. Indeed, Sleeping Beauty sleeps through her passage and Snow White learns housekeeping, but as Shakespeare notes in *A Winter's Tale*, "I would there were no age between ten and three-and-twenty, or that youth would sleep out the rest; for there is nothing in the between but getting wenches with child, wronging the ancientry, stealing, fighting" (III.iii). Considering the neglect or negative impressions of this time period, an attentive, objective treatment is a significant boon. But like all psychological maps, Hall's work unfortunately reflected his own prejudices (which were many) and was to a large degree performative; that is, in some measure it created what it purported to describe, becoming a paratext that set expectations through which society came to view the period between puberty and adulthood. His commitment to a *Sturm und Drang* view of adolescence that highlighted rebellion and conflict with parents, risky behaviors, and mood swings (incidentally consonant with that of Shakespeare's shepherd) has persisted and in many ways harmed our view of the creative potential of adolescents as well as the importance of the adolescent years for development toward capacious and generative adulthood. (Hall's work and its effects on LIS are explored in more detail in several other chapters in this volume.)

By far the most evocative pronouncement of the advent of adolescence that Cart notes, however, comes from Natalie Babbitt (1978: 140): "The category teenager itself is a new one, of course. It made its first appearance during the Second World War and was created partly by parents, partly by manufacturers, and partly by Frank Sinatra." Parsing this remark yields interesting results. The manufacturing part accords with Carter's comments that post–World War II industry required a more specialized and well-trained workforce, necessitating prolonged education, particularly in math and science, in order to meet demand for and development of enhanced technologies. But the role of parents in creating adolescence is more complex. During the wars, many women had seen their fathers, lovers, and brothers taken away from the home, only to return broken and traumatized, while they stayed home and attempted to do their part by conserving and going without luxuries in their domestic life. The response of those who were able to do so was to create homes that were havens for these wounded warriors as well as protect their own sons and daughters from the awareness that the world could be that awful and tenuous. The Donna Reed/Harriet Nelson stereotype was at least in part an attempt to provide for a softer transition between childhood and adulthood, a space of care and attention that resolutely shut out the horrors of the parents' own adolescent experience of tragedy, loss, deprivation, and uncertainty. The appeal of these idealized media images was undeniable, and even though the ideal was problematic on its face as well as simply out of reach for many Americans, it became a fetishized ideological model that set the terms of desire for many viewers. For some, mostly middle-class white families, the ability to create such tranquil domestic spaces was enabled by the postwar economic boom that afforded these children the luxury of not having to contribute to the family's income, to be pampered consumers for longer periods of time rather than taking on the mantle of financial responsibility that inaugurates adulthood. According to Swiss-Israeli psychologist Carlo Strenger (2004), this well-meaning parenting style understandably resulted in widespread narcissism on the part of these well-cared-for children who were the center of their parent's attention, a phenomenon also noted by historian and social critic Christopher Lasch (1979). Lasch charted the progression of character types that have dominated American capitalist culture from the rugged, boot-strapping individualist of the prewar period through the company man of the world war era to the pathological narcissist of the boomer generation. Today, the children and grandchildren of boomers feel the effects of having been reared by narcissists in ways that are important to consider as we imagine what today's teens are like and what they value. On the one hand, narcissistic parenting may result in emotional and/or physical neglect as parents pursue their own concerns, but on the other hand, it may lead to the kind of hovering that we have come to call "helicopter" or "Velcro" parenting, where parents are overly invested in their children's success as an extension of their own. The consequences of the former form of narcissistic parenting for LIS youth services means that teens will bring unmet emotional needs to the library—needs for personalized attention and engaged relational pedagogy to discover the kinds of books and materials that attend to their specific coping styles. However, neglectful parenting can also result in the need for youth service professionals to establish clearly defined boundaries, as these teens in taking their parents as unconscious models may be looking for relationships that transcend the professional in order to meet their own narcissistic needs for connection.

The latter model of narcissistic parenting, where parents project their successes and failures onto their teens, results in a different set of circumstances. Strenger (2004) points out the tremendous pressure on today's youth to be fabulous; ordinary lives and ordinary bodies are unacceptable as parents consciously and unconsciously communicate their narcissistic needs for their children to be wildly successful, viewing that success as a reflection of their parenting skills. These ramped-up expectations are conveyed in the increasingly common idiom that is heard everywhere these days: "This is going to be the *best* day/party/prom/school year/game *ever!*" Obviously, teens will respond to such pressures in dynamic and unpredictable ways.

For instance, on the one hand all some teens may want from a library is a place to escape the pressure cooker; designated places of enforced peace and quiet, though seemingly old-fashioned and traditional, still have their role in youth services for teens who need the respite. On the other hand, however, they may have internalized from their high-powered parents an expectation of specific outcomes for the time they spend in the library, so the opportunity to participate in community outreach and service-oriented programming that can go on a college application becomes a priority.

In either case, knowing that the problem of narcissistic parenting is likely to be a feature of teens who are using the library can run as a sort of background program to the LIS professional's reading and recommending of young adult (YA) fiction. Teens situated between the desire to be fabulous and the disappointments of overbearing parents feature in many YA novels, such as Jessica Warman's *Between* (2011), Robin Friedman's *Nothing* (2008), and Jen Violi's *Putting Makeup on Dead People* (2011). Even a biography like Susan Goldman Rubin's *Music Was IT: Young Leonard Bernstein* (2011) can offer sustenance for teens, as it emphasizes Bernstein's father's strong and continuous disapproval of his son's ambitions. The reading needs and preferences of teens with narcissistic parents can be ambiguous, however, and depend on what style of coping they have developed. While some might gravitate to fantasy or humor, others may prefer to face the problem head on, as in books like A. S. King's *Everybody Sees the Ants* (2011). In any case, a theoretical knowledge of contemporary parenting styles can be helpful in the service of readers' advisory.

What remains to be considered of Babbitt's pronouncement is the reference to Frank Sinatra. What does it mean to say that a singer had a part in creating modern adolescence? Scholars in the sociology of music have written extensively about the relationship of teens to their music, and how it acts to secure both individual and group identity particularly between the ages of 14 and 18 when music preferences tend to form and solidify. In addition to its identity-bearing function, Simon Frith (1987) notes that music helps teens express and even experience emotion in more complex and satisfying ways. The intensity of first love, the depth of sadness or loneliness, the rage of a perceived injustice, the elation of a really good mood—these are all rendered rather banal by the ordinary language we have to express them. But put a beat and some soulful instruments behind metaphorical lyrics and a song can make emotions more available, and their expression more adequate, to the experience.

The specific context of Sinatra surely refers to his appeal to adolescent girls, who made him the first teen singing idol. But I read Babbitt's quip as a metonym for the representation and validation of specifically adolescent concerns in literature as well as music. When we consider the development of YA literature offered by Michael Cart (1996) in light of Lasch's overview of dominant personality types, we note a similar progression of plot preoccupations and characters, with perhaps only a small mismatch between texts and the historical moments as Lasch delineates them. For instance, Mark Twain's *Adventures of Huckleberry Finn* (1885) and Howard Pease's *The Tattooed Man* (1926) feature rough-edged individualists, as do many of the boy's adventure stories of the early and mid-twentieth century. Similarly, novels for girls featured eponymous characters—Nancy Drew, Sue Barton, Cherry Ames—to emphasize their individuality. But there also grew alongside these popular novels works that featured group protagonists like the Rover Boys and the Adventure Girls who were defined by their affiliative identities rather than their individuality. The effect of both the rugged individualist and the organization man myths is to consolidate a specifically American identity that emphasizes allegiance to adult ideals of self-reliance, loyalty, and swagger in light of the notion of simply being American. Maureen Daly's *Seventeenth Summer* (1942) and the romances that followed, as well as the more or less realistic problem novels of the 1960s and 1970s, could be said to be driven by the growth in narcissistic concerns—the increasing desire to see oneself and one's experiences reflected in literature.

Were Lasch still alive, it would be interesting to hear his take on the dominant personality type that we find ourselves enacting today, but other social critics have taken up the task with interestingly parallel findings, even if they come at their work from different angles. In broadest terms, philosophers, sociologists, cultural historians, educators, theologians, and psychologists have traced an ideological shift from a romantic to a modernist to a postmodernist and now to a transmodern view of the self. These adjectival terms enact a kind of reductive shorthand, of course, encapsulating points of view that emerged from multiple sources, such as changes in economic and political systems, revolutions in religion, and literary innovations and interpretive stances. It is important to note that while these shifts can be said to have moments of emergence and even periods of ascendency or dominance, they are not confined to a particular time, nor are they progressive. Instead, they map attitudes or commitments that for most people exist along a continuum, a Likert scale of sorts if you will, that helps us sort out what we believe about what it means to be human— and in our more specific inquiry what it means to be a teen.

Thus, for instance, the romantic view, traditionally ascribed to Wordsworth and company in the late 1700s, configured the self as innate, complete, and glorious from birth, and rendered less so by growing older and less able to access our inborn connections to nature and the spiritual realm. According to Wordsworth (1807: V.vii) we come into the world "trailing clouds of glory" but soon devolve into less authentic creatures as we interact with polluted society. Even though this is decidedly an eighteenth-century conception, it could be said to have antecedent roots in the philosophy of St. Augustine, whose *Confessions* is arguably the first autobiography in Western literature and, if I may be forgiven for being a bit playful, may in fact be the first adolescent problem novel, chronicling as it does his teenage dissipation in a first person narrative. The salient point here is that his expressivist text espoused a romantic view of the self as a deep well of emotion, imagination, and perception, and posits that if one goes deep enough into self-understanding, one inevitably finds God as one's true source. The depths of sensibility that animate the soul connect the self to others and the natural world as well as to God, and have to be protected from the banalities of interaction and work in order to prioritize meditation and greater understanding of a self that already exists fully and needs only to be discovered. Harry Potter might be considered a touchstone of this type of character. Despite harsh treatment by his aunt and uncle and a significantly deprived childhood, Harry continually discovers depths of talent, strength, and compassion that amaze his friends and foes alike, and he possesses an innate, incorruptible goodness that enables him to resist the misuse of his considerable power.

The modernist self, on the other hand, was inaugurated largely by the work of John Locke, who rejected the idea of innate, preexisting depths of the self in favor of the view that the mind is a tabula rasa that takes in impressions from experience and then develops through reflecting and making associations. Rather than discovered, the self in modernist thought is formed through experience, then shaped and cultivated through rationality and reason. While some modernist thinkers also acknowledge the presence of a Freudian unconscious that harbors irrational drives and desires, those in the Lockean tradition favor developmental schema theories, believing in the possibility for continuous growth and progress in rational thought, impulse control, and intentional morality over the life span.

Andi Alpers, in Jennifer Donnelly's *Revolution* (2010), is representative of a modernist character. Her mental health is significantly compromised by the death of her younger brother, a death for which she feels responsible. But through reflecting on her own grief in light of the tragic fate of the young Dauphin in the aftermath of the French Revolution, she is able to slowly overcome her irrational desire to take her own life and instead embraces a moral imperative to help others through grief using her talent for music. Her relation to music acts as both a plot device and an affective metaphor, as she is studying a (fictional) composer known for his innovative use of the tritone, a note that was deemed "diabolic" because of its dissonant effect on the ear. The tritone, also known as an augmented fourth or diminished fifth, haunts as a sound out of place that requires resolution; the untimely death of Andi's brother constitutes such a restless interval in her life, a scary, oppressive time that she must resolve if she is going to remain alive and sane. Implicitly, the book enacts a patriarchal affirmation of rationality over the realm of emotion (traditionally associated with the feminine) by contrasting the character of her father, a Nobel Prize–winning geneticist, with her mother, an artist whose production becomes obsessive and dysfunctional following the death of her son. Andi's path could be said to reconcile and correct the two positions, but it clearly favors the paternal, modernist response of rendering grief functional through rational action.

Postmodern thought challenges both the romantic and the modernist conceptions of the self. Like modernity, it rejects a depth model, but it also critiques the optimistic notion of progress and the rejection of ways of knowing that are not embedded in empiricism, rationality, and reason. Most importantly, postmodernism rejects assertions of universal truth and essential humanity, calling these out as "grand narratives" that were never really adequate to define human experience, and thus became restrictive hegemonies that sought to stifle diversity in the service of institutional power. The monomyth of mid-twentieth-century American identity, for instance, is neatly summed up by Erving Goffman (1963: 128) in his book *Stigma: Notes on the Management of Spoiled Identity*: "In an important sense there is only one complete unblushing male in America: a young, married, white, urban, northern, heterosexual, Protestant, father, of college education, fully employed, of good complexion, weight, height, and a recent record in sports." Anyone who stands outside that string of attributes is judged against them and found wanting.

Consider how each character in S. E. Hinton's *The Outsiders* (1967) or Frank Bonham's *Durango Street* (1965) not only fails to meet more than one of those criteria as a teen, but is also positioned so that they can never achieve those ideals as an adult. Stories that bring these sorts of characters out of the margins and into a space of empathy within the teen reader sensitize the reader to the necessity of postmodern critique. It could even be said that the project to advance some sort of definition of what it means to be a teen in contemporary culture could be read as an attempt to erect a grand narrative that inevitably excludes and marginalizes those individuals who don't fit the mold. But conversely, the narrative that all teens are individuals with singular concerns and absolute ideological independence is just as suspect, as it depends on a contested view of atomic individualism. Still another popular narrative is the one that places teens in tribal identity groupings; that is, teens are seen to accord without personal exception with affiliative groupings or expectations organized around race, class, gender, ethnicity, and so on, based on the way they dress, talk, and look. Any of these narratives can be equally restrictive, as each may require teens to reject common understandings of and compliance with the dominant culture that may hold important components of their sense of self; in other words, they are put into ideological boxes that may not hold all of their various parts. The postmodernist argument thus calls on theorists of the self to move away from content-based assertions of what constitutes a mature self (such as coherence, integration, continuity of consciousness, etc., which may only have value in certain narratives) and focus instead on the dialogic processes by which one achieves a sense of self in contemporary culture.

The great divorce of the self from cultural monomyths and grand narratives forms the common core of these contemporary theories of the self.

For postmodern critics, the idea of a deep or authentic self is an illusion; such a sense of self is enabled by a certain kind of grand narrative that, because it is not shared by every culture, must have been constructed by one particular culture, and is therefore ideologically driven by the mechanisms of power that provide coherence and stability for that culture and may in fact be detrimental or oppressive for individuals. (I would be remiss if I did not point out that this position is itself ideologically driven—the grand narratives that provide stability and coherence for a culture can and do enable individuals to thrive as well; it is often the conditions of one's embodiment that place one at a particular point on the success/failure continuum.) On the one hand, untethering the self from grand narratives enables a sense of fluidity and freedom to fashion oneself as one wills; on the other it demands continual experimentation with cultural supports that act more as moving targets than fixed measures of success. The fact remains that the self is dialogic: it requires a dynamic feedback loop with a responsive culture to exist, and if not grand narratives, then the artifacts of popular culture provide that feedback.

What this means for LIS professionals endeavoring to understand their young clientele is that there is no longer the sense that there is a single path to a mature identity, nor is there a fixed idea of what that identity might ultimately look like. Though it seems by now a cliché, respect for diversity, broadly conceived, is key to understanding today's teens, because in today's reckoning diversity exists within the self as well as externally as a feature of identity politics. A teen may enjoy indie music, for instance, and incline more toward an evangelical Christian perspective than the goth or emo persona that musical preference may suggest to outsiders. Identity components are selected à la carte, rather than coming together as a prix fixe meal. Rather than rebelling against some fixed and restrictive notion of adulthood, teens today are using their access to global popular culture to experiment with niche identities that key to sometimes transient values. They then test and adjust these identities based on what kind of feedback they receive and how that makes them feel. Obviously, their skill and success at making these adjustments vary, and they are not always able to gauge the connection of their actions and self-presentation to the social consequences, but LIS professionals should understand that they themselves are part of the teens' feedback loop. They should also understand that experiments at self-fashioning sometimes fail, so that radical changes in a teen's presentation may be worth worrying about (for instance, when they seem to indicate self-harm) and at other times may not (when they suggest a new experiment in fashion or affiliation).

Postmodern theorists of the self analyze how this process of self-fashioning and developing niche identities came about and how it works. Philip Cushman (1995), for instance, argues that postwar advertising and therapeutic culture consciously set out to construct the self as empty, so that they could offer consumer-based products to fill it. Cushman's assessment of adult culture has filtered down to advertising and therapies aimed squarely at teens: Libba Bray's darkly hilarious send-up of teen pageant and reality show culture, *Beauty Queens* (2011: 37), contains a commercial that ends with the tagline, "Because there's nothing wrong with you...that we can't fix," and more and more YA lit features characters with mental health and disability issues, such as E. Lockhart's Ruby Oliver books, Donnelly's *Revolution* (2010), Beverley Brenna's *Wild Orchid* (2005), Jennifer Roy's *Mindblind* (2010), and any number of books with characters struggling with eating disorders. While books that feature rampant consumerism run the gamut between celebration (e.g., Cecily von Ziegesar's *Gossip Girls* [2002]) and critique (e.g., Janet Tashjian's *The Gospel According to Larry* [2001]), contemporary books about mental illness and disability seek to normalize those characters' experience, to show them coping and healing when they need to but otherwise living functional lives.

Strenger's fabulous teens are also well represented in YA literature but are again given differential treatments: superachieving Parker in Friedman's *Nothing* (2008) turns to bulimia in an attempt to escape his father's overbearing pressure, while Carlos in Bil Wright's *Putting Makeup on the Fat Boy* (2011) realizes his dream of becoming a teen makeup artist for a reality TV star. Danny's dilemmas in *Mexican Whiteboy* (2008) and Junior's in *The Absolutely True Diary of a Part-Time Indian* (2007) offer more nuanced reflections on the pressures of being exceptional. Other theorists focus on the process of self-fashioning as pursuing the self as a work of art (Foucault, 1997) or the outcome of a series of gender performances (Butler, 1990). The former is foregrounded metaphorically in Paul Fleischman's *Whirligig* (1998) and *Mind's Eye* (2001), where the characters craft their sense of self through identification with artistic styles, while the latter is arguably present in all YA fiction, but perhaps most visible in books that feature transgressive gender performances, such as Julie Ann Peters's *Luna* (2004) and Cris Beam's *I am J* (2011).

Another compelling theory of the self in contemporary culture is offered by Kenneth Gergen (1991) in his book *The Saturated Self: Dilemmas of Identity in Contemporary Life*. Like the other theorists I have mentioned, he agrees that young people have been set adrift from grand narratives into a sea of competing and ever-proliferating messages that are increasingly difficult to sort through. It is not that youth today face an attention deficit; rather, it is that they pay attention to everything, and no message stands out as particularly compelling or foundational—there is no authoritative voice that helps them sort opposing messages into categories of useful or trivial, right or wrong. The self, then, is fully dependent, and admittedly so, on the images and discourses that swirl around it from birth demanding attention and response. M. T. Anderson's *Feed* (2002) is exemplary of this type of media and social saturation; with the Internet wet-wired into people's heads, there is no escape into a space of Augustinian contemplation but rather a constant relational matrix to negotiate. And while *Feed* offers a cautionary tale of being constantly online, its warning seems almost anachronistic as social networking has become ubiquitous. The self is no longer at the center of activity but is displaced by the social relationships that one must continually develop and maintain. Consider Facebook in this regard: The continual updates are without question narcissistic, but they are narcissistic in the service of maintaining relationships with others.

Indeed one of the most interesting facets of these theories seems to be that they implicitly rehabilitate narcissism from its negative connotations. Because the new form of the self is not inwardly focused or dependent on exclusive or oppressive metanarratives, a narcissistic focus on the self encompasses a broader space, a space of relationship, community, and interdependence that renders narcissism expansive: when I am looking at myself, I see all of the others who are in conversation with me and I am performing for those others. David Levithan creates the quintessential postmodern subject in *Boy Meets Boy* (2003). Infinite Darlene is transgendered and is both the star quarterback of the football team and the homecoming queen. She thus embodies multiple and fluid subject positions, and her sense of self is fully relationship-oriented:

She seems very full of herself. Which she is. It's only after you get to know her better that you realize that somehow she's managed to encompass all her friends within her own self-image, so that when she's acting full of herself, she's actually full of her close friends, too. (Levithan, 2003: 41)

But even though today's teens are relationship oriented, that does not mean that they have lost the value of thinking for themselves, of claiming their individuated right to do things that run counter to parental and societal desires and expectations. Donna Parisi, the protagonist of Jen Violi's *Putting Makeup on Dead People* (2011), offers a powerful example of many of the traits identified by the theorists I have cited. She is grieving the death of her beloved father and has pulled back emotionally from the rest of her family, but she still feels the pressure to make her life extraordinary. She discovers within herself a willingness to do what many people would not be capable of doing—loving the dead and supporting the living by standing alongside them and preparing bodies for funerals. This is certainly countercultural in terms of gender performance and teen performance; her mother is particularly resistant to the idea, interpreting it as a morbid response to the loss of her father. But Donna knows better. She knows that this is a way of honoring her own experience, of claiming the intensity of what happened to her and remaking it into a loving service for others.

Other characters insist on their right to resist the pull of social saturation, as Scarlet does in *The Six Rules of Maybe*:

I never understood why it was somehow superior to be a joiner. Being an introvert is judged in some extreme way, as if you're lacking some ability to cope because you don't drink beer and smoke pot in Macy Friedman's basement. In our society, introversion as an alternate lifestyle gets less respect than any other alternate lifestyle, in my opinion. You could be gay and go to homecoming with your girlfriend or boyfriend, you could go drunk, you could go and ditch your partner mid-dance, but if you didn't go at all, you were a loser. Introversion is distrusted—it makes people nervous. Maybe it seems like we've got secrets. They think the secret is that you're depressed or something, that's why you don't seek their company, when the secret is really that you're happy and relieved and almost flying at the near-miss escape of not having to be in their company. You're looked at like you're seriously lacking, when the only thing you feel lacking in is the ability to be an introvert in peace. (Caletti, 2010: 69)

But even Scarlet is absorbed in her small network of friends and neighbors whose lives intersect with hers and whom she feels a desire to help and protect. Similarly, nearly all of the 70 YA authors who participated in the *Dear Bully* anthology, edited by Megan Kelley Hall and Carrie Jones (2011), emphasize their current adult status as surrounded by a group of loving friends as an implicit (and sometimes explicit) measure of their self-worth, which was called into question by their adolescent experience with bullying.

The guiding principles of the self in postmodern society for teens as well as adults, then, are fluidity and dialogism; our sense of self is marked by continual responsiveness to the feedback of others rather than a stubborn adherence to an abstract ideal that might set us apart from our peers. As a result, we can feel somewhat fragmented and at times compromised or inauthentic, but it is the embrace of flexibility that enables us to confront rapidly changing technologies that both force and enable us to engage in the social networks that have come to define us.

Interestingly, this kind of flexibility and fluidity is, and perhaps always has been, a hallmark of teen identity. As we turn now to examine the key developmental tasks of the teenage years, it is important to note that the life skills necessary to negotiate contemporary technologies, such as identity fluidity, peer orientation, incessant interactivity, a fascination with cool, adaptability to the new, and risk taking, have long been viewed as teen behaviors that we should ideally grow out of as we achieve a more serene and stable adulthood; in contemporary culture, however, they are a destination rather than a stage you pass on the way.

The Emerging Adult

The challenge for many adults thinking through these postmodern challenges is that many of us do experience a strong, stable sense of self based on what we believe are core values, and we do not think of ourselves as fragmented and plastic; we believe that achieving a stable and secure identity is a good thing, and we want that for our teens as well. In short, we both believe in and value a lot of the things that postmodernism critiques about romantic and modernist conceptions of the self. We believe in progressive intellectual and moral development, although we may reject lockstep, age-defined categories such as those identified by Freud, Piaget, Erikson, and Kohlberg, among others. We believe in fostering critical thinking, although we may insist on a place for emotional response as a complement to a mechanistic rationality. We believe in encouraging the ability to make and keep commitments, even though we want to hold open space for flexibility when life circumstances force change. Indeed, these values were all part of the dialogue that we engaged in as we grew up, and therefore they helped shape the dialogic selves we now uphold as ideal.

How, then, can we hold on to and pass on to our teens what we value while taking the critiques of postmodernism seriously? How do we preserve what we believe to be important in the face of cultural and ideological change? Paul Vitz (1995) coined the term *transmodern* to indicate a view of the self that reaches across prior understandings and transforms them. The answer to many of the critiques of the modernist and postmodern versions of the self lies in reintroducing the body into the discussion. In terms of imagining the teen, then, we have to consider not only social environment and immersion in the contemporary cultural moment but also the special circumstances of teen embodiment.

Recent research in brain development has yielded information that surprised the scientists if not the parents of teens. What they discovered is that teen brains do not work the same way as adult brains, and therefore their responses to situations tend to be different as well. Specifically, there is an overproduction of gray matter in the area of the prefrontal cortex just prior to puberty. Hence, new capacities in the area that is known as the chief executive officer (CEO) of the brain stand ready to be reinforced or pruned, depending on experience during the next several years. The prefrontal cortex is believed to be responsible for mental activities such as planning, organizing, strategizing, assessing risk, impulse control, and dispassionate reasoning. According to neuroscientist Jay Giedd (Spinks, 2002b), the overproduction of gray matter does not matter as much as the pruning down process that follows during the teen years. This is the time when the "use it or lose it" principle is most important, because "[t] hose cells and connections that are used will survive and flourish. Those cells and connections that are not used will wither and die." It might seem sad to "lose" certain capacities, but the pruning metaphor is not an idle one; just as in gardening, pruning away some pathways enables others to grow stronger.

Giedd notes that the cerebellum is also undergoing significant change during the teen years. Scientists have long believed that the cerebellum is responsible for coordinating physical movement, so new growth in that area may account for the frustrating clumsiness that some teens experience. But recent research indicates that the cerebellum is responsible for coordinating thought processes as well, so that social awkwardness or the inability to track complicated arguments or make cognitive connections may be related to the instability of the cerebellum as it grows and changes. The relative immaturity of these areas of the brain can account for teens' inability to connect their own behaviors with social consequences, but the presence of mirror neurons—that is, neurons that fire both when a person acts and when a person observes an action in others, as well as the ability to form emotional attachments with characters—may be instrumental in helping teens reflect on behaviors they read about in books. Although the scientific evidence for this is still in its infancy (see, for example, Vermeule, 2009), seeing how things work out for characters may then help build and reinforce the connections a teen needs to make in his or her own brain.

What is fully developed at this stage of life is the amygdala, the area of the brain that initiates emotional, gut responses. Because this area is well developed, because hormonal fluctuations augment emotional response, and because all of the connections to and from the frontal cortex are not fully functional yet, teens lead with their emotions. However, they are not always able to match the appropriate emotional response to the stimuli (Spinks, 2002a); this seems to require the full coordination of the cerebellum, the frontal cortex, and the amygdala, which as we have noted is not fully online yet.

While Giedd and others are cautious in translating their findings into recommendations for practice, several practical outcomes can be interpolated that are of use in our quest to think critically about how to imagine teens:

- It matters very much how people spend their time and energies during their teen years. It is not a time for sleeping as older texts suggest, but rather a time for experimentation with many different physical and mental activities so that they can find a few that they might want to specialize in.
- Most young people will need significant scaffolding to realize goals that require planning, organizing, and strategies. Depending on the genetic lottery, they may be full of creative ideas or have significant problem-solving abilities thanks to a well-developed corpus callosum, but their frontal lobes are simply not yet ready to figure out and implement the series of steps that will secure the success of their endeavors.
- Reading engrossing fiction may help scaffold increased emotional intelligence as well as help students develop an awareness of cause and effect.
- As much as we want to encourage reading, we need to ensure that teens get up and get moving. The new findings regarding the cerebellum indicate a correlation between sluggish bodies and sluggish minds.
- Their responses will not always accord rationally with the stimuli that prompt them.

Combining these findings with what we know about "zones of proximal development" should prompt us to think carefully about the kinds of support teens need. They need the opportunity to participate in diverse, experimental activities that engage both mind and body. For instance, LIS professionals can build such activities into their programming by inviting community experts to offer one-off workshops specifically for teens in which nothing is dismissed as too weird or uncool, because it might be just right for someone looking for a new niche identity component or skill set to try.

The brain research should also remind us that while they are not exactly *other*, teens are also not exactly like us, and hence we should be careful not to be dismissive of the things that are important to them, even if they seem ephemeral or melodramatic. The teenage years appear as something of a paradox in our usual ways of sorting experience: it is a time that is both crucial and temporary, urgent and important. We have to remind both them and ourselves that the impermanence of this stage of life in no way negates its importance.

Besides embodiment, Vitz (1995) posits two other elements that are essential to understanding the transmodern self—our embeddedness in community and the centrality of language to both crafting and communicating identity. These elements, he contends, are in fact human universals, but they are also infinitely variable across cultures. In order to translate his concept into a model that we can use to better understand both ourselves and our teens, I turn to the work of Mark Bracher (2006). Bracher cites the work of Heinz Lichtenstein (1977) and Norman Holland (1985) to support the claim that development and maintenance of one's identity is the most basic of all human needs. He ties this insight to current thought in education that the primary goal of education is no longer socialization, as it was in previous eras, but individual identity formation (Chickering and Reisser, 1993). Bracher then goes on to advance a theory of identity that, though drawn specifically from the psychoanalytic theory of Jacques Lacan, resonates with the theory of the transmodern self. Like the transmodern self, Bracher's theory of identity consists of three basic elements: the affective/emotional register, which correlates most closely with the experience of embodiment; the imagistic/perceptual register, which is composed of ideal images of the self and others and which privileges one's body image and capabilities as the site of agency; and the cognitive/linguistic register, which revolves around the signifiers that a person identifies with and finds valuable. Too often, Bracher argues, we who work with young people focus overmuch on this latter category. We are educators, after all, who have been trained to see our arena of influence as the information-processing dimensions of the human mind. We give short shrift, then, to aspects of our teens' personalities that are in fact very important to them, namely, the development and maintenance of their body image and nonlinguistic competencies and the validation of their emotions. He also urges us to be aware that we ourselves have similar identity needs in each of the three areas, and when they are neglected or come into conflict with our students' identity needs or the goals of our programming, we will all be hindered from achieving those goals.

But conflict can arise between the registers as well. For instance, an exceptionally tall black male teenager may be expected, because of his embodiment and his cultural positioning, to desire to be a basketball star and hang out with friends, when the signifiers and activities he actually values include being a good poet and spending time with his grandfather. While his friends and coach seek to use him to serve and validate their identity needs or the needs of the school sports program, his needs go unrecognized. When this happens, he may try to compensate for unmet needs in one register by engaging another; for example, he may retreat into music to alter his feeling state or may sabotage his basketball playing by injuring himself. The point is that when teens act out inappropriately, they are usually driven by unrecognized needs in one area or another and are seeking to compensate for the lack of recognition of their identity, because even negative recognition, or recognition for negative things, is better than not being recognized at all.

Admittedly, it is difficult to withhold judgment for behaviors that we consider negative, and sometimes we should not; after all, as adults we can perceive consequences in ways that teens may not, either because of brain development or a lack of historical perspective. But honest self-reflection is key here: If we understand the teen self as dialogically engaged with his or her culture, we must also recognize that we as adults are acting in dialogue with our cultures as well. Often our judgments are based in nostalgia or unexamined ideological notions that came from a culture that no longer functions as it once did. As the culture changes, then, so does the dialogue and its outcomes; our goals are not necessarily their goals. But this does not mean that our opinions and insights do not matter, because we are part of the dialogue as well. Engaged YA librarians and LIS scholars can and should critically examine current cultural trends, delaying judgment while measuring them against their likely consequences and outcomes, and then find ways through book and media talks and discussion groups to engage teens in critical conversations about their world as well.

As librarians and educators, we have a wealth of resources at our disposal to help our teens find recognition for their identity components. As I have argued in this essay, thinking theoretically matters. We must recognize that today's teens live in a world that demands they be spectacular and that sometimes glosses over their individuality in favor of their identity group affiliation. We must stay abreast of current brain research, which teaches us that teenaged bodies are in a state of flux that can be confusing and painful, but that most importantly recognizes their brain development drives them to process information differently from children or adults. We must be aware that they are constantly immersed in a swirl of language and social connection that requires organization and sorting skills they may not yet possess but that we can help scaffold through connecting them with the literature that will expand their understanding of characters and situations. We must engage in serious self-reflection such that our own unmet needs are not visited on our clients in negative ways. And then we must find ways to turn our theoretical knowledge into practical programming that encourages healthy experimentation, provides appropriate and effective feedback, and supports diversity, even diversity within the self. This project requires that we be our best adult selves—attentive, supportive, creative, and generative. If we succeed, then we can help our teens develop through a more informed and self-aware dialogue with their culture toward what *they* consider a desirable destination.

Primary Sources

Alexie, Sherman. 2007. *The Absolutely True Diary of a Part-Time Indian*. New York: Little, Brown.

Anderson, M. T. 2002. *Feed*. New York: Candlewick.

Beam, Cris. 2011. *I am J*. New York: Little, Brown.

Bonham, Frank. 1965. *Durango Street*. New York: Dutton.

Bray, Libba. 2011. *Beauty Queens*. New York: Scholastic.

Brenna, Beverley. 2005. *Wild Orchid*. Markham, ON: Red Deer Press.

Caletti, Deb. 2010. *The Six Rules of Maybe*. New York: Simon Pulse.

Daly, Maureen. 1942. *Seventh Summer*. New York: Dodd, Mead.

Donnelly, Jennifer. 2010. *Revolution*. New York: Delacorte.

Fleischman, Paul. 1998. *Whirligig*. New York: Henry Holt.

———. 2001. *Mind's Eye*. New York: Henry Holt.

Friedman, Robin. 2008. *Nothing*. New York: Flux.

Hall, Megan Kelley, and Carrie Jones. 2011. *Dear Bully*. New York: HarperTeen.

Hinton, S. E. 1967. *The Outsiders*. New York: Viking.

King, A. S. 2011. *Everybody Sees the Ants*. New York: Little, Brown.

La Pena, Matt de. 2008. *Mexican Whiteboy*. New York: Delacorte.

Levithan, David. 2003. *Boy Meets Boy*. New York: Knopf.

Lockhart, E. 2005. *The Boyfriend List*. New York: Delacorte.

Pease, Howard. 1926. *The Tattooed Man*. New York: Doubleday.

Peters, Julie Anne. 2004. *Luna*. New York: Little, Brown.

Roy, Jennifer. 2010. *Mindblind*. Tarrytown, NY: Marshall Cavendish.

Rubin, Susan Goldman. 2011. *Music Was IT: Young Leonard Bernstein*. Watertown, MA: Charlesbridge.

Tashjian, Janet. 2001. *The Gospel According to Larry*. New York: Henry Holt.

Twain, Mark. 1885. *Adventures of Huckleberry Finn*. New York: Charles L. Webster.

Violi, Jen. 2011. *Putting Makeup on Dead People*. New York: Hyperion.

Von Ziegesar, Cecily. 2002. *Gossip Girl #1: A Novel*. New York: Poppy.

Warman, Jessica. 2011. *Between*. New York: Walker.

Wordsworth, William. 1807. *Poems: In Two Volumes*. London: Longman.

Wright, Bil. 2011. *Putting Makeup on the Fat Boy*. New York: Simon and Schuster.

Scholarly References

Babbitt, Natalie. 1978. "Between Innocence and Maturity." In *Young Adult Literature in the Seventies,* edited by Jana Varlejs. Metuchen, NJ: Scarecrow.

Bracher, Mark. 2006. *Radical Pedagogy: Identity, Generativity, and Social Transformation*. New York: Palgrave Macmillan.

Butler, Judith. 1990. *Gender Trouble: Feminism and the Subversion of Identity*. New York: Routledge.

Campbell, Patty. 2000. "The Sand in the Oyster: Middle Muddle." *Horn Book* 76 (July–August): 483–485.

Cart, Michael. 1996. *From Romance to Realism: 50 Years of Growth and Change in Young Adult Literature*. New York: HarperCollins.

Carter, Betty. 1994. *Best Books for Young Adults: The History, the Selections, the Romance*. Chicago: American Library Association.

Chickering, Arthur W., and Linda Reisser. 1993. *Education and Identity*. 2nd ed. San Francisco: Jossey-Bass.

Cushman, Philip. 1995. *Constructing the Self, Constructing America: A Cultural History of Psychotherapy*. Reading, MA: Addison-Wesley.

Foucault, Michel. 1997. *Michel Foucault: Ethics, Subjectivity, and Truth*. Edited by Paul Rabinow. Vol. 1 of *Essential Works of Foucault, 1954–1984*. New York: NYU Press.

Frith, Simon. 1987. "Toward an Aesthetic of Popular Music." In *Music and Society: The Politics of Composition, Performance, and Reception,* edited by Richard Leppert and Susan McClary, 133–150. Cambridge, UK: Cambridge University Press.

Gergen, Kenneth. 1991. *The Saturated Self: Dilemmas of Identity in Contemporary Life*. New York: Basic Books.

Goffman, Erving. 1963. *Stigma: Notes on the Management of Spoiled Identity*. New York: Simon and Schuster.

Hall, G. Stanley. 1904. *Adolescence: Its Psychology and Its Relations to Physiology, Anthropology, Sociology, Sex, Crime, Religion and Education*, vols. 1 and 2. New York: D. Appleton.

Holland, Norman N. 1985. *The I*. New Haven: Yale University Press.

Lasch, Christopher. 1979. *The Culture of Narcissism*. New York: Norton.

Lichtenstein, Heinz. 1977. *The Dilemma of Human Identity*. New York: Aronson.

Nilsen, Alleen, and Kenneth L. Donelson. 1993. *Literature for Today's Young Adults*. 4th ed. New York: Harper.

Spinks, Sarah, writer, producer, and director. 2002a. "Interview: Deborah Yurgelun-Todd." *Frontline: Inside the Teenage Brain*. WGBH Boston. Accessed June 30, 2011. http://www.pbs.org/wgbh/pages/frontline/shows/teenbrain/interviews/todd.html.

———. 2002b. "Interview: Jay Giedd." *Frontline: Inside the Teenage Brain*. WGBH Boston. Accessed June 30, 2011. http://www.pbs.org/wgbh/pages/frontline/shows/teenbrain/interviews/giedd.html.

Strenger, Carlo. 2004. *The Designed Self: Psychoanalysis and Contemporary Identities*. Hillsdale, NJ: The Analytic Press.

Vermeule, Blakey. 2009. *Why Do We Care about Literary Characters?* Baltimore, MD: Johns Hopkins.

Vitz, Paul. 1995. "A Christian Theory of Personality: Interpersonal and Transmodern." In *The Nature and Tasks of a Personalist Psychology*, edited by J. M. Dubois, 23–26. Lanham, MD: University Press of America.

Zangwill, Israel. 1896. *Without Prejudice*. London: T. Fisher Unwin.

Crossing Over

The Advent of the Adultescent

Michael Cart

A comprehensive collection of literature meeting the unique developmental needs of its young adult population remains a fundamental aspect of library service. This chapter addresses the question of how library professionals select these materials and how they define the term *young adult*? Furthermore, this chapter argues that reviews remain a core guide to selecting suitable materials for a dynamic young adult population that is changing as society redefines its parameters, which now extend to age 25. Reviews are also changing, migrating from print media to online sources as they become increasingly targeted at young adults themselves instead of the traditional audience of adult professionals. The impact of these changes on reviews and collections will be the major focus of this chapter.

The years from 18 until 25 and even beyond have become a distinct and separate life stage....

—LEV GROSSMAN (2005)

Surely the term *young adult* should be as dynamic as the population it defines. Yet since 1991 the Young Adult Library Services Association (YALSA) has continued to define young adults as young people ages 12 to 18. It is time to change this definition to recognize the rapidly changing nature of this population, for today's young adults are now widely regarded as being as old as 25. This dramatic change clearly impacts young adult library services. One area most heavily impacted is that of materials selection and collection development. In making purchasing decisions librarians need to recognize that there now are or should be three young adult literatures: (1) middle school literature for readers 10 through 14 years of age, (2) teen literature for readers 13 to 19, and (3) young adult literature for readers 19 through 25. These are not hard and fast categories, for the long-established barriers that for years rigidly defined a book's intended audience are becoming more fluid every day. That said, the new categories I propose generally define potential readerships that will guide professionals in providing materials relevant to the service population's interests and needs.

This new definition impacts not only librarians and libraries but also publishers and book reviews and reviewers. Though sometimes intimidating, change is a necessary part of library service. Recognizing and managing this redefinition of young adults and its practical implications for collection development is one of the major challenges confronting young adult librarians in the twenty-first century.

The New Young Adult

The mainstream media call them "adultescents," "kidults," "twixters," or "boomerangers," but whatever you call them, they're a new generation that is redefining the traditional library meaning of young adult. For today's young adults may, it is claimed, be as old as 25. How is this so? The short answer is that they are a generation influenced by the Peter Pan syndrome: they simply won't grow up! But that is not entirely accurate. Instead, consider that nearly 20 million, or 30 percent, of America's nearly 70 million 18- to 24-year-olds are still living at home with their parents, delaying marriage until their late twenties, and often not finding a career path job until their early thirties (AP, 2009).

There are a number of reasons for this: a principal one is the distressed nature of the current economy and the corollary shortage of jobs, and a second is the fact that knowing their life expectancy is now 77.9 (CDC, 2011) and their retirement age may be at least 68 or even 70, these young people are in no hurry to assume the responsibilities and, some might say, burdens of adulthood. Finally, today's youth are children of a generation of "helicopter parents" who are concerned for their children's well-being and have hovered over them like, well, a helicopter.

Meanwhile, these new young adults continue to be heavily invested in teen and traditional young adult (YA) popular culture, shopping at the same stores, wearing the same clothes, going to the same movies and concerts, and being similarly devoted to every aspect of the burgeoning social media. They simply won't grow up.

The prevalence of this new generation has actually inspired at least one movie, *Failure to Launch*, a romantic comedy starring Matthew McConaughey as a 35-year-old still living at home with his parents. His two best friends are also still living at home to the considerable distress of their parents. Two recent television programs—both comedies—also address this situation: *$#*! My Dad Says* and *Big Lake*. Like the McConaughey movie, both feature young men still living at home and failing to launch themselves into adulthood.

Since the early twenty-first century, a growing number of developmental psychologists, sociologists, and neuroscientists have been studying this age group (18–34), particularly the segment ages 18 to 25, and have concluded that it constitutes a new, distinct life stage that leading expert Dr. Jeffrey Jensen Arnett calls "emerging adulthood."

A professor of psychology at Clark University in Worcester, Massachusetts, and author of the book *Emerging Adulthood: The Winding Road from the Late Teens through the Twenties,* Arnett recently told the *New York Times* that what is happening now is analogous to what happened a century ago when social and economic changes helped create adolescence (Henig, 2010).

During that time of social and economic changes, G. Stanley Hall, the first American PhD in psychology and first president of the American Psychological Association, published his massive two-volume work, *Adolescence: Its Psychology and Its Relations to Physiology, Anthropology, Sociology, Sex, Crime, Religion, and Education*. It might be said that Hall created this new category of human being; certainly his theories about the storm and stress that typified this season of life were enormously influential among youth service workers, educators, and developmental psychologists.

Once the idea of the adolescent was established, the concept of a specific stage of adolescence, the teenager, was not far behind. In fact, by the end of the 1930s a youth culture was fast emerging, thanks in part to the Great Depression that had dried up the job market for youth and sent them to high school in record numbers.

With the advent of World War II, these newly minted teenagers began to acquire money of their own (in part because so many adults were involved in the war effort that new jobs for younger people were once again available). This, in turn, resulted in the establishment in the late 1940s of Eugene Gilbert's Youth Marketing Company, the first market research firm to analyze the enormous commercial potential of this group.

Meanwhile, Hall's theories continued to resonate nearly half a century later in the work of developmental psychologists Erik Erikson and Robert J. Havighurst, both of whom asserted that two of the stages of human development were (1) adolescence and (2) young adulthood. Erikson defined them as the years 12 to 18 and 19 to 40, respectively. Havighurst opted for 13 to 18 and 19 to 30. Despite these relatively small chronological differences, it is clear that both believed that full adulthood did not arrive until age 30 (Cart, 2010: 7).

To attain such full adulthood, Havighurst, in the late 1940s, posited the notion that young people must successfully complete seven rites of passage, or as he called them "developmental tasks." They were (1) achieve new and more mature relations with age mates of both sexes, (2) achieve masculine or feminine social roles, (3) accept their physiques and use their bodies effectively, (4) achieve emotional independence of parents and other adults, (5) prepare for marriage and family life, (6) prepare for economic careers, and (7) acquire a set of values and an ethical system as a guide to behavior.

"To accomplish the tasks," Havighurst asserted, "will lead to happiness and to success with later tasks, while failure leads to unhappiness in the individual, disapproval by society, and difficulty with later tasks" (Cart, 2011d: 61).

To help young people accomplish these tasks educators turned to books for youth. A leading expert in the field, G. Robert Carlsen, led the way, equating stages of reading development with Havighurst's stages of personal development. In Carlsen's (1980) *Books and the Teenage Reader*, originally published in 1967, he identified three such stages: (1) early adolescence, or ages 11 to 14; (2) middle adolescence, ages 15 to 16; and (3) late adolescence, ages 17 to 18. He then developed a series of book categories that were appropriate to each stage and asserted that early adolescents would enjoy animal, adventure, and mystery stories; middle adolescents would prefer war stories and historical novels; and late adolescents, searches for personal values and books of social significance.

It is worth noting that Hall, Erikson, and Havighurst had all labeled as "adolescents" youth from ages 12 to 30 or even 40. Carlsen, on the other hand, limited his interest to what he called "teen-age[rs]," perhaps to signify that his classification was less inclusive than the former and was consistent with the age of high school students.

As for librarians who were discovering this population segment and beginning to develop collections and services for them, the professional term was *young adult*, one that has remained until recently. In fact, the term *young adult* appeared in library literature as early as 1944 and became formalized in 1957 with the American Library Association's formation of the Young Adult Services Division (YASD), the precursor to today's YALSA.

Like Carlsen, YASD from its beginning tacitly defined young adults as being ages 12 to 18, though it was not until 1991 that the division, in concert with the National Center for Education Statistics, formally defined young adults as "those individuals from 12 to 18 years old."

Clearly, the driving force in both Carlsen's and YASD's definitions was the age of the junior high and high school populations. The problem with this, however, was that it made youth who turned 19 into what might be called "instant adults" who were no longer eligible for young adult services. And so it remained, for good or ill, until the turn of the twenty-first century when the definition of YA once again began to broaden as many observers of the field started to argue that YA should now be regarded as youth ages 12 to 25 or even 12 to 34. How did this come about?

As is the case with so much in this material world, a root cause was economic and was vested in the bursting of the stock market bubble in 2000. The result of this fiscal disaster was a dramatic dip in the economy, which in turn caused the job market to dry up as it had in the 1930s. And so when today's high school and college graduates began entering the job market in 2003–2004, there were not enough jobs to go around, and rather than starve (not a happy prospect) many of these young people moved back home to live with their parents. This situation continues, as a recent Rutgers University poll found that fully 30 percent of recent college graduates had not found employment six months after graduation (Wolverson, 2011).

By 2004, a total of 52 percent of America's 18- to 24-year-olds were still living at home (Clifford, 2005). One indication of the significance of this phenomenon is that *adultescent* was chosen by the editors of *Webster's New World College Dictionary* as Word of the Year for 2004.

A second cause of the expansion of adolescence was neurological/physiological. For years scientists had believed that the human brain was fully formed shortly after puberty (typically age 12). However, thanks to a major longitudinal study sponsored by the National Institute of Mental Health, scientists recently discovered—to their surprise—that the brain is in fact not fully developed until the age of 25 or older. The final areas of the brain to mature are the prefrontal cortex and cerebellum, which govern emotional control and higher-order cognitive functions. In other words, young people remain adolescents until the age of 25 or thereabouts (Henig, 2010).

In addition to economic and physiological causes, at least one cultural cause should be considered—the creation of MTV in 1981. In the years since, the so-called MTV demographic—those ages 12 to 25—has become a commonplace element of branding, marketing, and to be a bit redundant, demography. While these numbers are certainly more arbitrary than those of, say, a Havighurst or Erickson, they do suggest a commonality of interest between 12- and 25-year-olds. "The age at which Americans reach adulthood is increasing," psychologist Robert Epstein told the magazine *Psychology Today.* "Thirty is the new twenty and most Americans now believe a person isn't an adult until age twenty-six" (Cart, 2011d: 119).

While there may be some uncertainty among the general public about the age range occupied by adultescents, there is none among the members of the medical profession. Between 1994 and 2005, nearly one thousand doctors were certified in a new subspecialty: adolescent medicine. As *Newsweek* magazine observed, "The old view of adolescence was that it ended at 18 or 19. Now, with many young adults in their early twenties still struggling to find their foothold in the world, doctors call the years from 18 to 28 'the second decade of adolescence'" (Kantrowitz and Springen, 2005).

During this second decade of adolescence, more and more young people seem to be taking time off from completing school and/or getting jobs to pursue interests for personal satisfaction or because they feel the experience will look good on their résumés; some of these experiences in fact consist of unpaid internships, an increasingly common phenomenon that saves employers the cost of hiring a regular employee. These life experiences are being called "gap years" or "the timeout" and may recall the nineteenth-century custom of the *Wanderjahr*, a period of wandering that typically saw wealthy young Englishmen heading to Europe to broaden their life experience (Finder, 2005).

Like the first period of adolescence (12 to 18), the members of this new period have an array of developmental tasks to negotiate, though in their case only five instead of seven. They are (1) finishing school, (2) moving out of their parents' home, (3) getting a good job with benefits, (4) getting married, and (5) having a child (Henig, 2010).

Offering these five choices, *Time* magazine interviewed an array of adultescents asking them, "What makes you an adult?" (Grossman, 2005). A total of 22 percent said it was having their first child; another 22 percent said it was moving away from home, though surely not to buy a home of their own (the *Kansas City Star* has reported that the average age of first-time homebuyers has climbed from 29 to 33 in the last decade [Montgomery, 2005]). Nineteen percent opted for getting a good job; 14 percent said it was getting married (the median age for a first marriage in the 1970s was 21 for women and 23 for men, and by 2009 it had grown to 26 for women and 28 for men), and 10 percent said it was finishing their education (though more and more students are taking five years to complete their undergraduate education and 23 percent of *Time* respondents said they were at least 24 or older before they finished).

As a follow-up question *Time* also asked, "How would you describe yourself?" To this question 61 percent replied "an adult." However, 29 percent said they were just entering adulthood, and 10 percent said they were not yet out of school.

When *Time* then asked of the 29 percent why they didn't consider themselves adults, 35 percent replied it was because they "were just enjoying life the way it is." Another 33 percent said it was because they weren't yet financially independent, and 13 percent said it was because they weren't out of school.

The consideration of financial independence brings us back to the economy. Going to school poses a major financial burden. A total of 52 percent of those interviewed said they owed money when they finished. How much? Well, 66 percent said it was over $10,000, 23 percent owed more than $30,000, and 5 percent owed a whopping $100,000. And that is not all; there is also credit card debt to be considered. According to public policy group Demos, credit card debt for 18- to 24-year-olds more than doubled from 1992 to 2001 (Grossman, 2005: 45). Small wonder so many of these young people are returning to the parental nest.

On the other hand, the fact that this relieves them of virtually every economic burden, including repaying student loans, means the new adultescents have a fairly significant amount of disposable income. *Time*'s survey asked these boomerangers' opinion of what they might spend more on than most people do. Their responses: 32 percent said "eating out," 26 percent said "clothes," 17 percent identified "going to or renting movies," and 12 percent said "computers and software."

Not surprisingly, this new market has resulted in the establishment of a new market research firm called Twentysomething Inc. It is the first such company to offer research on adultescents to corporate America (shades of the 1940s Youth Marketing Company). David Morrison, president and founder of the company, confirms the new buying power of adultescents, telling *Time*, "They are the optimum market to be going after for consumer electronics, Game Boys, flat screen TVs, iPods, couture fashion, exotic vacations, and so forth" (Grossman, 2005).

On the other hand, Morrison also notes: "Young adults are the first to feel the brunt of a bad economy and the last to feel the benefits of a recovering economy" (AP, 2009). It's worth noting that a firm called Twentysomething should use the term *young adult*. This appears to reinforce this writer's own redefinition of the term.

Despite this somewhat gloomy observation, it is surely likely that if and when the economy recovers and viable jobs become more readily available, a good number of those who are presently adultescents will assume full adult responsibilities. However, according to Morrison enough will remain to ensure that this new stage of life continues to be a sociological, psychological, and cultural phenomenon. Many young people will continue to drift along enjoying life; many will remain financially dependent ("The stigma of depending on your parents is gone" [Montgomery, 2005]); and many will simply remain unsettled. *Time* discovered that half of its respondents had worked at anywhere from two to six different jobs in the preceding three years. Another 25 percent had lived at three different addresses in the previous five years, while 22 percent had lived at four or more.

The existence of this new, distinct life stage surely demands new library services to meet its members' personal needs—psychological, emotional, and developmental—just as service to the new category of human being called young adult did 50-some years ago. Though there must be many different kinds of library service to meet these various needs, our focus in the remainder of this chapter will be on materials and their selection.

A New Literature for a New Category of Users

Historically, library collections for young adults have been pegged at users ages 12 to 18. To expand this user base to include 19- to 25-year-olds would require a similar expansion of the collection to include what we have traditionally called adult books. Of course, there is nothing necessarily new about such inclusion. American Library Association (ALA) has been including adult titles on its lists of best books for teenage readers since 1930 when it established its Young People's Reading Round Table (young people in this context translates roughly to today's definition of young adult). Because there was no YA literature then, the Round Table's annual list of best books included a sometimes uneasy mix of adult and children's books, ranging from Will James's *Lone Cowboy* to Edna Ferber's *Cimarron*.

This situation continued until 1948 when, acknowledging that the members of the new category of user called young adult had no interest in children's books, the list name was changed to Adult Books for Young People. In 1966 it was changed again to Best Books for Young Adults (BBYA), though the list continued to be one of exclusively adult books until 1973 when ALA's Young Adult Services Division (YASD) finally included young adult books (though to be fair YA literature as we know it today was still a newly minted genre, not having launched until 1967 with the publication of S. E. Hinton's *The Outsiders* and Robert Lipsyte's *The Contender*).

Since that time there has been considerable discussion (some of it heated) over the proper proportion of adult and YA titles to be included on the BBYA list. Some have suggested that adult titles should be eliminated altogether, so that the list would be exclusively YA titles stressing the importance of YA literature in meeting the life needs of its target audience and of encouraging publishers to issue more books in the genre. While this debate has yet to be resolved, in the late 1990s YALSA did establish a new award relevant to this discussion. The Alex Award honoring pioneering YA librarian Margaret Alexander Edwards consists of an annual list of the ten best adult books of the year for young adults.

Adult is not the only non-YA (12–18) category to be included on the BBYA list; for some years it has also included what are now being called "middle school" books for readers in grades five through nine and ages 10 to 14. As a result—at least in BBYA terms—YA literature could theoretically if not practically be said to appeal to readers anywhere from ages 10 to 25. But this, of course, is a ridiculously broad range, impossibly broad when one considers the differences in developmental needs between a reader of age 10 and a reader of 25.

Recognizing this, I suggested in my *Booklist* column "Carte Blanche" for January 1, 2005, that we now divide YA literature into three categories. The first would be middle school literature for 10- to 14-year-olds; the second category would embrace the traditional 12 to 18 readership but instead of being called young adult would be called "teen books"; and the third category for those 19- to 25-year-olds would now be called "young adult." These would not be rigidly fixed categories, of course, since there is always some overlapping in such arrangements, tacitly acknowledging the differing rates of development.

Practical Considerations: The Crossover Book

Adopting and implementing a new definition of young adult—turning the theoretical into reality—requires attention to a number of practical considerations. Among these are the types of books and other materials that might be included as well as placing increasing importance on the selection and acquisition of reviews and review media.

If we acknowledge that 19- to 25-year-olds are indeed young adults with specific developmental needs, we also need to acknowledge that simply adding more traditional and even classic adult books to the collection will not meet those needs. Happily, however, a new kind of fiction is now available that might.

Thanks to the multigenerational popularity of J. K. Rowling's Harry Potter books, publishers have begun experimenting with the publication of other titles having similar multigenerational appeal. Called "crossover books," these titles are being published as either YA or adult, but in either case they have intrinsic appeal to both traditional teens and to the new young adults. They are almost all coming-of-age stories and many recall Carlsen's type of novel suggested for late adolescents, though they are significantly more sophisticated in theme, language, and incident.

An early example of this type of book is Stephen Chbosky's *The Perks of Being a Wallflower*, the story of a troubled 14-year-old boy who finds his future in friendship. This was published as an adult title by MTV/Pocket Books, but in the dozen or so years since its 1999 publication it has become a modern YA classic in the same way that J. D. Salinger's *The Catcher in the Rye* did for an earlier generation of young adults.

Another interesting early example of the crossover novel is Mark Haddon's *The Curious Incident of the Dog in the Nighttime*. Though first published in England in two simultaneous editions, one adult and the other YA, the American edition of this memorable book about a boy with Asperger's syndrome was published only as an adult title. Another example is Yann Martel's *Life of Pi*. Though published here in hardcover as an adult title, its publisher, Harcourt, recognized that the unusual survival story of a boy and a tiger had crossover appeal and subsequently published a paperback edition specifically targeted at a YA readership.

Australia is a hotbed of such simultaneous publications; some of the authors whose work falls into this category are Markus Zusak (*The Book Thief*), Sonya Hartnett (*What the Birds See*), and Margo Lanagan (*Tender Morsels*). Interestingly, unlike Haddon and Martel all three of these authors are published here only as YA, though the fact is they could just as easily have been published as adult. Another case in point is American author Curtis Sittenfeld's first novel *Prep*, a coming-of-age prep school story that could easily have been published as YA but instead was issued as an adult title. The opposite, however, happened to author Margo Rabb, whose first book *Cures for Heartbreak* was written as an adult novel but was published here in the United States as YA. This raises the question: What does distinguish a traditional YA novel from a crossover? I would argue that the chief distinctions are that the crossover is character-driven rather than plot-driven; that the setting is more fully realized and far more than a static backdrop; that adult characters (those over age 25) may play significant parts, and the subject matter if not more sophisticated at least receives a more subtle treatment; and that the chances of ambiguity are greater. That said, two principal areas of commonality are the age of the protagonist relative to the readership and the coming-of-age nature of the narrative.

To demonstrate that crossovers move up as well as down, we should note that many titles that have been written and published as YA could nevertheless have been published as adult. Two examples that immediately come to mind are M. T. Anderson's two-volume novel *Octavian Nothing* and Aidan Chambers's *This Is All.*

Lastly, consider that an increasing number of established adult authors are now writing and being published for YAs, authors like Joyce Carol Oates, Francine Prose, Julia Alvarez, Alice Hoffman, and others. That these authors are now writing for YAs may attract their built-in adult audience to the dynamic exercise that YA has become.

Clearly, the long-established barriers that for years rigidly defined a book's intended audience are becoming more fluid every day. This is a great boon for readers but also a bit of a challenge to both book selectors and reviewers.

It would simplify a complexity of issues if publishers were to recognize the "new" young adult (the 19- to 25-year-old) and begin publishing books specifically targeted at this readership, but so far they have not. Librarians are not without influence in the world of publishing, and therefore need to make their new needs known and apply pressure to encourage publishers to begin meeting these needs. Librarians also would benefit from a better understanding of modern publishing. Knowledge, as the old saying has it, is power. So for example librarians need to recognize that publishers seem to have a horror of trying anything new, a horror that rivals that of the motion picture industry. There's no surprise about that, of course, since most publishers are owned by giant conglomerates that also own motion picture studios. The ramifications, however, are widespread, and explain why publishing for young readers has become "event publishing"—witness the search for the next big thing in the wake of Harry Potter that can then be turned into a media event.

Another challenge to implementing a new kind of crossover book is managerial and economic: if a new YA line were to be created by a publisher, for example, the question arises of who would control it—the adult division or the juvenile? Alas, there is no opportunity for joint publication since both divisions would be in competition for profits. The same situation abounds in chain bookstores, especially Barnes and Noble, where no book can be shelved in more than one place; for example, despite its YA appeal *The Curious Incident of the Dog in the Nighttime* could be shelved only in adult fiction. Otherwise two departments of the store would have to share profits, an impossibility since each is an independent profit center in competition for sales dollars with the other. And while we're speaking of economics, the simple answer to the often-articulated question of who decides if a book will be published as a YA or as an adult is the sales and marketing department of the publisher (with minimal editorial input). Often this decision may be vetted by Barnes & Noble, since the market for YA (old and new) has since the turn of the twenty-first century migrated from the traditional institutional market to the retail one.

The point of our brief excursion into the land of the bottom line is to point out that any book selector who is trying to establish a collection for the 19- to 25-year-old constituency will have to be familiar with both adult and juvenile publishing. This is no easy feat since upwards of 5,000 YA retail titles are published each year, not to mention the equally large number of curriculum-related nonfiction titles issued by the remaining institutional publishers. And the number of adult titles is exponentially larger. To stay abreast of this avalanche of books is nearly impossible for the individual reader, and this is why reviews are more important now than ever.

Reviews and Reviewing for a New Generation of Readers

The three major young adult review media—*Booklist, School Library Journal* (*SLJ*), and *VOYA*—all feature reviews of adult books for young adults but present them in different ways. *Booklist* adds a note to adult titles deemed to be of interest to this readership; *SLJ* features a separate section of adult books for young adults in its Book Review section. And *VOYA* uses the code "A/YA" to identify "adult-marketed books recommended for YAs."

That all three review media use different methods is secondary to the fact that each does give specific attention to adult books that are suitable for and of interest to teens and young adults. There is nothing new here; all three have been providing this reader service for a number of years and it has served its purpose well. It is also a great help to those doing retrospective collection development.

Unfortunately, none of the journals identifies YA books suitable for adult readers (crossover trickles up as well as down after all). Considering the increasing number of these books, however, it would seem time for this added annotation to be considered, as it is singularly important for those attempting to build collections for the new YA reader. To understand the type of book I envision as being appropriate for this, I offer one example, Aidan Chambers's landmark novel *This Is All*. This writer happened to review this title for *Booklist* and thinking it relevant to this discussion I have included it here (Cart, 2006).

This Is All, by Aidan Chambers

Nineteen-year-old Cordelia Kenn records the story of her life for the daughter with whom she is pregnant, planning to present it to the girl on her sixteenth birthday. The form Cordelia chooses for her tale is unusual: she is writing—or constructing—a pillow book (a la the tenth-century Japanese "Pillow Book of Sei Shonagon"), in which she not only records a narrative but also jots down poetry, ideas, observations, lists (she's a compulsive list-maker), musings and more. Cordelia is such an acute observer and has such a lively, inquiring mind that ultimately her pillow book becomes six books. Each one has its own structure and narrative strategy. Book 2, for example, is actually two stories—one fills the left-hand pages;

the second, the right-hand pages. Readers must choose the order in which to read them. Some will complain about this; others will complain about the novel's great length. But the curious, the patient, and the adventurous will treasure the novel's challenges and savor its great rewards.

Arguably, the book offers the most complete character study in all of young adult literature, showing readers the life, mind and soul of a teen-age girl, while also giving readers full-dress portraits of her baby's father, her friends, her family, and—most satisfyingly—her English teacher and mentor, Julie. Cordelia records not only her love for these people but also for Shakespeare, for poetry, for words. Unsparingly honest and candid, she never flinches from exploring the realities of her body or from recounting the sexually explicit details of her affair with an older man and her terrifying ordeal when she is kidnapped and threatened with rape. Cordelia records it all, because she wants to understand it all; she wants to know everything about herself, and her way of understanding is writing. Thus, she explores the why of things as well as the what and the how. In so doing she's by turns captivating and maddening, for she loves to analyze and to discover ambiguities.

And so her story challenges—but it will grow richer and larger with each reading. Ultimately, this ambitious and multilayered novel is more than a mere pièce de résistance; it is the masterpiece of one of young adult literature's greatest living writers.

Yes, I liked the book quite a lot, and I wouldn't hesitate to recommend it to the most sophisticated adult readers, especially since Cordelia is 19, the lower end of the new YA range.

As noted earlier, none of the review journals, like publishers, specifically identifies books for 19- to 25-year-old readers either, although since late 2004 this writer at least has been reviewing such books for *Booklist* magazine. I include two sample reviews (including their YA "tags" at the end) here (Cart, 2004, 2011a).

PREP, by Curtis Sittenfeld

"The world was so big!" 17-year-old Lee thinks in wonder as she prepares to graduate from Ault, the tony East Coast prep school that provides the setting for this bittersweet coming-of-age novel. A scholarship student from South Bend, Indiana, the relentlessly introspective and self-absorbed Lee has always regarded herself as an invisible outsider, "one of the mild, boring, peripheral girls." No wonder she's astonished when the most popular boy in class shows up in her bedroom one night, and they begin an increasingly intimate affair that lasts throughout their senior year. It's no surprise at all, however, that it should end badly. For the denouement, like so much else in this first novel, is simply too predictable. Saving the book from formula, however, are some fine writing and assorted shrewd insights into both the psychology of adolescence and the privileged world of a traditional prep school.

YA. Teens are clearly Sittenfeld's audience, despite her book being published as an adult novel. MC

The Borrower, by Rebecca Makkai

Lucy, a twenty-six-year-old children's librarian, has a favorite patron, a bright, book-loving ten-year-old named Ian. The trouble is the boy's fundamentalist mother insists he read only books "with the breath of God in them." When the parents enroll their son in a behavior modification program designed to "cure" him of his nascent homosexuality, the boy runs away and Lucy decides she must help. "Borrowing" (some might say kidnapping) the boy, Lucy and he—two fugitives now—hit the road. But who is really running away? Is it Ian or is it actually Lucy replicating the experience of her émigré parents who, years before, had run away from their Russian homeland? And is America, as a friend of Lucy's family claims, truly a nation of runaways but with no place left to run? Time (and considerable driving in Lucy's ancient car) may tell. An accomplished short story writer, Makkai has written a splendid first novel that cleverly weaves telling references to children's books into her whimsically patchwork plot. Larger-than-life characters and an element of the picaresque add to the book's delights. Best of all, however, is Lucy's absolutely unshakeable faith in the power of books to save. From her lips, readers, to God's ear.

YA. Teen readers will identify with Lucy's desire to help Ian and will enjoy the plot's many twists and turns. MC

The Sittenfeld review—published in January 2005—was the first this writer did of a crossover novel. Note that the two reviews feature protagonists who are at either end of the adultescent stage: Lee is 17 and Lucy is 26, the outer limit of the new YA. Both novels feature female protagonists who are experiencing delayed rite-of-passage experiences, and both novels are by women. All of these factors are quite typical of the new crossover novel.

Not all crossovers are targeted at YAs. Some are simply traditional adult novels that have significant appeal to readers of all ages. I include here a review of one of those (Cart, 2011b).

Jamrach's Menagerie, by Carol Birch

When he is eight years old, Jaffy Brown, a nineteenth century London street urchin, finds himself in the mouth of an escaped tiger. While he survives that unpleasantness, the experience does change his life when the tiger's owner, Mr. Jamrach, an importer of exotic animals, gives him a job. Seven years later the boy—along with this best friend Tim—finds himself aboard a whaler headed for the South Seas. Their assignment:

(continued on next page)

(continued from previous page)

capture a fabled dragon for Mr. Jamrach who will then sell it to a wealthy and eccentric collector. Things do not go as planned and the result is an almost unbearably suspenseful story of adventure and survival. But it is also a story of madness, malevolence, and an almost palpable evil. And as the story advances, a powerfully pervasive sense of melancholy takes hold of the reader as the tiger did young Jaffy and one wonders if it will ever let go. Though Mr. Jamrach is based on a real historical figure and Jaffy's voyage on that of the ill-fated whaler Essex, the story is entirely Birch's own and her principal characters her own wonderful invention. She is, moreover a brilliant stylist and reading her is like Christmas, every word being a gift to the reader. Though Birch is an established writer in England, this is her first novel to be published in the U.S. One fervently hopes it will not be the last!

YA. The wonderful narrative sweep of Birch's story will captivate teen readers as will Jaffy and his friend Tim. MC

Nonfiction is an essential part of the new YA collection, as well, so I include a review of this type of book (Cart, 2011c).

The Winter of Our Disconnect, by Susan Maushart

Australian journalist and single parent Maushart reports on her family's decision to take a figurative six-month voyage into an unplugged life—easier said than done when your family consists of three teenagers! No wonder she describes the "voyage" as "The Caine Mutiny" with her playing Captain Queeg. As it happens, the voyage is relatively storm free, though there are some squalls at the beginning. Maushart nearly goes through withdrawal after turning off her iPhone and finds that her work takes twice as long without a computer. In a way the kids are more adaptable (perhaps because their mother offers them various bribes). They quickly learn how to do homework without access to Wikipedia and discover such joys as playing the saxophone and having sing-alongs. Interspersed with the family's experience is a great deal of timely information about the impact of electronic technology on Generation M (8- to 18-year-olds) and not all of it is pretty. Nevertheless, the entire family is relieved when the experiment is over but delighted to discover that it has introduced them to "life itself."

YA. Though some teens will view this as a horror story, others will find it thought-and discussion-provoking. And, yes, it will be great for classroom use. MC

Book Reviewing 2.0

Ironically, the growing importance of reviews comes at the same time—thanks to the economy and the migration of print to the web—that some traditional review media are in danger of becoming extinct, newspapers being the first to feel the impact. A major reason is once again economic. Understand that as print has increasingly migrated from paper to digital form, many long-established newspapers have folded while the survivors have dramatically reduced staff and content to cut production costs. Others have created as yet unprofitable versions of the newspaper online. As a result, only one weekly book review section survives in print form in America, that of the *New York Times*; all of the others have been discontinued, though in some cases truncated versions survive online (such as the *Los Angeles Times* and the *Washington Post*).

Another new electronic phenomenon that is changing the world of book reviews is blogs. Though as recently as five years ago blogs about children's and YA books were a rarity, the field has since exploded. A June 2011 search of the website Kidlitosphere Central reveals a strapping total of 900 active blogs, up from 300 in January 2010 (http://www.kidlito sphere.org/members/).

While many blogs do not feature traditional book reviews, the highly personal, mostly unedited, idiosyncratic, sometimes controversial, sometimes ill-informed commentary they do include is already changing the way many people would define reviews and reviewers. In fact, in today's wired world everyone with a computer can become a self-styled book reviewer. Fortunately, all of the major newspapers that have launched websites include at least one blog as part of their book coverage—the *New York Times* "Papercutz" is one of the best—as do the major professional book review media. At least these blogs are more reliable sources of information and opinion than the self-created, independent versions.

In the meantime, the major professional review sources like *Booklist*, *SLJ*, and *VOYA* have all licensed their reviews to the two major online bookstores, Amazon and Barnes & Noble, for reprint at their sites. This is certainly convenient for librarians who are spared searching a variety of different sources to find reviews. However, it also means that reviews originally written for professional readers are now being read by the general public, many of whom are visiting these commercial websites in search of books to purchase. Since it is the positive review that sparks sales, there is some professional concern of the influence these behemoth online sellers may bring to bear on the nature and content of reviews to drive sales, bringing economic pressure on review media (e.g., threatening the loss of their license) to make reviews more positive and books being reviewed more attractive. In late 2012, Amazon began culling reviews on its website but did not provide specific guidelines for deciding which reviews would be pulled.

Certainly, the online bookstores have already introduced another less than salutary phenomenon to the world of book reviewing: the self-posted reader review. Just as anyone with a computer can start a blog, so can anyone visit Amazon or Barnes & Noble and post a review of any book. It almost goes without saying that the quality and reliability of these reviews vary wildly, and that many of them are written by people who haven't read the book, are friends of the author, or even the authors themselves posting pseudonymously.

On a more positive note there are a number of online sites that offer a lively, reliable mix of book news, features, and reviews. Several that focus on adult books and publishing are Galleycat, Bookforum, and Bookre porter.com. Such online magazines as Salon.com, Slate.com, and "Book Beast," a department of Tina Brown's The Daily Beast, also are worth following. As for sites specializing in books for young readers, two of the best are Teenreads.com and Kidsreads.com—both services of the Book Report Network. Each offers more reliable online reviews since they are edited and written by professionals. They offer the added benefit of being aimed at teens and young adults themselves. And being online the reviews are more likely than print reviews to be found by teens and young adults who are, famously, habitués of the online world. Finally, being online these reviews can be more timely than those that have to go through a print process.

That said, the next major home for book "reviews" is now predicted to be the various social networking sites—both generic ones like Facebook and MySpace and also more subject-specific ones like Goodreads.com and Librarything.com. Goodreads is arguably the largest social network for readers in the world. According to its website it boasts 5,500,000 members who recommend books, compare what they are reading, form book clubs, and so on. LibraryThing is an online service that both helps people catalog their books easily and helps them connect with others having the same taste in books, swap reading suggestions, and so on.

But here, too, the problem remains one of reliability. Consider that if you do a Google search for the phrase "children's and young adult book reviews," you will be overwhelmed with 14,200,000 hits. Learning how to select from among this surfeit of "stuff" and how to evaluate one's findings is clearly becoming a fundamental part of every nascent librarian's education. And speaking of fundamentals: this avalanche of book reviews and other book-related information on the Internet suggests that the single most important aspect of the book review today is the credentials of the reviewers themselves.

Meanwhile, the long-standing and often-criticized problem with reviews—their too brief length—may someday be resolved by the burgeoning presence of blogs, which do allow for more discursive discussion of individual books. When these blogs are features of established, creditable websites like Booklistonline.com or Publishersweekly.com, this could represent a positive change. For the moment, however, most traditional professional reviews remain brief (seldom longer than 200 words, if that), and may be getting briefer as production costs continue to escalate because the number of books being published also soars. For the reviewer, this means an endless exercise in economy and self-discipline. In the world of traditional book reviewing, less really is more—particularly now when more books are being published than ever before. According to R. R. Bowker, the number of new juvenile (children's and YA) book titles and editions published in 2008 was nearly 30,000! For older librarians who remember when this total was closer to 2,500, such a statistic is startling and begs careful analysis. Thus, librarians must become more conversant with the world of publishing and with trends in the field. They must cultivate a new group of readers—the new young adults—to determine their reading tastes and interests, for there is no question that the last five years have seen more books for young readers published than ever before in US history, and the growth rate has been particularly steep in the YA area, growing from approximately 500 to 5,000, according to YALSA.

No matter how much YA books and the young adults who read them change, one thing will surely remain constant: the essential importance of reviews. Good reviews are essential not only to ensure that good books never go overlooked but, in a larger sense, also to guarantee that by identifying and analyzing excellence in books for young readers, reviewers will stimulate young people to read better books and publishers to issue more works of enduring quality and interest to our new category of young adult, the adultescent.

Conclusion

Over the course of the last several years the traditional definition of young adult as individuals ages 12 to 18 has changed dramatically. Both researchers and cultural observers have concluded that young adulthood now extends to age 25. Thus far, libraries have failed to recognize this phenomenon, and as a result no new collections of materials speaking to this new group's personal, intellectual, and developmental needs have been created. It is important that librarians consider there are now three YA literatures: middle school literature, teen literature, and literature for the new young adults ages 19 to 25. In developing new collections for this new service group, librarians need to be particularly aware of crossover books, those books with multigenerational appeal. Finally, librarians need to become thoroughly familiar with new sources of reviews, many of them online.

Numerous challenges remain. The online world of information about and reviews of books can be extremely unreliable, since anyone who has a computer can become a blogger and self-styled reviewer with no credentials whatsoever. Another major challenge is determining who will be responsible for creating, organizing, and managing new collections for the new young adult. Paying for these collections is another significant challenge, as is the problem of space—where the new collection will be located and how much space can be allocated to it—how it will be introduced to the community, and so on.

Changes and challenges can be intimidating, but they are definitely worth the prize: recognizing and serving a new community of users.

References

AP (Associated Press). 2009. "Goodbye Jobs, Hello Mom and Dad, Say Young Adults." *USA Today*, November 24. http://usatoday30.usatoday.com/news/nation/2009 -11-24-boomerang-kids_N.htm.

Carlsen, G. Robert. 1980. *Books and the Teenage Reader: A Guide for Teachers, Librarians, and Parents*. 2nd ed. New York: HarperCollins.

Cart, Michael. 2004. "Prep." *Booklist* 101, no. 8: 709.

———. 2006. "This Is All." *Booklist* 102, no. 22: 66.

———. 2010. *Young Adult Literature from Romance to Realism*. Chicago: ALA Editions.

———. 2011a. "The Borrower." *Booklist* 107, no. 17: 66.

———. 2011b. "Jamrach's Menagerie." *Booklist* 107, no. 18: 23.

———. 2011c. "The Winter of Our Disconnect." *Booklist* 107, no. 7: 8.

———. 2011d. *Young Adult Literature: From Romance to Realism*. Chicago: American Library Association.

CDC (Centers for Disease Control and Prevention). 2011. "Life Expectancy." http:// www.cdc.gov/nchs/fastats/lifexpec.htm.

Clifford, Jane. 2005. "Refilling the Nest." *San Diego Union Tribune*, August 20: E1.

Finder, Alan. 2005. "For Some College Graduates, a Fanciful Detour (or Two)." *New York Times*, October 23: 23.

Grossman, Lev. 2005. "Grow Up? Not So Fast." *Time*, January 16: 42.

Henig, Robin Marantz. 2010. "Why Are So Many People in their 20s Taking So Long to Grow Up?" *New York Times*, August 18.

Kantrowitz, Barbara, and Karen Springen. 2005. "A Teen Health Gap." *Newsweek*, December 11: 65.

Montgomery, Rick. 2005. "The Elastic State of Growing Up: More Young Adults Stay Longer in the Nest." *Kansas City Star*, April 24: 1.

Wolverson, Roya. 2011. "NowWhat?" *Time*, June 13. http://www.time.com/time/magazine/article/0,9171,2075326,00.html.

PART II

From White and Marginal
to Civic Partners

"The Library Is Like Her House"

Reimagining Youth of Color in LIS Discourses

Kafi D. Kumasi

In the library and information science (LIS) field, scholarly discourses and practices tend to overlook or marginalize the unique backgrounds, identities, and literacy practices of youth of color, or youth from historically underrepresented racial/ethnic backgrounds. In this chapter, I use some of the hallmark themes of critical race theory (CRT) to interrogate the ways in which the LIS field sees and positions youth of color against the backdrop of the mainstream white cultural norms and institutional practices. In keeping with the CRT theme *voice*, I argue that it is just as important for LIS scholars to understand how youth of color view and experience libraries and librarians as it is for LIS scholars to contemplate new ways of seeing and defining young adults. I conclude by offering a series of critical questions that might help LIS scholars move toward more culturally sensitive conceptualizations of youth.

If the charge of this volume is to examine the broad question of how the LIS field should define or envision young adults (YAs), then the specific goal of this chapter is to examine that query as it relates to youth of color. The repositioning of this question, I believe, helps place issues of race, power, and white privilege more squarely at the forefront of LIS scholarship, which to the present has not received such critical examinations

(Honma, 1995). One of the goals of this chapter is, therefore, to help LIS scholars develop a more critical, reflexive stance that would enable them to understand how whiteness and white privilege function in their own lives and ultimately how they envision youth of color in libraries. I contend that the current (and historical) vision of youth in libraries is one that has been framed primarily by Eurocentric cultural norms and aesthetics. Everything from collection development policies, rules of library usage, library programming, and hiring practices, to views about what constitutes literacy has been historically constructed by and for whites (Pawley, 1998).

Another goal of this work is to insert the voices and experiences of youth of color into the conversation, particularly as it relates to their experiences in libraries. Doing so will help offset an often one-sided conversation about what libraries can do for youth of color that does not include their own voices and experiences. Critical race theory (CRT) is a promising interpretive lens through which to examine this topic, because it holds whiteness and white privilege up to scrutiny while foregrounding the voices of people of color as a legitimate point of entry for examining these issues (Delgado and Stefancic, 2001). Therefore, in this chapter I use three hallmark themes of CRT—voice, interest convergence, and whiteness as property—to help frame a discussion about the ways in which libraries can better envision and define youth of color.

Voice

"The library is like her house."

—HOPE, 15-year-old African-American female

Sample evidence from my dissertation research with a diverse group of African-American youth confirms the notion that some youth of color experience feelings of cultural disconnect with their school and public libraries and librarians. The above quote was taken from a segment of transcript gathered during a book club conversation I helped to facilitate (Kumasi, 2008). The youth were being asked some preliminary questions about their library usage and reading habits. Hope's statement that "the library is like her house" seems to capture a certain view that some library spaces reflect the cultural norms and values of the librarians who operate them. Moreover, her choice of the word *house* is significant because it carries certain implicit references to words like *ownership*, *comfortability*, and *exclusivity*.

To further dissect Hope's statement from a CRT perspective, one might ask questions such as the following: Would you ordinarily feel welcomed in her house? Are there any symbols or cultural things in her house that remind you of home? Do the rules that seem to govern her house seem similar to the rules your family keeps at home? Could your family afford a house like hers and do your neighbors look like you? Would living at her house enable you to attend a desirable school? And finally, do you think her house was ever been broken into? If so, how swift do you think the police would respond?

CRT provides the interpretive power to ask these kinds of provocative questions since it looks at the more systemic issues that underlie current racial inequalities. Through the construct of "voice," CRT scholars recognize the centrality of the experiential knowledge of people of color and view this knowledge as legitimate, appropriate, and critical to understanding, analyzing, and teaching about racial subordination. Therefore, from a CRT perspective, the statement that "the library is like her house" would not be dismissed simply as one person's subjective opinion. Rather, as a CRT analysis it would acknowledge the ability of a person or a group to articulate experiences in ways that are unique to that person or group (Dixson and Rousseau, 2006). Through storytelling and counter-narratives, disenfranchised people are provided the intellectual space to name their own realities in areas such as academia, where they may have been previously marginalized.

Interest Convergence

Interest convergence is another hallmark CRT theme that can help library scholars question the way they see (or don't see) youth of color in libraries. Interest convergence is a thesis proposed by Derrick Bell that maintains the white majority group tolerates advances for racial justice only when it suits its interests to do so. This thesis plays out subtly, often requiring multiple theoretical tools to fully unpack. It has been used most notably by leading CRT scholar Bell to explain the real impetus behind the passage of the Civil Rights Act of 1964 (Wright, 2005). Through his research, Bell found that the motivating factor behind the bill's passage was to protect the national reputation of the United States amid a tense political climate during the Cold War (Bell, 1980). The world was watching the United States, and leaders in the US government knew that they could not very well take a moral stand against other countries that were facing human rights dilemmas if their own country did not afford Black citizens basic equal rights. Therefore, the advancement of civil rights for African-Americans coincided with the dominant white political interest of the US government to be seen as a leader in the global political landscape. Without this convergence of interests, Bell and others argue that the so-called civil rights gains we now celebrate may not have occurred were they not also in the immediate interest of the dominant white political powers.

The question is, How does this understanding relate to the ways in which libraries envision youth of color? One way it relates is in how librarians conceptualize youth of color and their literate potential. For example, if librarians hold a cultural deficit perspective toward youth of color, they might only see their so-called problems without recognizing their unique talents and gifts. They may also hold stereotypical views toward youth of color based on representations they see in the mass media. If a librarian holds a cultural deficit perspective toward youth of color and masks this belief system, but at the same time capitalizes on efforts to promote diversity with youth of color, then that can be seen as interest convergence. Because of the liberal ideology within the LIS profession that uncritically celebrates diversity efforts (Balderrama, 2000), a librarian could benefit personally from implementing a diversity initiative with youth of color. On the other hand, no one might question how such initiatives position youth of color as objects of study and divert attention away from the role libraries and librarians play in maintaining the status quo of racial oppression through established institutional practices and belief systems.

The interest convergence principle can help librarians take a critical look at their own perspectives about youth of color. They might ask themselves questions like these: Do I capitalize on youth initiatives that promote diversity and equality while subconsciously holding a cultural deficit perspective about youth of color themselves? Do I view youth of color as unfortunate victims in a fundamentally just society? Do I transfer the stereotypical images that play out in the media about youth of color onto those whom I might encounter in my library? Do I believe that *all* children can succeed provided the right support and opportunities?

The LIS field has traditionally taken a more pluralistic approach to diversity that avoids dealing directly with race and racial inequities. The problem with the more pluralistic or multicultural initiatives is that they seek to accommodate so many facets of diversity that they often wind up having little or no real impact on any particular group. CRT scholars have made similar critiques about the ineffectiveness of multicultural approaches. Ladson-Billings and Tate state:

> *The multicultural paradigm functions in a manner similar to civil rights law. Instead of creating radically new paradigms which ensure justice, multicultural reforms are routinely, "sucked back into the system"; and just as traditional civil rights law is based on a foundation of human rights, the current multicultural paradigm is mired in a liberal ideology that offers no radical change in the current order. (quoted in Dixson and Rousseau, 2006: 25)*

Thus, from a CRT perspective it is important for librarians to not just study youth of color as objects under the gaze of a predominantly white librarian workforce. Rather, it is incumbent upon librarians to look reflexively at the library's institutional policies and practices to see how they uphold certain cultural norms and worldviews that might marginalize the home and community literacy practices of many youth of color (e.g., rap, spoken word, code-switching, or tagging). Or, it might mean looking at how and why funding and other resources are disproportionally allocated to libraries in affluent (mostly white) suburban communities. A project such as this would not likely get agency funding, but these are the very deep-seated issues that need to be addressed if libraries and librarians are to move beyond a monolithic vision of youth of color that is based primarily on white cultural frames of reference that promote white self-interests.

Whiteness as Property

Understanding the CRT concept of "whiteness as property" can help LIS scholars reframe any number of questions that are taken up in LIS by critically analyzing the way that whiteness has been framed as both the preferred and normal state of being. The principle of whiteness as property maintains that people with white skin have been afforded a set of unearned rights and privileges since the period of slavery. As the ultimate form of property, one who "possesses" whiteness can enjoy (1) the rights of disposition, (2) the right to use and enjoyment, (3) reputation and status property, and (4) the absolute right to exclude (Ladson-Billings and Tate, 1995). Thompson (2001) offers several methodological approaches for helping unmask whiteness in both professional and institutional discourses as well as on a personal level.

Related to discourses around youth in the LIS field, some questions that we might ask ourselves are the following: Do I participate in the "othering" of nonwhite youth by inadvertently assuming a white audience as the default norm in my various library practices (e.g., promotional signage, book displays, collection development, etc.)? Do the rules I support and enforce in the library primarily cater to the cultural and linguistic norms of whites (e.g., rules of noise levels, etc.)? Questions such as these help unmask whiteness as the invisible norm or reference point for thinking about any number of questions taken up in the LIS field.

The principle of whiteness as property can also be applied to examining how the concept of literacy is conceived in YA library discourses and the impact such a stance might have on how youth of color participate in and are viewed in libraries. The way literacy is conceived in the LIS field tends to privilege the literacy practices of white youth, which are often rooted in cognitive and autonomous forms of knowing. This conceptual stance often comes at the expense of supporting the literacy practices of nonwhite youth, which are rooted in sociocultural frameworks of understanding (Langer, 1991). The notion of whiteness itself has been linked to the development of scientific rationalist thinking, which privileges "mind over body, intellectual over experiential ways of knowing, mental abstractions over passion, bodily sensations, and tactile understanding" (Kincheloe, Steinberg, and Hinchey, 1999).

Information literacy, which is the intellectual domain of librarians, falls within this cognitive and positivist tradition of learning (Kapitzke, 2003). This approach begins from a standpoint that students come to the library with specific information problems that arise out of their personal, workplace, or academic concerns. The librarians' role is then to help these youth develop skills in solving these information problems by teaching them how to access the most current, reliable, and authentic information through the library's resources. Yet, this approach leaves librarians at the periphery of the learning experience and positions them more as resource providers than teachers. Thus, there is little room for librarians to help youth address anything other than mundane information problems rather than larger social and cultural concerns they may face (e.g., poverty, unemployment, racial discrimination, etc.) (Kumasi-Johnson, 2007).

Yet, unless the majority white librarian scholarly base is exposed to more expansive perspectives on literacy such as those that frame literacy as a social practice, then those newer approaches will remain on the periphery. Moreover, because there is not a critical mass of library scholars researching literacy from a sociocultural perspective, the dominant view of literacy as a cognitive skill is the only view that can take up "residence" in the LIS field—to use the metaphor of whiteness as property. This may seem like a tangential matter, but I would argue it is a very pressing issue that can have significant implications for how librarians view and engage youth of color. For example, if librarians were to expand how they define literacy to include home and community literacy perspectives, then library instruction might take on a very different form. Instead of doing activities centered on evaluating websites and other static exercises bounded to libraries, librarians might instead take up a more activist role and go into communities and help youth uncover what their real world information concerns are and encourage them to develop skills at posing questions and finding solutions to these real-life issues.

A Note on Intersectionality

As a matter of disclosure, I write this chapter from a social location as a thirtysomething, upper-working-class Black female who is a fifth-generation college graduate. Despite being both self-identified and outwardly labeled as Black, I have probably benefitted from and participated in whiteness in my daily life. The reason a person of color can participate in whiteness is because, as Thompson (2001) notes, "whiteness does not refer to a biological but to a socially constructed category" (under "Differences in Theoretical Focus and Approach": para. 6). Thompson goes on to explain that Black or academics of color who internalize white-privileging institutional norms may be said to benefit from and participate in the promotion of institutional whiteness. Insofar as African-Americans, Latinos, and other nonwhites aspire to material privileges that are coded as white *and* insofar as they see material well-being as earned through individual merit (rather than through a system that excludes all but a few people of color), they may be said to participate in material whiteness. As a Black academic who aspires to achieve a level of success in higher education, I am somewhat caught up in the trappings of whiteness. I do not, however, ascribe to the myth of "Ameritocracy" (Akom, 2008), but rather I recognize that I am a fortunate exception to the implicit rule in higher education that says only so many people of color can gain access to higher-level positions at predominately white institutions. While I do believe that I have *earned* the position I occupy, I recognize that there are many more people of color who are just as deserving but who will not be given this opportunity because there are so few spaces available for faculty of color in the academy.

Similarly, we are all privileged and oppressed to differing degrees. This is what CRT scholars describe as intersectionality, or interlocking systems of oppression. Thus, white librarians who read this should not come away with a sense of guilt or shame about benefiting from and participating in whiteness. By understanding each of our layers of privilege and penalty, we can begin to locate ourselves on the stratum of race, power, and privilege as a first step at being reflexive and self-aware, which can ultimately lead to social transformation.

Understanding one's layers of privilege can also be useful in disrupting negative stereotypes about nonwhite people. One of the first things to recognize when it comes to youth of color is that their racial identity is only *one* facet of their identity and it may *not* be the primary lens through which they view and experience the world. Still, I would argue that taking a "colorblind" stance toward seeing youth of color is not helpful. Most youth of color are aware of the way society views them and how people of color are positioned in the social stratification of society in the United States. To ignore race or to create an atmosphere in libraries that seems to minimize cultural differences and aim for a more colorblind goal could be just as damaging on a subconscious level for some youth of color. It is important to celebrate cultural differences and maintain a healthy balance between promoting mainstream colorblind perspectives and race-conscious world-views in our work with young adults (Carter and Kumasi, 2011).

Conclusion

The question at the heart of this chapter is, How might the LIS field better imagine youth of color in order to embrace their situated identities, their culturally based literacy practices, and their unique social histories? The answer, I believe, lies in looking reflexively at how whiteness functions in the library and scrutinizing how it is operationalized through certain institutional policies and personal belief systems. This work must occur on both the conceptual and the structural levels. Conceptually, the librarian workforce must engage in the messy and tenuous work of holding up to scrutiny our own beliefs, practices, and worldviews about people of color to see how these constructs might privilege white ways of knowing and being. Structurally, we must look at the ways libraries historically (and still today) upheld whiteness through various institutional practices and poli-cies, such as collection development, resource allocation, training, staffing, and so on. Finally, we might all benefit from keeping several questions at the forefront of our minds as we strive for a more culturally inclusive vision of youth in LIS. Some of those questions might include the follow-ing: How might I disrupt static and binary conceptualizations of youth that position white youth as the default normative cultural frame of reference? How might I avoid "othering" nonwhite youth by making them objects of study only in the context of "special" projects (e.g., closing the black-white achievement gap)? How might I help examine and transform the institu-tional practices of libraries that uphold racism in a profession that prides itself on being colorblind and accessible to all people? We might also direct some of our questions toward youth of color themselves and ask them:

- What would your ideal library look like?
- How would you feel when you entered it?
- What might you see and what kind of rules would you want enforced?
- What are the ways you think libraries have been organized with the needs of white youth in mind?
- What are some of the needs you see that black youth have that could be better met by libraries or librarians?

References

Akom, Antwi A. 2008. "Ameritocracy and Infra-racial Racism: Racializing Social and Cultural Reproduction Theory in the Twenty-first Century." *Race, Ethnicity, and Education* 11, no. 3: 205–230.

Balderrama, Sandra Rios. 2000. "This Trend Called Diversity." *Library Trends* 49, no. 1: 194–214.

Bell, Derrick. 1980. "*Brown v. Board of Education* and the Interest Convergence Dilemma." *Harvard Law Review* 93: 518–533.

Carter, Stephanie, and Kafi Kumasi. 2011. "Double Reading: Young Black Scholars Responding to Whiteness in a Community Literacy Program." In *Urban Literacies: Critical Perspectives on Language, Learning, and Community*, edited by V. Kinlock, 72–90. New York: Teachers College Press.

Delgado, Richard, and Jean Stefancic. 2001. *Critical Race Theory: An Introduction*. New York: New York University Press.

Dixson, Adrienne D., and Celia K. Rousseau. 2006. *Critical Race Theory in Education: All God's Children Got a Song*. New York: Routledge.

Honma, Todd. 1995. "Trippin' over the Color Line: The Invisibility of Race in Library and Information Studies." *InterActions: UCLA Journal of Education and Information Studies* 1, no. 2: 1–28.

Kapitzke, Cushla. 2003. "Information Literacy: A Positivist Epistemology and a Politics of Outformation." *Educational Theory* 53, no. 1: 37–52.

Kincheloe, Joe, Shirley Steinberg, and Patricia Hinchey, eds. 1999. *The Post-formal Reader: Cognition and Education*. New York: Falmer.

Kumasi, Kafi. 2008. *Seeing White in Black: Examining Racial Identity among African American Adolescents in a Culturally Centered Book Club*. Ann Arbor, MI: Proquest.

Kumasi-Johnson, Kafi. 2007. "Critical Inquiry: Library Media Specialists as Change Agents." *School Library Media Activities Monthly* 28, no. 9: 42–45.

Ladson-Billings, Gloria, and William F. Tate. 1995. "Toward a Critical Race Theory of Education." *Teachers College Record* 97: 47–68.

Langer, Judith. 1991. "Literacy and Schooling: A Sociocognitive Perspective." In *Literacy for a Diverse Society: Perspectives, Practices, and Policies,* edited by E. Hiebert. New York: Teachers College Press.

Pawley, Christine. 1998. "Hegemony's Handmaid? The Library and Information Science Curriculum from a Class Perspective." *The Library Quarterly* 68, no. 2: 123–144.

Thompson, Audrey. 2001. "Summary of Whiteness Theory." Whiteness in Cross-Race Classroom Relationships, University of Utah, Spring 2008. Accessed December 8, 2011. http://www.pauahtun.org/Whiteness-Summary-1.html.

Wright, Susan. 2005. *The Civil Rights Act of 1964: Landmark Antidiscrimination Legislation.* New York: Rosen Publishing Group.

5

Misfits, Loners, Immature Students, and Reluctant Readers

Librarianship in the Construction of Teen Readers of Comics

Lucia Cedeira Serantes

This chapter focuses on how librarianship constructs teen readers of comics. This analysis contributes to a body of work exploring denigrated materials such as series books or video games. It also makes inferences about how teen librarians understand their role as reader's advisors. Using a social constructivist approach and applying discourse analysis to professional literature from the last ten years, this chapter demonstrates how librarianship collaborates in the perpetuation of stereotypes about comics reading in particular and about teen readers in general.

Introduction: Situating the Topic

In 2002, the journal *Young Adult Library Services* published an article by a school librarian who explained her experience creating a comic book club (Halpern, 2002). She claimed no expertise with these materials, recognized that comics helped her build stronger relationships with students, and focused the article on the process of recruiting students for the club.

According to Halpern (2002: 41), the potential membership for this group would most likely be:

- students who were "not the popular, academic, socially mature" type and
- students who "did not care what other people thought about them."

She based this target population on the one student who replied to her advertisement of the activity. Always in a general positive attitude toward the activity and her relationship with students, she described the new recruits as "misfits, loners, and kids just a little too immature to go to school dances (God bless 'em)" that "were proud to belong somewhere" (Halpern, 2002: 41). One is surprised by her confinement of comics readers to a very particular subset of the high school population: teens who are not sociable, do not have any other interests or groups to join, and essentially are not accepted anywhere else. Consequently, several questions arise: Does this group of readers represent the only group of comics readers in the school or just an actualization of how this librarian imagines comics readers? Why did she decide that comics readers were "not the popular, academic, socially mature" students? Is this a practical approach to the difficulty of recruiting teen participants for her activity? What do her descriptions say about teen readers of comics?

It is difficult to reconcile this fracture between the positive effects Halpern found using these materials in her library work and the condescending stereotype she applies to readers of these same materials. The article by Halpern (2002) is just one example of how graphic novels and their readers are currently being constructed in library and information science (LIS) professional journals. Librarians actively seek advice about acquisition, organization, and programming with these materials; graphic novels have become a "token" material to attract an evasive teenage population to the library. However, the way comics readers are presented in these same articles is harder to qualify in a positive manner.

Librarians' imagery of readers of "scorned reading materials" (i.e., series books, romance novels, comics, among others) has always been controversial. Wayne Wiegand (1997: 314) in his widely cited article "Out of

Sight, Out of Mind" alludes to the tradition in librarianship of "slighting certain kinds of reading" and points to the lack of information about the readers of these materials as a problem that sustained pejorative behavior by library professionals. He says, "We have never bothered to investigate seriously why people want to read them." Is a lack of information the only problem to unfold in the way librarians present comics readers? Certainly there is a lack of research about comics readers, but through LIS professional literature one can also identify a distinctive way of constructing comics readers, one that perpetuates historical discourses and stereotypes and lacks a self-reflective approach to the understanding of teen readers specifically and teen patrons in general.

The purpose of this chapter is to analyze how recent LIS professional literature constructs teens within the context of the discourse on comics. If the construction of teen readers of comics is understood as a spectrum with positive and negative poles, the aforementioned example by Halpern (2002) would belong at the extreme negative pole. However, it is not difficult to find more moderate examples that still fall on the negative side of this spectrum. By exploring and analyzing these dominant discourses, this chapter will shed light on the question of how recent professional LIS literature is constructing young adult readers within the context of discourse on comics. These dominant discourses not only perpetuate historical stereotypes about comics reading but also construct a negative image of contemporary teen readers.

The relationship between librarianship and comics goes back to the 1930s; therefore, it is necessary to locate this study in the basic historical discourses. From this vantage, we can explore the developments, continuities, and differences in our more modern discourses. By analyzing past discourses, I hope to show how many conceptualizations of comics and their readers have stagnated, and point at the need to critically engage with the way libraries construct their relationship to actual and potential teen users. The core of this chapter examines LIS professional literature from 2000 to 2008 focusing on multiple aspects of the relationship between comics as a medium and libraries—definition, content, highlighted characteristics, and roles. Many of these matters connect directly and indirectly with the examination of the teen readership of comics, thus illuminating the contemporary discourse about readers. The following section illustrates the methodology I followed to identify and narrow the professional literature. Also, since numerous approaches to discourse analysis exist, I briefly introduce the approach selected for this project.

Research Data and Tool for Analysis

First of all, two issues need to be clarified. The terminology about comics is abundant and usually confusing for beginning readers. In this chapter, the term *comics* is used as an umbrella concept for comic books, graphic novels, and other forms that employ sequential art. Also, graphic novels will be heavily used in the fourth section correlating with their heavy use in LIS professional literature. I use the term *comic books* more often in the historical section since comics books were the main form of comics production at that particular historical moment. The textual data presented in this chapter comes from a previous research endeavor (Cedeira Serantes, 2010a, 2010b). The reference section provides the information for LIS professional literature cited in this chapter.

I limited my literature search to a list of journals that would help identify the prevailing definition and use of comics in libraries: *Booklist*, *Library Journal*, *Voice of Youth Advocates*, *Young Adult Library Services*, *School Library Journal*, *Children and Libraries*, *Knowledge Quest*, and *Library Media Connection*. It immediately became obvious that between 2000 and 2008 there was one major player in the development of the discourse about comics: the regular column by Kat Kan published in the journal *Voice of Youth Advocates* (*VOYA*) since 1994.

Excluding *VOYA*, one can see how the number of articles doubled between the period 2000–2004 and 2005–2008 from 41 to 93. This increase is explained in the publication of three regular columns about graphic novels in *Knowledge Quest* (2002), *School Library Journal* (2003), and *Library Media Connection* (2007). The year 2002 is clearly relevant. One hundred seventy librarians participated in the Getting Graphic @ Your Library American Library Association (ALA) preconference, becoming one of the most successful ever organized by the Young Adult Library Services Association (YALSA) ("Graphic Moments," 2002). This event

Articles on Comics in LIS Journals, 2000–2008

The following table shows the number of articles that focus on the topic of comics published in LIS professional journals between the years 2000 and 2008.

	2000–2004	2005–2008
Voice of Youth Advocates	31	24
Rest of journals	41	93
TOTAL	72	117

proved to be a catalyst for the interest in comics among librarians and youth services librarians in particular.

In his use of discourse analysis, James Paul Gee differentiates between discourse and Discourse. The first is language-in-use, "connected stretches of language that make sense, like conversations, stories, reports, arguments, essays" (Gee, 1990: 142). This discourse is always part of Discourse. In contrast, Discourse encompasses a larger meaning: "Discourse is a socially accepted association among ways of using language, of thinking, feeling, believing, valuing, and of acting that can be used to identify oneself as a member of a socially meaningful group or 'social network,' or to signal (that one is playing) a socially meaningful 'role'" (Gee, 1990: 143). Because of this understanding of Discourse, Gee believes that its analysis should go beyond the description, rather seeking to "illuminate and gain evidence for our theory of the domain" and especially to "contribute, in terms of understanding and intervention, to important issues and problems in some 'applied' area (e.g., education) that interests and motivates the researcher" (Gee, 2005: 8). This research project will contribute to the understanding of how librarians construct and understand teen readers of comics, and it will support future interventions in order to increase the awareness about the overall literary value of these materials and the diversity in comics readership.

How does one apply discourse analysis according to Gee? First, it is necessary to identify a situation where language is used. As conceived by Gee (2005: 97), a situation involves a series of connected components that might be singled out through some building tasks: significance, activities, roles or identities, relationships, politics, connections, sign systems, and forms of knowledge. In the case of this project, I analyzed a sample of professional literature that offers guidance and information about comics for the library community. From these seven building tasks, four tasks have been identified as relevant for the overall purpose of this project: significance, identities, relationships, and connections. Although the questions connected to these tasks will not surface in the text of the analysis, they were pivotal during the process of interrogation, supporting the evolution and enrichment of questions and shifting perspectives. For instance, how are graphic novels understood and defined? What is their role in the library and how is this role expressed? What discourses are relevant (and irrelevant) in the construction of comics readers? How are these discourses made relevant (and irrelevant), and in what ways? What sort of relationship or relationships is this piece of language seeking to enact with others (present or not)? (See Gee, 2005: 10–12.)

Historical Discourses: Their Origin and Scope

The task of summarizing and highlighting relevant historical trends in the discourse about comics, especially concerning their readers, is not an easy and straightforward endeavor. The literature that informs this topic is diverse in origin and is not very extensive; however, three trends can be identified. First, one can recognize the crucial role that Sterling North and Fredric Wertham had in shaping the popular negative discourse about comic books in the period between the 1930s and 1950s. Second, the literature not only points to the strength and prevalence of this same negative opinion among librarians but also to the development of a relatively positive or at least neutral discourse. Finally, a slow process of acceptance and inclusion of graphic novels in the library is described in two secondary sources (Ellis and Highsmith, 2000; Horner, 2006) that examine the decades between the 1960s and 2000s.

Sterling North published "A National Disgrace" in 1940. More than 40 newspapers and magazines reprinted the editorial, and the *Daily News*, source of the article, reported receiving "twenty-five million requests for reprints of the editorial for distribution in churches and schools across the country" (Nyberg, 1994: 116). North's attack was virulent and focused on cultural aspects: the quality of the comics and the repercussions of reading them for the cultural taste and habits of innocent children. North (1940: 3) claimed that comic books' "hypodermic injection of sex and murder [made] the child impatient with better, though quieter, stories" and that the only "antidote to the 'comic' magazine poison [could] be found in any library or good bookstore."

Fredric Wertham picked up the idea of innocent readers and made it central to his offensive against comic books. From the title of his main work, *The Seduction of the Innocent* (1954), to a speech where he addressed librarians, "Reading for the Innocent" (1955), Wertham evidenced a deep worry for the vulnerable reader. He reinforced the metaphor of reading comic books as a disease, claiming that it helped spread the general "literary avitaminosis" suffered by American children (1955: 612), and that comic books were "virulent and harbor the virus of violence" (1955: 610).

North and Wertham presented readers as passive receivers of the comics' "disease." Evidently influenced by North and Wertham along with their role as literary gatekeepers and culture guardians, librarians reinforced this hegemonic discourse about comic book reading (Beaty, 2005: 106). Tilley's doctoral thesis (2007) contains a rich and detailed discussion of the relationship between youth services librarians and comic books from 1938 to 1955. She concludes that the characterization of librarians' reactions to comics as "another instance of the profession's distaste for light reading...obscures the complex social and cultural currents that specifically shaped librarians' responses in this instance" (Tilley, 2007: 244). This chapter's modest approach to the topic does not attempt to elude this contextual complexity; however, an in-depth analysis is out of scope. In order to remedy this situation to some extent, it is necessary to create a spectrum of positive and negative discourses, thus establishing a wide and solid framework that allows one to point to continuities and breaks in LIS in relation to comics readership. The examination of librarians' historical attitudes toward comics and their readers attracts researchers in LIS and other disciplines (Beaty, 2005; Ellis and Highsmith, 2000; Nyberg, 2002; Springhall, 1998; Steele, 2005; Tilley, 2007; Wright, 2001). Professional articles chronicling librarians' historical perspective can be divided in three groups: contrary to comics, supportive of comics, and utilitarian.

This first group of publications overwhelmingly represents a negative angle on comics. The majority of these articles are opinion pieces based on personal observations. They are rich in metaphors of disease and addiction similar to those previously advocated by North and Wertham. Often they were shocking and alarmist (Nyberg, 2002: 171). Stanley Kunitz (1941b: 670), a poet and editor of the *Wilson Library Bulletin*, called libraries to arms against the comics menace: "A child conditioned by the jerky, jig-gling, inflamed world of the comics is a damaged child, incapacitated for enjoyment of the more serene pleasure of the imagination." Jean Gray Harker (1948: 1705), a librarian, called upon youth services librarians to defeat comics and who described them as a cultural threat that "rob[s] our future generations the ability to think, to talk, to read, to act with intel-ligence." These are just two examples of the many publications that con-demned comic book reading. Numerous examples can be found in Beaty (2005), Nyberg (2002), and Tilley (2007). Librarians' writings agreed with the construction of a passive young reader who was impoverished by com-ics. This reader was not an agent who decides what to read but rather one whose preference for comics was highlighted as a weakness and as an example of the influence of the power of mass culture.

A second group of publications represents a much less prevalent but positive attitude toward comics. Tilley's PhD thesis (2007) points to some positive statements made during the University of Chicago's 1943 "Con-ference on Reading." Frances Henne, a well-known advocate of children librarianship, connected comic books with children's literature through picture books and asserted that "people have tended, for different rea-sons in different times to consume this form of communication" (Tilley, 2007: 60). Josette Frank described comics as "an expression of our times, a folk lore [*sic*] of today. I, for one, refuse to believe that so many millions of readers can be wrong" (Tilley, 2007: 60). In contrast with North and Wertham's conceptions of readers, Frank and Henne pointed at readers as active agents and reflected on this predilection for comic books rather than simply criticizing or ignoring it.

A third approach to comics brings a pragmatic or utilitarian approach to the relationship between comics and libraries. The goal of this approach is to reconcile practical strengths and applications of comics for the library without directly opposing the general negative discourse. This third group proves particularly insidious in the way it bridges historical and present discourses. For instance, Elizabeth Margulis (1949) in her article "The Comics Dilemma" is concerned with the violent and explicit content of comics; however, she realized that comics attract readers who "cannot read" or are "lazy" (4). Margaret Brady's article "Comics—To Read or Not to Read" (1950) represents an effort to introduce the topic of comics in a balanced manner. On the one hand, Brady notes that comics cultivate lazy readers, and she objects to the "wild fantasy" that they embody. She also articulates a still prevalent notion about comics reading and youth: comics are something temporary for a young reader, "likely to be out-grown as older and more important interests arise" (Brady, 1950: 664). On the other hand, she indicates positive attributes in comics: they teach concentration; the adaptations of classics help young readers to connect to the original work; they are good at providing an escape from reality; and in general they stimulate reading since "boys and girls read the words as well as the pictures" (Brady, 1950: 665). This article exemplifies the complex and contradictory discourse around comics, reading, and libraries. These arguments are in some ways positive or supportive in light of the general rejection of comics at the time. It is intriguing to note that these same posi-tive statements are mirrored in current articles in LIS professional literature about comics, especially the conceptualization of the comics reader as "a reader who lacks."

Historically, the discourse about comics and their readers is not an easy topic to draw defined boundaries around. This brief review of the literature shows that between the extremes of blunt criticism and uncon-ditional support, there were many librarians who struggled with several contending ideas: the quality and value of comics as a reading material, the definitive and passionate interest from readers, and the different practical applications that comic books have in libraries. In many and less overt ways than in the past, these same struggles will be examined in the analysis of the current literature about comics.

Continuities, Practices, and Challenges of Teen Readers of Comics

This section provides an analysis of LIS professional literature from 2000 to 2008 about comics. This analysis examines the following aspects of the relationship between the comics as a medium and libraries: definition, content, highlighted characteristics, and roles. Through the analysis of these aspects three issues emerge:

- The reader of comics is characterized as one "who lacks": a reluctant reader, a visual reader, or an English as a second language (ESL) student.
- It is difficult to reconcile a complex medium with a young readership.
- Stereotypes about the medium directly affect the image of the reader.

The following examples illustrate the general discourse that connects comics, libraries, and teen patrons/readers. Mooney (2005: 20) sees in graphic novels a tool to hook reluctant readers "into becoming interested and enthusiastic readers" as well as to lead them down "the path to lifelong learning." Those are high hopes for a reading material whose content and quality are still a major concern, as will be discussed later in this section. Wilson (2006) insists on a connection between graphic novels and reluctant readers as well as their appropriateness for ESL students and visual learners. Crawford comments on the experience of two librarians that reinforces the connection between reluctant readers and graphic novels. The first librarian, Kay Hones at John O'Connell High School, places graphic novels near magazines or with drawing books to create a "magnet area for reluctant readers" (Crawford, 2004c: 26). Elaine Moskowitz from James Denman Middle School highlights the popularity of graphic novels among students with "limited English proficiency" (Crawford, 2004c: 26). Gorman (2002: 47) maintains that comic books are "especially attractive to reluctant readers" and, because of this, recommends that comic books be placed near "magazines, CDs, or Cliffs Notes." Knop (2008: 41) explains that her manga club offers a place to "belong" for "students who might not otherwise join an after-school club to meet with their friends and talk about a unique common interest." At this point, the image of teen readers of comics projected by librarians in their articles is that of readers who lack; librarians refer to reluctant readers or nonreaders, students with limited English proficiency, or teens who do not make friends or have difficulties integrating in the school community.

A recurrent topic in LIS professional literature about comics and youth is the reluctant reader. Interestingly enough, very few authors actually attempt to set clear boundaries around this unclear term. One can certainly assume that writers and readers share the same conceptualization of what a reluctant reader is, at least in the realm of teen readers and comics. Snowball (2005) attempts to tackle this conceptual problem in her article about reluctant readers and graphic novels. This attempt points to the reality of how this term is employed, for the most part with negative implications. An alternative approach comes from the discipline of education. Reeves (2001: 13) understands reluctant readers as those who "will not read just for the sake of reading." These readers are "highly selective" in choosing their reading materials and read only when they have found something they connect with (Reeves, 2001: 13). This critical approach to the reading experience is often interpreted as negative in teens, assuming that their criteria or tastes are not yet adequately developed.

Lyga (2006) problematizes the reluctant reader discourse by expanding the discussion to the realm of different types of learners: those incapable of visualizing, those visually dependent, the ever-present reluctant readers, and those students who like to cross gender lines. Lyga's approach can certainly be presented as an improvement; however, three of the learners she mentions are reluctant, incapable of doing something, or dependent on the visual aspect of the comics. Again, these comments project a restrictive understanding of graphic novels and their readers.

Bergin (2005) offers a different view from the reader who lacks. Through informal observation and a survey, she explores the diversity of manga readers in her institution to find out that:

- both readers and nonreaders are attracted to manga;
- students interested in anime and Japanese culture read this type of comics;

- avid readers as well as reluctant readers are attracted to titles recognizable from current anime on TV; and
- readers make reading and discussing manga part of their social experience.

According to her informal research attempt, virtually any teen can be a manga reader. One of her most revelatory reflections points at how students' self-descriptions do not match those others give to them. Bergin does not identify who these "others" are (adults in general, librarians, or maybe teachers), but it is highly relevant that she finds a dissonance between how these manga readers are constructed and perceived and how they see themselves. This idea of misrepresentation is not unique. Bauer (2001), a teenager who writes for *VOYA*'s column "Notes from the Teenage Underground," in commenting on manga, anime, and otaku culture expresses some opinions highly critical with adults' perception of this material. She highlights the negative portrayal that "media watchdogs" construct and transmit about manga, summarizing this negativity with the following statement: "Anime, it seemed today, [is] the New Crack" (Bauer, 2001: 187). In contrast, she defends its complexity and attractiveness with a passion not frequently seen. For example, about the title *Ranma ½*, she says: "the classification most often given to *Ranma ½* is 'martial arts love comedy,' a distinction giving one a pretty good idea of its gender demographic (or lack of thereof)" (Bauer, 2001: 187).

In many cases, graphic novels are presented as tools that solve many issues: low circulation numbers or library attendance, poor reading skills, and social inclusion issues. Gorman (2002: 42) sees graphic novels as a material that "transcend[s] apathy and the lack of coolness" associated with reading and libraries, and so graphic novels can be used to "lure and engage" teenagers. Ty R. Burns, co–head librarian at Spring High School and chairperson of the YALSA 2003 Quick Pick for Reluctant Readers Committee, affirms that since his library introduced graphic novels into the collection, not only have their circulation numbers risen but also this material is "attracting students to his library who might not have otherwise stopped by to check out a book for independent reading" (Gorman, 2003: 20). Other authors also highlight the connection between graphic novels and increasing circulation numbers (Ching, 2005; Neace, 2005).

Professional literature is not just reflecting the utilitarian role that librarians have already found for graphic novels but also actively reinforcing it. Another classic example of this utilitarian role is that of graphic novels as a stepping stone to some "better reading." Dickinson (2007: 56) uses this controversial idea in a discussion about where to shelve graphic novels; in order to support the recommendation of interfiling these materials with other forms of literature, she writes: "deep down, some of us want the reading of graphic novels to lead to 'real books.'"

Foster provides a rich example of this inherently contradictory position of librarians toward comics and their readers:

> [Graphic novels are] appealing to readers of all ages and intensely popular with adolescents, but they have many other redeeming qualities. Educators have discovered that comic books have proven useful in getting reluctant readers to read....[Graphic novels] are able to teach readers about literary techniques such as plot, conflict, setting, character, and even foreshadowing and flashbacks. (Foster, 2004: 32)

In this excerpt, Foster both challenges and reinforces stereotypes about comics and their readers. She presents a rather inclusive concept of comics readers, and although the connection with reluctant readers is reinforced, she justifies it based on the literary attributes of comics. However, one cannot avoid discussing the use of "redeeming" to qualify these positive characteristics; Foster seems to imply that comics are at fault and need to compensate for their intrinsic weaknesses. Indeed, library professionals like Foster seem to perpetually link comics to an imagined reluctant reader in what these professionals view as a mutually redemptive relationship: comics may redeem their readers and thereby are themselves redeemed as a medium worthy of a place in the library. In the end, what do comics need to redeem themselves for? Are they not "real books"? And if comics are not "real books," how then shall we call their readers?

Alternatively, some exceptions arise. Seyfried (2008) qualifies graphic novels as "educational heavyweights"; these texts provide his students with "rich and rewarding literary experience" at a moment when "the duration, vocabulary, and style of prose masterpieces cannot." He cites a seventh-grader who says, "We didn't just read the story; we read the story behind the story" (Seyfried, 2008: 46).

Seyfried's positive attitude is often exhibited by Kat Kan in her *VOYA* column "Graphically Speaking." Kan shares a holistic concept of what a graphic novel reader is. First, she barely talks about reluctant readers; she prefers to distinguish between young readers and mature readers, or readers familiar with the medium or not. She also connects graphic novels to other media that might interest readers, understanding reading as part of the cultural consumption patterns of teen library patrons. For instance, she recommends particular titles to readers of Roald Dahl and Lemony Snicket (2001b), or viewers of police shows like *Law and Order* and *CSI* (2004a). Beyond recommending graphic novels, Kan (1995, 1996, 2009) helps librarians to connect graphic novels with other media, supporting the reading habits of contemporary teens whose hierarchy of value and media boundaries often differ from adults'. Apart from this open conceptualization of the reader, Kan also does not confine the medium to a particular gender or age. For example, she has written articles reviewing titles for girls (Kan, 2001a, 2002a, 2005), for boys (Kan, 2004a), all ages (Kan, 2003a, 2004b), and middle-schoolers (Kan, 2001b). To summarize, Kan reviews graphic novels as any other reading material; she does not need to validate or justify the need for graphic novels but simply assesses and recommends titles that might be interesting, challenging, and appropriate for teen readers.

Librarians describe the content of graphic novels as clearly different from the classic comic books, and they consider this shift a positive one. St. Lifer (2002) situates this development in "the scope and diversity of the graphic novel [that] has broadened to include much more sophisticated subject matter." Graphic novels represent the maturity of the medium. However, this evolution crashes against the still prevalent idea that comics are a reading material for youth and all that this notion implies. Graphic novels bring a certain sophistication in art and text that does not match the expected audience's reading maturity. "Edgy" graphic novels are a regular topic in Kan's column (2000, 2001b, 2002a, 2003b, 2008). She describes these titles in an extremely positive manner: they "can offer mature-minded teens a fantastic array of stories and styles to delight their minds—and perhaps their souls" (Kan, 2002a).

Nevertheless, many librarians and parents are worried that mature graphic novels might end up in the hands of children or tweens. To support the selection process, most articles include some sort of bibliographic selection where reviewers tend to summarize the virtues and shortcomings of these materials. In some cases, the concern about the content is marked with visual aids added in some of these reviews. For example, Crawford has established the asterisk as a symbol to note graphic novels that have mature themes. A closer analysis of Crawford's articles (2002, 2003a, 2003b, 2004a, 2004b, 2005a, 2005b, 2005c, 2006, 2007) reveals that the section labeled "Young Adult Literature" has a higher number of titles with asterisks, becoming the unofficial section for graphic novels with mature and probably controversial titles; however, this is not made explicit in any of the articles. On the other hand, the section "All Ages" is described as "free of excessive violence, profanity, and adult situations" (Crawford, 2004c). Therefore, there are comics that contain these elements in an excessive manner, and because of that the discussion often moves to topics of age appropriateness and censorship.

This concern tends to be linked to the preconceived idea that comics are only meant to be read by children. This situation is described by Pawuk (2002) as an "archaic notion" and a "potential stumbling block" when both library staff and the community are "shocked" to find content that is not suitable for a young reader. Gorman (2002) extends the fear to genres of graphic novels that can potentially be a target of parental and community objections: horror, the supernatural, crime and punishment, satire and dark humor. It seems that the profession is actively trying to reconcile the development of the comics medium with some of the lasting stereotypes about comics readers, especially young readers. The recent interest in the younger reader has also increased attention paid to the violent and sexual content in graphic novels. However, Rudiger and Schliesman (2007: 57–58) offer a sound piece of advice when they say that graphic novels might present content, situations, and images that readers, parents, and teachers might find upsetting or offensive, just as some novels, picture books, or nonfiction works have dialogue, distressing images, or shocking topics. In the same way that librarians do not embrace or reject other mediums as a whole, they should also evaluate graphic novels individually.

In this section, one can see the multiplicity of elements impacting the discourse about teen readers of comics and how these elements in most cases contribute to creating an image of a reader who lacks. However, the possibility for change exists and should be exercised. Flagg (2003: 988) comments on how exposure to diverse, demanding, and stimulating media "has accustomed [teen readers of comics] to more complex narratives and a less clear-cut morality." This quote explores one alternative portrayal of comics and their readers and serves as an introduction to the reflection offered in the following and final section of this study.

Conclusion: Discourse and Its Implications

In the articles analyzed for this chapter, the implicit goal of most authors was to find a role for graphic novels that validates and justifies their presence in libraries, especially in front of educational or library boards and parents. This issue is complicated, since parents and boards might not be friendly to this inclusion. Comics were born as an entertainment product for youth, but they were quickly considered a corruptor of innocent minds and were banished from any reading-sanctioning institution (i.e., libraries and schools). However, as noted in the historical review, some librarians found positive arguments for inclusion of comics in their collections, pointing to their usefulness as literacy tools for reluctant and poor readers and also as potential springboards into traditional literature. These arguments were conceived more than 60 years ago, but they are still present in the discourse about comics in libraries today.

More recently, comics have gained a certain cultural status, especially around the creation and dissemination of the idea of the graphic novel. For the general public, and many librarians, the graphic novel embodies the evolution of the sequential art from childish entertainment to serious literary form. On the one hand, the inclusion of graphic novels in the collection means that libraries and librarians support and validate the cultural and reading tastes of the current generation. On the other hand, the connection between graphic novels and validation is still made through these same ideas of evolution and maturity, in this case of the medium itself.

This idea of evolution brings a major collateral issue: the reconcilement between the challenges and tensions of a medium increasingly acknowledged as complex in content on the one hand and a young readership on the other. In this process of reconcilement, preconceptions and misconceptions about teen readers surface. Even though graphic novels are increasingly characterized as rich, complex, challenging, diverse, and multilayered reading materials, the commonplace is to present teen readers of comics as misfits, loners, reluctant readers, and patrons who lack reading skills or discriminatory taste. The richness of the material should potentially imply a similar richness in its readers, but this is not true in the literature. Teen readers—and by extension teen patrons—could be portrayed as savvy, complex, experimental, multimedia readers. They could be easily characterized as readers who have busy lives and are strategic about their reading selections; their reading agendas are packed with compulsory materials from school, and thus their reading for pleasure choices might vary tremendously from a challenging and complex novel to a satisfying and enjoyable series book.

What does need to change? The discipline's shift echoed in Wayne Wiegand's (2003) idea of "the library in the life of the user" might inform this struggle. Librarianship looks at the graphic novel as a tool to bring teen patrons to the library, as a solution to library problems. In the process, teen patrons and readers have been constructed to fit what the library needs, rather than identified by how the library fits into young readers' lives or how youth actually imagine the library. The way graphic novels are discussed in the literature symbolize an effort to make them fit into current library practices, especially as a bait to attract teens to reading or "good reading" and to lure them into the library. Once teens are in the library, it is assumed they will discover the wealth of resources, services, and programs that the library has to offer them.

Keeping Wiegand in mind, an alternative interpretation suggests that graphic novels can be more than bait, that they can represent an actual shift. From teenagers' viewpoint, graphic novels signal a response by libraries to actual teen interests. Instead of understanding graphic novels as a panacea that remedies the difficulties between libraries and teens, graphic novels should be understood as important only in so far as they represent and intersect with teen interests. The main distinction lies in whether we want to keep problematizing teens as reluctant readers and library users, or whether we shift the discourse and constructively criticize the library as not responding to teens' developments and interests.

References

Beaty, Bart. 2005. *Fredric Wertham and the Critique of Mass Culture*. Jackson, MS: University Press of Mississippi.

Brady, Margaret E. 1950. "Comics—To Read or Not to Read." *Wilson Library Bulletin*, no. 24: 662–667.

Cedeira Serantes, Lucia. 2010a. "From Virus to Bait: Comic Books, Graphic Novels, and Their Readers in Library Science Professional Literature (2000–2004)." Paper presented at 3rd New Narrative Conference: Narrative Arts and Visual Media, Toronto, ON, May 6–7.

———. 2010b. "From Virus to Bait: Comic Books, Graphic Novels, and Their Readers in Library Science Professional Literature (2000–2008)." Paper presented at the Library Research Seminar V: Integrating Research into Practice. College Park, MD, October 6–9.

Ellis, Allen W., and Doug Highsmith. 2000. "About Face: Comic Books in Library Literature." *Serials Review* 26, no. 2: 21–43.

Gee, James Paul. 1990. *Social Linguistics and Literacies: Ideology in Discourses*. New York: Falmer.

———. 2005. *An Introduction to Discourse Analysis: Theory and Method*. New York: Routledge.

"Graphic Moments from the Getting Graphic @ Your Library Preconference." 2002. *Voice of Youth Advocates* 25, no. 4: 252–255.

Harker, Jean Gray. 1948. "Youth's Librarians Can Defeat Comics." *Library Journal*, no. 73 (December): 1705–1720.

Horner, Emily C. 2006. *Librarians' Attitudes and Perspectives Regarding Graphic Novels*. MSLS, University of North Carolina at Chapel Hill.

Kunitz, Stanley J. 1941. "The Roving Eye: The Comic Menace." *Wilson Library Bulletin* 15 (June): 846–847.

———. 1941b. "The Roving Eye: Libraries, to Arms!" *Wilson Library Bulletin* 15 (April): 670–671.

Margulis, Elizabeth S. 1949. "The Comics Dilemma." *New Mexico Library Bulletin*, no. 18: 3–5.

North, Sterling. 1940. "A National Disgrace." *Illinois Libraries*, no. 22 (June): 3.

Nyberg, Amy Kiste. 1994. "Seal of Approval: The Origins and History of the Comics Code." Unpublished doctoral dissertation, University of Wisconsin–Madison.

——. 2002. "Poisoning Children's Culture: Comics and Their Critics." In *Scorned Literature: Essays on the History and Criticism of Popular Mass-produced Fiction in America*, edited by Lydia Cushman Schurman and Deidre Johnson, 167–186. Westport, CT: Greenwood Press.

Reeves, Anne. 2001. "Reading This and Refusing That: Case Studies of High School Students' Patterns of Reading and Resistance." Paper presented at 91st Annual Meeting of the National Council of Teachers of English, Baltimore, MD.

Springhall, John. 1998. *Youth, Popular Culture and Moral Panics: Penny Gaffs to Gangsta-rap, 1830–1996*. New York: St. Martin's.

Tilley, Carol L. 2007. "Of Nightingales and Supermen: How Youth Services Librarians Responded to Comics Between the Years 1938 and 1955." Unpublished doctoral dissertation, Indiana University, Bloomington, IN.

Wertham, Fredric. 1954. *Seduction of the Innocent*. New York: Rinehart.

——. 1955. "Reading for the Innocent." *Wilson Library Bulletin*, no. 29 (April): 610–613.

Wiegand, Wayne A. 1997. "Out of Sight, Out of Mind: Why Don't We Have Any Schools of Library and Reading Studies?" *Journal of Education for Library and Information Science* 38, no. 4: 314–326.

——. 2003. "To Reposition a Research Agenda: What American Studies Can Teach the LIS Community about the Library in the Life of the User." *Library Quarterly* 73, no. 4: 369–382.

Wright, Bradford W. 2001. *Comic Book Nation: The Transformation of Youth Culture in America*. Baltimore, MD: Johns Hopkins University Press.

References from LIS Professional Publications

Bauer, Megan. 2001. "Anime, Manga, and Otaku Culture: A Quick Study Guide for the Uninitiated." *Voice of Youth Advocates* 24, no. 3: 186–187.

Bergin, Melissa. 2005. "Who Is Reading Manga? One High School's Story." *Young Adult Library Services* 3, no. 4: 25–26.

Ching, Alison. 2005. "Holy Reading Revolution, Batman! Developing a Graphic Novel Collection for Young Adults." *Young Adult Library Services* 3, no. 4: 19–21.

Crawford, Philip. 2002. "Graphic Novels: Selecting Materials That Will Appeal to Girls." *Knowledge Quest* 31, no. 2: 43–45.

——. 2003a. "Beyond 'Maus': Using Graphic Novels to Support Social Studies Standards." *Knowledge Quest* 31, no. 4: 41–42.

——. 2003b. "Graphic Novels of 2002: Superheroes and More." *Knowledge Quest* 31, no. 5: 46–47.

——. 2004a. "Graphic Novels for Elementary School Libraries." *Knowledge Quest* 32, no. 3: 35–37.

———. 2004b. "Notable Graphic Novels of 2003." *Knowledge Quest* 32, no. 4: 43.

———. 2004c. "A Novel Approach: Using Graphic Novels to Attract Reluctant Readers and Promote Literacy." *Library Media Connection* 22, no. 5: 26–28.

———. 2005a. "The Fantastic Worlds of P. Craig Russell." *Knowledge Quest* 33, no. 4: 30–31.

———. 2005b. "Moving Beyond Collection Development: Recent Professional Books about Graphic Novels." *Knowledge Quest* 34, no. 1: 36–38.

———. 2005c. "Within the Realms of Faerie: Modern Fairy Tales for Older Teens." *Knowledge Quest* 33, no. 3: 50–51.

———. 2006. "Americana Popular Culture and the Comics: Studying American Culture Through Comics and Graphic Novels." *Knowledge Quest* 35, no. 1: 50–53.

———. 2007. "'Oooh! I Must Be Dreaming!' The Delightfully Strange and Marvelous Worlds of America's Great Fantasist, Winsor McCay." *Knowledge Quest* 35, no. 5: 58–61.

Dickinson, Gail. 2007. "The Question: Where Should I Shelve Graphic Novels?" *Knowledge Quest* 35, no. 5: 56–57.

Flagg, Gordon. 2003. "Not Your Father's Superheroes." *Booklist* 99, no. 11: 988.

Foster, Katy. 2004. "Graphic Novels in Libraries: An Expert's Opinion." *Library Media Connection* 22, no. 5: 30–32.

Gorman, Michele. 2002. "What Teens Want: Graphic Novels." *School Library Journal* 48, no. 8: 42–44.

———. 2003. "Graphic Novels and the Curriculum Connection." *Library Media Connection* 22, no. 3: 20–21.

Halpern, Julie. 2002. "Ten Geeks, One League of Power, Many Butt-Kicking Comics! Francis W. Parker School Comic Book Club." *Young Adult Library Services* 1, no. 1: 41–43.

Kan, Kat. 1995. "Slip-Sliding Through the Media…Novels and Movies about Superheroes." *Voice of Youth Advocates* 18, no. 3: 207–208.

———. 1996. "Slip-Sliding Through the Media, Part II: About Some Favorites, Old and New." *Voice of Youth Advocates* 19, no. 3: 203–204.

———. 2000. "Strange Sojourns: Graphic Novels." *Voice of Youth Advocates* 22, no. 6: 400–401.

———. 2001a. "Girls Rule! Graphic Novels with Female Protagonists." *Voice of Youth Advocates* 23, no. 6: 418–419.

———. 2001b. "Great for Middle School." *Voice of Youth Advocates* 24, no. 4: 270–271.

———. 2001c. "Weird and Wonderful." *Voice of Youth Advocates* 24, no. 2: 116–117.

———. 2002a. "Girls Still Rule!" *Voice of Youth Advocates* 25, no. 5: 370–371.

———. 2002b. "On the Edge." *Voice of Youth Advocates* 24, no. 6: 430–431.

———. 2003a. "Fun for All Ages." *Voice of Youth Advocates* 26, no. 2: 124–125.

———. 2003b. "On the Edge." *Voice of Youth Advocates,* 26, no. 5: 386–387.

———. 2004a. "Let's Hear It for the Guys." *Voice of Youth Advocates* 27, no. 2: 118–119.

———. 2004b. "More All Ages Fun." *Voice of Youth Advocates* 27, no. 5: 374–375.

———. 2004c. "Titles Too Good to Miss!" *Voice of Youth Advocates* 26, no. 6: 480–481.

———. 2005. "The Girls Have It!" *Voice of Youth Advocates* 28, no. 1: 32–33.

———. 2008. "Pirates, Zombies, Racing, and Being a Stranger in a Strange Land." *Voice of Youth Advocates* 31, no. 1: 36–37.

———. 2009. "Slip-Sliding Through the Media...Again." *Voice of Youth Advocates* 31, no. 6: 20–21.

Knop, Kathi. 2008. "Graphic Novels—Join the Club!" *Library Media Connection* 27, no. 3: 40–41.

Lyga, Allyson W. 2006. "Graphic Novels for Really Young Readers." *School Library Journal* 52, no. 3: 56–61.

Mooney, Maureen. 2005. Graphic Novels for the Elementary School Audience." *Library Media Connection*, January.

Neace, Melissa. 2005. "Building a Graphic Novel Collection." *Library Media Connection* 23, no. 7: 52–5.

Pawuk, Michael. 2002. "Creating a Graphic Novel Collection @ Your Library." *Young Adult Library Services* 1, no. 1: 30–35.

Rudiger, Hollis Margaret, and Megan Schliesman. 2007. "Graphic Novels and School Libraries." *Knowledge Quest* 36, no. 2: 57–59.

Seyfried, Jonathan. 2008. "Reinventing the Book Club: Graphic Novels as Educational Heavyweights." *Knowledge Quest* 36, no. 3: 44–48.

Snowball, Clare. 2005. "Teenage Reluctant Readers and Graphic Novels." *Young Adult Library Services* 3, no. 4: 43–45.

St. Lifer, Evan. 2002. "Graphic Novels, Seriously." *School Library Journal* 48, no. 8: 9.

Wilson, Rachel. 2006. "Multicultural Graphic Novels." *Library Media Connection* 24, no. 6: 32–33.

6

Beyond Coaching

Copiloting with Young Adults

Wendy Schaetzel Lesko

Imaginative open-minded librarians serve as catalysts and create a conducive atmosphere unlike any other environment for young adults in our age-segregated society. This chapter explores the idea that librarians who are brimming with curiosity and inquiry can engage young adults as real decision makers who can have a real impact on organizational development. Youth-led and adult-supported programs such as the Youth Activism Project and School Girls Unite serve as examples of ways that librarians can encourage minors' substantive participation in the public policy arena.

Society at large needs to put both feet in the water when it comes to seeking input, ideas, and involvement from young adults. Librarians deserve credit for sustained efforts to engage teens, but our age-segregated culture still permeates every institution. A seismic adult attitude adjustment that moves from authoritative to collegial is essential. Multiple entry points and trajectories invite a broader swath of young adults to participate in cocreating libraries. Envision truly open-minded librarians who usher in a new era of collaboration with young adults and together concoct a smorgasbord of activities and services that attract people of all ages and backgrounds.

The mantra "Don't make decisions for youth without youth" implies shared decision making but typically is limited to engaging teens on peripheral issues or parallel efforts to those of adults, often in a subordinate advisory role. The primary objectives of these programs include increasing self-esteem, real-world learning, and leadership skills. These deeply held attitudes must undergo a dramatic shift in order for young adults to assume pivotal roles in the ongoing innovation of libraries and civic engagement. The aim is for diverse young adults to be fully engaged as real decision makers who have real impact on organizational development with positive youth development as a by-product. This paradigm does not demand that new structures or initiatives be created, nor does it displace the critical job of professional librarians, but it does require intentional strategies.

The prerequisite is an adult mind-set of authentic appreciation and commitment for exchanging views with youth. The onus is on grown-ups to demonstrate their interest and intent to learn from and with teens. A can-do philosophy coupled with nimble and fast-paced strategizing are trademarks of successful multigenerational teamwork. The library universe represents one of the best community hubs to move from dabbling to copiloting with young adults. In addition to describing these opportunities, other approaches for this transformative model are drawn from my firsthand experiences.

For nearly two decades, the Youth Activism Project has served as a national clearinghouse to encourage minors to participate in substantive ways in the public policy arena. We urge young people to influence their peers as well as their elected officials. For example, a tenth-grader called our toll-free hotline several times a week while he organized a successful campaign to expand the state board of education to include two student representatives. A 13-year-old wanted to start a teen center in her town and we suggested she contact several youth in another rural community who won their mayor's support to use an abandoned movie theater. Over a period of ten years, my two sons channeled their anger over the tobacco industry's marketing tactics and were instrumental in getting a county ordinance passed that banned cigarette vending machines and a second law requiring all tobacco products be placed behind the counters. In contrast to being the parent on the sidelines, terrific collaboration occurred while I coauthored *Youth! The 26% Solution* with Emanuel Tsourounis, who was 19 at the time.

In 2004, my attention moved to the global south, where millions of girls are denied an education because of their sex. I shared my outrage with a half a dozen seventh-graders and young African women. Together, we launched School Girls Unite, which combines philanthropy and political advocacy. Thus far, my greatest learning and most satisfying experience can be traced to working with four cofounders of School Girls Unite who were paid interns over the summer. Together, we designed all components of a national campaign for global gender equality called Day of the Girl. My role was as copilot rather than as coach.

Favorable Culture and Climate

Libraries have several distinct advantages to shift from age-segregated traditions to new modes of interaction and operation. Librarians represent a rare species different from most adults and many teachers. Even librarians who work in school media centers offer an oasis from the classroom grind of tests and grades. Unlike most youth programs where there are unspoken boundaries when it comes to questioning authority or conventional wisdom, no such limits exist in libraries.

Openness is a hallmark of the profession. Fighting censorship is a given. Curiosity and eccentric interests are embraced. Close ties with community leaders and organizations help youth make connections to pursue their own interests and passions. Awareness of current trends in the youth culture erases the outdated stereotypes of librarians. This acceptance of free thinking and eagerness for exploration creates a truly unique environment.

Gifted young adult (YA) librarians, like most youth workers who are underappreciated and underpaid, often say one reason they do not quit is because of a special energy they gain from intergenerational exchange. There is an addictive quality derived from out-of-the-box brainstorming and the pace of action that contrasts to often sluggish adult decision-making processes. This space for freedom and exploration exists to a far larger extent in a community-based setting like a library. When a project takes off, it can be absolutely magical for all involved. For example, School Girls Unite received a minigrant to write a booklet about the reasons why millions of girls don't go to school. Soon the publication blossomed into a 100-page bilingual action guide titled *Girls Gone Activist! How to Change the World through Education* with contributions from our sister organization in Mali, West Africa. Five US high school students each took responsibility for writing one chapter, another team collaborated with our graphic designer on photos and fonts, and my main role was organizing meeting spaces and managing a team of volunteer translators. Imagine this type of intergenerational project with young poets or novelists.

Building on YA Programs

Libraries are miles ahead of many youth-serving organizations in terms of giving young people opportunities to steer the ship. Youth advisory councils, reading clubs, Teen Wii, and other creative outlets translate into a core of regulars who are at home at the library. Months of shared experiences provide a collegial foundation. Assuming good group dynamics, more reticent youth become comfortable speaking their minds. Encouragement for proposing untried or wacky ideas becomes the norm. Even without a teen space complete with giant bean bags, an atmosphere charged with imaginative inquiry makes the library a hot spot.

In the youth empowerment field, typically the first step is for young adults to focus on the issues they themselves identify as paramount. This approach puts them in the driver's seat. It signals permission to abandon established programs or conventions. There are plenty of young adults eager to invent, including new ways to transform library services. This open-ended invitation is often just what it takes to unleash unorthodox thinking. Initial brainstorming should not be weighted down by a review of sacrosanct programs, library policies, or funding restrictions; however, these issues need to be discussed before blueprints for change take shape. Otherwise it may be regarded as a futile exercise. Similarly, these young architects need to understand the entire process for proposing their recommendations as well as the chain of command. This awareness of the library decision-making machine will guard against disappointment and likely cynicism if their ideas collide with existing YA services or get vetoed by the powers that be.

Another pillar of positive youth development and empowerment is peer education. The motto is that youth know best what will interest other youth. This categorical assumption denies the vast differences in every community, even towns with only one traffic signal. Luckily, librarians know there is no such thing as a monolithic generation and offer eclectic teen activities. Official structures like youth advisory boards as well as ad hoc groups are given the reins to plan events. They create the buzz and can take a lion's share of the credit for attracting people to the library.

With all the increasing demands on librarians, it makes sense to stick with a tight-knit group and put these individuals in the position of charting the future path for YA services. This comfort zone spells continuity and building on the past, but the risk is too great that the library menu will become stale and the library will fail to attract new patrons.

Importance of Individual Interactions

Even though teen space is familiar and often preferred by young and old alike, this form of quarantine has consequences. What about those youth who are not interested in YA programs or opt not to be around their near-peers who frequent the library? Think about the hordes of students who are turned off by their student government, extracurricular clubs, athletics, or other prescribed activities? In the library, do independent-minded youth feel welcome outside the teen-designated zone? Are other librarians and staff ready and eager to interact with them? What about the policies for free meeting spaces for young adults with no group affiliation? Imagine these and other situations and consider whether the library encourages freedom of movement and thought.

The shift to age-blind attitudes comes into play. Every single young adult who uses the library should feel as though he or she is a respected member of this public institution. This heightens the importance of even brief encounters with all staff from reference desk librarians to security guards. One-to-one interactions are an undervalued strategy. Without being too intrusive, chatting with people individually to learn about their interests can lead to encouraging them to share ideas, whether it is about a community issue or pertains to services the library might offer. Impromptu conversations between young people and adults should be part of the library climate, as long as the adults are actively listening to what the young people are saying.

Another intuitive yet intentional strategy is for adults not to always put young people on the spot to respond to questions. The different "dance step" is to start by sharing one's own interests. If you are excited about a new graphic novel or fuming about a banned book, talk about it. Invite young adults into your circle.

The following statements from my manual, *Maximum Youth Involvement: The Complete Gameplan for Community Action* (Lesko, 2006), reveal some subtleties of intergenerational collaboration in contrast to the stark labels of youth-led or adult-directed decision making. More often than not, the outcomes are due to each of the individuals involved rather than the degree of youth independence versus adult intervention:

- "I love it when adults tell me they don't know."
- "Some adults surprise and inspire me. I am drawn to those who have not completely forgotten their adolescence and its open-mindedness."
- "Encourage us. Build on our ideas. That gives us the confidence we need."
- "Lead us to the cliff and trust us!"

Nothing beats honesty and authenticity. Young people detect insincere interest or fake praise, as described by a high school student who served on a nonprofit board: "The adult smirk is a half smile and slight nod as a young person speaks and silently thinks that the ideas being presented are unrealistic, have been tried in the past, or are plain stupid." Remember when you were young and didn't reveal your opinions because of the expectation that grown-ups would dismiss your ideas. This patronizing attitude can poison the atmosphere.

Young people aren't fooled when they are being asked to rubber-stamp a decision. "Adults think if they feed us pizza, that's all it takes," is a telling reminder by an eleventh-grader. Imagine being put in the uncomfortable and untenable position of being the token representative to pontificate about what "kids" in the community want. Think about serving as a youth board member who is the only one not to have a vote.

We need to call out adults who speak about "using kids." Another phrase that should make us wince is "their little project." This attitude is all too common, even among well-intentioned librarians who cannot click with a challenging mix of personalities. Every mismatch undermines job satisfaction and sabotages potential youth and adult synergy.

The Scarce Resource

Time is the four-letter word that explains why there is so little substantive youth influence with organizations, including those with a mission to empower youth. Minors have minimal control over their waking hours. Many students juggle multiple activities such as the school newspaper, a part-time job, or family responsibilities. This is one reason for erratic attendance at Teen Advisory Group meetings or library events. Staff need to be sensitive to young people's time, and one way is not to seek input on trivial issues or ask for feedback on significant matters without providing the necessary background material or adequate discussion time. For example, the Board of Young Adult Commissioners in New Haven, Connecticut, was considering the merits of a proposed curfew and an aide to the police chief shared information he had compiled for them that compared ordinances in dozens of other cities. This analysis enabled these high school students to rely on more than local and anecdotal information, and they proposed a modified curfew that ultimately was adopted by the city council.

Even if the mix of personalities and brainpower is awesome, there is another inevitable frustration. One or several of the most involved young adults take a break, drop out, or move. It could be something like the student is grounded or cannot miss any theater rehearsals or team practices. Snail mail, texting, e-mail, and Facebook are all strategies of patient persistence. After a one-year hiatus during the first year at college, four young adults who started an international initiative with me back when they were in the seventh grade transitioned from volunteers to paid interns. This experience proved remarkable in several ways. All of us went up the learning curve together. We increased our efficiency by dividing up in pairs and interviewing candidates for our social media manager. Designing a website and generating content was a team effort. Daily osmosis in our campaign meant that two of the interns were completely prepared to meet with White House staff when I was out of the country. In addition to concrete accomplishments, collaborating with smart, committed young colleagues exceeded all expectations.

Providing opportunities and venues for young adults to spend time at the libraries where they are in the loop and steeped in the issues on an ongoing basis enables them to truly participate as partners. Paid internships that come with real responsibilities can be one of the best investments to get solid input, especially when it comes to cocreating libraries. Internships also provide a critical rung on the ladder of engagement. An eighth-grader can imagine such a role three to five years into the future. Part-time staff and paid internships need to become the norm to promote youth infusion with professional librarians to replace separate or parallel activities.

Community Central

YA librarians have another distinct advantage over most adults that positions them as ideal copilots. As infomaniacs, librarians are constantly networking with community-based youth organizations, schools and universities, government agencies, advocacy groups, and so on. Electronic discussion lists, meetings, conferences, and rallies produce a stream of opportunities that might be of interest to young adults. Too often, we assume that teens won't be interested or busy schedules cause adults not to have the time to share current debates or upcoming events with teens.

Being deliberate about bringing news of community happenings, especially those beyond the school walls, can result in young adults participating in unexpected ways. I remember sharing a research study with School Girls Unite students that revealed one in seven girls worldwide are forced into marriage. An upcoming forum in the US Congress on this human rights issue peaked interest more. Within the week, one student wrote an article for her high school newspaper. Several tenth-graders decided to produce a video petition in favor of legislation that would include child marriage as one of the criteria evaluating every country in the US State Department's annual human rights report. Within a two-week period, students completed a clever video with sound bites from girls and boys expressing horror at forced marriage. It was shown at the forum and used by the students in their meetings with congressional staff, which led to their two senators and representative agreeing to be cosponsors on the bill. This example simply shows the potential of sharing information and the impact that can surprise everyone involved.

This strategy for broadening the bandwidth of young adults who depend on the library as information central can include policies and proposals that directly impact young people. In addition to battles over library funding, so many issues under consideration by the city or county council, board of education, parks and recreation, state legislature, and Congress are not on anyone's radar screen. Rarely are young people aware of when and where they could present their views and perhaps influence the outcome. Instead of a passive role, libraries could alert young adults to a school board hearing on changes to the zero-tolerance policy, a vote in the state senate on student voting eligibility, or immigration legislation in Congress. Using the library's connections to so many organizations, advocacy groups, and elected officials, this information hub could foster more meaningful civic engagement.

This approach ignores the reality that most minors believe they don't wield any influence whatsoever with the decision makers, especially those marginalized who are likely to feel disenfranchised well into adulthood. Storytelling, especially local history, can inspire young people to envision themselves as change agents whether in their library or the larger community. A case in point involved how few of the youth who visit the stunning Salt Lake City Public Library know about the East High School students who tried to start a Gay-Straight Alliance club in 2000. When initially rejected by the city board of education, students sought legal help and an antidiscrimination lawsuit forced the board to shut down all extracurricular clubs. This decision angered even more people and caused the school board to approve the student proposal. With a bit of digging in every community, there are true stories of ordinary youth accomplishing extraordinary things that prove there is no minimum age for leadership.

Another rich research area for student interns or perhaps a teen council is to survey libraries in other cities in search of innovative programming and cost-effective approaches. Browsing library websites and Facebook pages is bound to fuel fresh ideas. Follow up with individual libraries to learn more details as well as the resources required gives young adults ownership of the information. This investigation also enables them to gain more equal footing with adults involved with the library's strategic planning process.

Conclusion

We know every young adult is not always a joy to be around, and the feeling is usually mutual. But widespread negative stereotypes can be an excuse not to engage. Another attitude that interferes with meaningful partnership involves the standard benchmarks for cognitive abilities for specific adolescents by age. Plenty of middle school students demonstrate critical thinking skills and maturity that surpass high school students. Online skills and social marketing savvy also are obvious reasons to tap the brains of young adults. From the standpoint of longevity, offering opportunities to very young teens in the ongoing mission of revitalizing the library can result in years of involvement, with the added benefit of valuable institutional memory.

Every organization knows the tug-of-war between continuing to deliver services that have withstood the test of time and moving beyond the comfort zone to avoid becoming obsolete. Not only do young adults need to be actively involved in transforming YA services, but this multi-generational engagement also can help the entire library system be on the cutting edge. The next generation by virtue of age sees the future in ways that adults cannot fathom. It is incomprehensible not to take advantage of the ideas of a very diverse group of young adults to ensure libraries remain not only relevant but also a magnet in the community.

Combating inertia and resistance is no easy task. The common and unfortunate assumption when discussing the involvement of young people in organizational decision making is that youth are uninterested, unprepared, and uniformed. Staff time and precious resources are already stretched. As a result, most organizations only involve young people in minor volunteer roles or as program recipients. Providing paid internships for discrete projects as well as ongoing activities can begin this process in a sustained and deliberate way.

Youth infusion does not occur as an add-on or afterthought but is integral to the continual process of reinventing our libraries and community participation. Instead of should young adults be involved, the question should be, How can young adults be involved? This philosophy means valuing and respecting young people beyond an intrinsic future value and more as unique individuals who can make important contributions today.

New committees or structures are not necessary, but rather a systemic library-wide attitudinal shift. Not only do many adults need to transform their own perceptions, but young people also need to be convinced that authority figures and those in power will not be patronizing but genuinely seek to involve them as equal partners. Margaret Mead (1970: 73–74) describes the complexity of this paradigm:

> *The young, free to act on their initiative, can lead their elders in the direction of the unknown. The children, the young, must ask the questions that we would never think to ask, but enough trust must be re-established so that elders will be permitted to work with them on the answers.*

The creativity between generations has the potential to reduce our age-segregated institutions. Flexible and relentless strategies are necessary to engage young adults, including those who rarely or never use the libraries. This advancement will not happen until adults—all library staff—shift their thinking from being coaches to copilots with young adults. The involvement of the next generation as architects and advocates is essential to the ongoing process of reinventing libraries to ensure their relevance and popularity as vital and irreplaceable centers in communities across America.

References

Lesko, Wendy Schaetzel. 2006. *Maximum Youth Involvement: A Complete Gameplan for Community Action.* Youth Activism Project. http://www.youthactivismproject .org/.

Mead, Margaret. 1970. *Culture and Commitment: A Study of the Generation Gap.* New York: Natural History Press.

PART III

Beyond Youth Development and
Questions of Intellectual Freedom

7

Tribalism versus Citizenship

Are Youth Increasingly Unwelcome in Libraries?

Mike Males

Young adult spaces, which are populated by racially and ethnically diverse youth, challenge the assumption that libraries can accommodate only traditionally narrow "tribal" uses. This chapter addresses the question of whether these generational divisions between young adults and elder society members are so irreconcilable that libraries must physically separate young people from older patrons, perhaps to the point of restricting or banning youth from library spaces. In addition, this chapter explores how the fear-based movement in the larger society creates barriers between older Americans and young people and complicates notions of library citizenship.

Startling demographic and technological changes have combined to shake traditional views of libraries as passive cellulose (i.e., book and printed material) repositories occupied by patrons whose shared citizenship valued quiet studiousness, the ordered partitioning of specialties, and segregation of child from adult. As will be discussed in detail, libraries are a microcosm of larger society's increasing refusal to reconcile elders, still viewing society through their tribal lens, with emerging, multicultural youth adept in global technology. Segregative movements, wielding threats to defund libraries along with other publicly shared institutions, are likely to become more intense as age demographics continue to diverge. One counterforce—modern young adult (YA) library spaces populated by more racially and ethnically diverse youth populations and equipped with activist, integrated technologies—challenges these segregative forces and assumptions that libraries can enforce such traditionally narrow "tribal" uses, ironically, by segregating youths from adults!

Are generational divisions so irreconcilable that libraries must physically separate young people from older patrons, perhaps to the point of restricting or banning youth from adult library spaces or libraries themselves? The fear-based movement in larger society to create barriers between older American "citizens" and younger "invaders" complicates notions of library citizenship as well. While I advance the argument that in an era of rapid change, young people now make better citizens than older adults, my larger thesis is that the theoretical underpinning of library policy should recognize that the general features of old and young are not oppositional, but symbiotic; that is, libraries are in a unique position to boldly lead the way to redefine youth as genuine citizens.

Generational Decorum

The legacy of my dozen years of working with youth in community and wilderness programs is that I have scores of photos of teenagers. There are pictures of teens sitting around campfires, celebrating work project completions, watching rangers' evening talks, wrapped in sleeping bags on the porch of a remote cabin, perched on high mountain ledges, standing in lines, saying hello, saying goodbye. Where there are teens in groups, their most striking feature is their physicality. They tend—not universally but as a general rule—to cram closer together than adults do even in the most routine circumstances.

Teenagers' physicality bothers many grown-ups, who confuse it with sexuality. This has led to infamous "two-feet apart" and "anti-PDA" (public displays of affection) rules mandating corporeal distance. In libraries, the rule emerges in so many words as "one butt to a chair." One library banned patrons, clearly meaning young ones, from "grooming each other" (Kelly, 2007).

One could ask how the mere fact of chair-sharing—which has practical utility when, say, maximizing eyes on a computer screen during busy hours—or brushing someone else's hair thwarts any important library goal. But such behaviors clearly offend many elders' sense of what is "appropriate" in shared library culture. Few libraries have gone to the extremes of Maplewood, New Jersey's, which simply closed its doors during after-school hours until the mostly black, allegedly rowdy middle-schoolers had dispersed (an edict later reversed after negative publicity) (Kelly, 2007). While libraries may not originally have intended to use separate teen/young adult spaces to address generational decorum rifts, the soberly considered placement of a YA space today would be away from the sight lines of aging patrons.

Why are such dramatic generational rifts occurring at this time? Step back and consider America's gathering "demographic revolution." The concern that age segregation is a sign of more serious demographic fear is an extension of Margaret Mead's (1970) conclusion in *Culture and Commitment* (and less starkly, Alvin Toffler's popular *Future Shock*) 40 years ago: adults, bound to tradition, cannot handle the jolting pace of modern racial and technological change and become irrationally alienated from younger generations they see as embodying an unwanted present and future. "In this new culture it will be the child—and not the parent and grandparent—that represents what is to come.... The alienation of the young is emphasized, while the alienation of their elders may be entirely overlooked" (Mead, 1970: 62, 68).

While Mead (1970: 63) argued the modern, post-1960 "generation gap" was "deep, new, unprecedented," few seem to appreciate just how this simple-sounding idea foretold an accelerating evolutionary shift. Prior to the modern era, elders held power by virtue of harboring the knowledge and skills necessary to the survival of their tribe, and elder and younger generations were tied by the common kinship, race, customs, and traditions derived from homogeneity and assurance that the future would be much like the present and past. But in diversifying, fast-changing modern societies, the grown-ups "do not know how to teach these children who are so different from what they themselves once were, and the children are unable to learn from parents and elders they will never resemble" (Mead, 1970: 66).

Today's generation gap, whose ominous implications are just now being perceived in mainstream discussion, has a stark fault line. The 2010 census details the demographic revolution. Among children, youth, and young adults ages 19 and younger, 47 percent are nonwhite: Hispanic, African-American, Asian-American, or Native American, or of other or mixed race. By the 2020 census, American youth will have no racial majority. Among adults ages 50 and older, just one-fourth are of color. Compare this to the 1950 census, when approximately 85 percent of youth and over 90 percent of elders were white of European origin; that is, the kids looked like the parents (US Bureau of the Census, 2011).

The United States is rapidly becoming an all-minority country, with the arrival of a nonwhite majority predicted by the 2030s. An Associated Press story on June 23, 2011, notes (or warns) that a majority of children under age two in the United States now are minorities. Most cities have already undergone the transition, and states herald the multicultural future. In 2010, Texas, Florida, Arizona, Nevada, Georgia, and Mississippi joined California, New Mexico, and Hawaii with all-minority youth populations. New York, Illinois, Delaware, Oklahoma, Colorado, Louisiana, North Carolina, and South Carolina will soon follow suit, and then a dozen other states.

This hypothalamus-rattling demographic revolution has occurred in the space not of centuries, but within a single individual's life span— indeed, dramatic changes have and will continue to take place during the professional lives of most librarians today. The color wave is rising from young ages upward. The trend is setting off evolutionary alarm bells, and the reaction against it—though coded—has been virulent. Efforts to restrict immigrants, reverse advancements in minority rights, and banish young people from private and public spaces have burgeoned as nativist movements led by the Tea Party, heavily comprised of aging whites, gains influence. Generational conflict, coextant with racial and ethnic rifts, were most evident in states like Arizona, Florida, and California, where unusually large aging white populations confront unusually large minority youth populations. Libraries situated at the intersections of inner cities and old-wealth districts, in increasingly minority older suburbs and newly gentrifying neighborhoods, and in rural communities where employers have brought in Hispanic and other migrant laborers—in short, everywhere

where races are in flux—are likely to face pressures to shield older patrons from younger ones of varying colors, speaking unknown languages, and presenting the visible menace of difference.

One largely noncontroversial result—in that it has proven popular among both conservative and liberal officials—has been a sweeping movement to banish young people from public spaces, especially where older folks gather. Our studies at the Center on Juvenile and Criminal Justice and research reviews of juvenile curfews find they're not effective at their ostensible goals of enhancing crime control or public safety (Males and Macallair, 1998). Curfew advocates, however, don't seem to care about research findings. Rather, they gain momentum in gentrifying areas such as Minneapolis's Mall of America, Oklahoma City's Bricktown, Pasadena's Old Town, and suburbs gaining minority populations, where black and brown youth are alarmingly visible in districts attempting to attract and maintain older, mostly white clientele.

Along with efforts to get darker youth out of sight, traditional measures to separate white youth from base underclass influences are being pushed with renewed vigor. As an information-dispersing and globally socializing force, the Internet is seen as a major threat to preservation of distinct, elder-controlled tribal cultures. Thus, the Internet is now being depicted in a cascade of identical press articles and interest-group forums as the font of dangerously ungoverned youth interaction and, therefore, atrocities. Libraries, as nodes of Internet technology as well as information-dispensing institutions in their own right, are subject to similar suspicions and retribalizing efforts.

Is, then, age segregation by means of youth spaces—a permutation of the sequester-youth impetus of larger American society reflected in juvenile curfews, mall and store banishments, separated venues founded in alcohol, pornography, or other "adults only" settings—the direction libraries ultimately want to go? My Youth in Transition class at the University of California–Santa Cruz, addressed that question to library youth-space specialist and Los Angeles Public Libraries TeenS'cape designer Anthony Bernier (see Bernier, 2011; Bernier, Chelton, Jenkins, and Pierce, 2005). His response was framed as a question of practicality: How can services to youth be maintained and expanded in the face of the growing desire on the part of elders to avoid young people? If forcing generations to occupy the same space results in conflicts leading to severe restrictions or even banishment of young people from libraries, how can libraries continue to serve youthful populations—at least for now, during the difficult transition from tribal to multiracial society—other than by benign, temporary age apartheid?

While to some extent youth spaces fulfill traditional library goals of organizing special collections and service areas around the interests of distinct populations, is their main function to get young people, with their generally darker skins and allegedly freer verbal and physical expressions, away from the gaze of nervous elders? If so, their proliferation raises troubling questions.

Unruly Trends

In formulating my idealism for libraries to boldly lead the way to redefine youth as full-fledged citizens rather than an object demographic whose status is defined by the metric of fear and disdain adult constituencies feel toward them, I had expected to make a standard pitch. To begin, I would concede: Look, we've learned too slowly and painfully to put aside what sociologist William Julius Wilson (1997) calls "statistical bigotry" and to admit to more or less full equality minority races, multiplying varieties of gender, and even statuses based on lifestyle. That is, because an African-American 40-year-old has a gun-homicide rate nine times higher than a corresponding white does not mean we should penalize 999 out of 1,000 middle-aged black men who will not be involved in gun murder for the one who is. Of course, Wilson should have said "selective statistical bigotry"; if the index were drug abuse instead of homicide, older white men might be saddled with the sundown curfew.

I had expected to continue by pointing out that the case for segregating adolescents and young adults from adults under a system of unique restrictions relies largely on statistical claims, along with "developmental" and "cognitive" (more crudely, "teen brain") arguments assembled to provide biological explanations for the statistics, of the type that would be rejected as prejudicial if applied to adult populations. Thus, the argument I expected to make was that even if teenagers as a class are statistically "worse" than adults it would be no more evidence for mass age-based partition than the even larger statistical differences between males and females, or between races, would justify gender or racial bigotries. Such a "civil rights for teens" case would carry the validity of banality, since no one to my knowledge argues for restricting men, older whites, or Mississippians because their group statistics tend to be alarming.

But it turns out that the actual argument against teen apartheid is stronger and stranger. First, the statistical and developmental arguments advanced to justify special restrictions and banishments of young people were dubious to begin with; resurrected psychobabble about teens' supposedly innate volatility, criminality, impulsiveness, and egocentrism disappears once the elementary stratum of socioeconomics is considered. Put a 40-year-old in the higher poverty brackets typically suffered by adolescents, and suddenly the middle-ager displays serious statistics regarding traffic crashes, guns, and alienation of the magnitude we typically blame on angsty kids (Males, 2010a). In fact, boomers are showing some dismaying behavior problems even though we're the richest demographic ever. Perhaps libraries should establish special boomer spaces stocked with that 1970 Sonny-Bono-on-quaaludes video and rehab-retirement posters.

To add insulting trend to injurious behavior, recent decades have brought distinct improvements in a wide variety of youth behaviors as the youth population has become more racially diverse and technologically interconnected—even as behaviors among much less diverse middle-aged and older adults have deteriorated alarmingly. Perhaps the most startling, relevant statistic is that today, the FBI (2011) *Uniform Crime Reports* shows more adults in their 40s are arrested for murder, rape, felony assault, drunken offenses, and all crimes than all juveniles under age 18, a truly shocking development given the distinct economic advantages midlife adults enjoy compared to youths. This renders statistical arguments that youths must be isolated and custodialized as a uniquely unpredictable, dangerous, "crime prone" population invalid on their face.

Marrying standards of basic equality to the force of modern trends, then, the argument for making young people full citizens is stronger than ever. But the argument for calling young people forth into citizenship and leadership roles is, to my mind, the most compelling of all when we consider what that actually might mean.

Are Age- and Generation-Based Qualities Irrelevant?

Pin down the two general, interrelated features of young people that are typically seen as negative: *inexperience* with complex tasks due simply to having lived fewer years, and *inefficient thinking* due to the proliferation of wide-open neural pathways in developing brains. In some situations, these are disadvantages. There aren't many 16-year-old National Football League (NFL) quarterbacks or high-specialty surgeons; in traditional societies, being old and versed in the traditional skills confer great power. But the trade-off, well discussed by social scientist Howard Sercombe (2010) and neuroscientist Tomas Paus, is that aging brains' rigidifying neural pathways result in narrower efficiencies at the expense of flexibility, openness to learning, and meeting new challenges.

As Mead (1970) pointed out more than 40 years ago, young people enjoy major advantages in a rapidly changing society. They grew up with the latest culture and technologies and don't tend to view change with the reflexive trepidation of their elders. Today's younger people also are more comfortable with diversity, displaying more racially integrated dating and friendship patterns and levels of tolerance appropriate to emerging multicultures. Youthful attitudes on immigration, gay rights, interracial marriage, religious tolerance, and the need for shared social investments are far more progressive than found among over-30 ages, as we document from analysis of numerous surveys (YouthFacts.org, 2010).

It's not just that elders are succumbing to more reactionary attitudes, including majority support for far-right-wing candidates who openly seek to dismantle shared public investment and concentrate wealth in older and richer cohorts, even to the point of threatening gunplay and secession. We are seeing massive deteriorations in the *personal behaviors* of older Americans, led by explosions in drug abuse, criminal arrest, imprisonment, and family disarray. Mead (1970) warned that the "alienation of the old" from their society, manifest in both attitudes and behaviors, would become more of a crisis than that of the young, and the rise of the modern Tea Party and reactionary politics driven heavily by over-45 white constituencies seem powerful evidence for concern.

The result, perhaps the temporary product of a wrenching transition from traditional, homogeneous population groups (tribes) to a global multiculture in which America harbors major representation from all five inhabited continents means that young people now make better citizens than older ones. That is, on balance, I suspect that the young today possess more skills necessary to the continuity of our society as it evolves into a worldly polyglot than do the old. This is unprecedented.

I don't propose a public campaign headlining this point, especially if a library's ultimate goal, like mine, is a more integrated approach and the organization of services around the most appropriate categories rather than ones dictated by fear and prejudice. To the extent that youth spaces are the products of ephebiphobia (the irrational fear of adolescents) rather than ideal allocation of library space, they need to be reexamined in terms of their integrative rather than segregative potential. This potential can be segregative in that as youth become more unwelcome in "adult" zones, the adult who uses a children's or YA space is likely to come under suspicion under the growing paranoia over pedophilia. An example of this dualized fear occurred in the San Jose, California, system in which a citizen's group complained that children who ventured into adult library areas were glimpsing "secondhand porn" on computer screens (Bernier, 2011; KCBS, 2007)—a panic that symbolized the larger fear of young people having uncontrolled access to information as the result of their presence in "adult" spaces and the corresponding access of adult pedophiles to children.

YA spaces are also justified on the professional grounds that adolescence, being a distinct and bounded time of life, has its own informational culture. There is a category dubbed YA literature, magazines that serve younger teens and grade-schoolers, and singular entry-level job, college preparatory, and other materials in which older adults presumably would have little interest. Seemingly, few adults would buy Miley Cyrus CDs or peruse *Tiger Beat* (and those who did would generate watchful anxiety). There may be some intersections of interest; for example, in today's market, adults are going back to school and exploring entry-level jobs in tandem with youth.

No, indeed, integrative pressures are not emanating from the oldsters. The big problem is seen as teen and tween precocity. While teens may form a distinct informational demographic, they also spill into adult library realms by consuming "adult" literature, visuals, research holdings, and other references too vast and varied to be maintained in a YA space. In fact, the teen "invasion" of adult territories is occurring across a wide spectrum of society, from having sex, drinking alcohol, and choosing independent lifestyles to checking out R-rated movies, steamy novels, racy magazines, and who knows what Internet sites.

Teenage incursions into adult spaces are generating society's greatest panics over "kids growing up too fast," followed by the harshest repressions. Yet, again, panic and repression are unrelated to the best measures of how teens are handling themselves as the invading force, which show young people have never been safer, healthier, and expressing better attitudes than they are now. This conclusion is based on our analysis of a wealth of long-term statistics on such topics as crime, violence, violent mortality, unwanted sexual outcomes, school performance and graduation, surveyed attitudes and behaviors, and other standard indexes, nearly all of which indicate most teenage "badness" is at or near all-time lows (Males, 2006). Emotional efforts to suppress teenage precocity and repel their invasion of adult life—typically founded in salacious anecdotes and panicky quips more than sober evidence—seem more related to the difficulties of a graying generation in a culture of change than to manifest youth troubles.

Are YA spaces functioning as cog in a systemic effort to maintain the juvenilization of adolescents then? At this juncture, several conclusions can be reached. Libraries' inadvertent contribution to the latest phase in a century-long effort to create a segregated teenage stage—ironically, one that contributed to the cementing of the very "youth culture" adults would fear as much as the prospect of teens lurking on the street corners of adult culture (Kett, 1977; Hine, 1999)—includes primitive efforts to separate adolescent from adult access to information via net filters, age-based restrictions on materials checkout, and more censorious policies on what items can appear in YA spaces than on adult shelves.

I don't mean to imply that the YA space functions as some kind of holding tank, only that it represents libraries' own version of resolving the tribal demand for generational separation. The ecology of the teen/YA space has recognized adults as the dominant species, allocated grown-ups the fullest library range in which to forage and graze on their interests as individual citizens. The child and adolescent niche species are given smaller, separate reserves with narrower ranges of materials on the assumption that their appetites are more uniform and circumscribed. Of course, few if any libraries actually fence the young out of adult spaces, though there have been some rumblings in that direction that are likely to grow louder as the demographic chasm between teen and grown-up becomes more pronounced over the next 25 years before receding. Left to themselves, the emotional "incident," the calls to "protect children" from adult materials, the intervention of herd journalism (which reflexively champions every new restriction on teens), and notions of "cognitive development" that insist adolescents generically are incompatible with adults, will continue to dominate. Assumptions (using curfews as a model) that the mere discomfort and fear of older patrons (the dominant species) toward the presence of young people (the unwanted vectors) justifies the latter's banishment are likely to be cited in favor of formal enforcement of age barriers within libraries. That libraries may not enforce the age divide as strictly as other institutions does not negate the utility of YA spaces and youth-specific polices in maintaining adolescent apartheid.

More practically, then, I would suggest that the theoretical underpinning of library policy recognize that the general strengths of old and young are not oppositional, but symbiotic, and that individuality, not demographic determinism, remains the salient characteristic of individuals of all ages. The biggest revolutionary advance is not just to treat teenagers as individuals—my impression in this regard is that libraries already are more advanced than, say, schools, police, media, and mental health interests (damnation by faint praise, perhaps)—but actually to *see* teens as individuals. That is, if a 50-year-old drunk man sprawls in the restroom, we don't crusade to lock the doors against citizen middle-agers or citizen males; we see him as a singular miscreant unreflective of his larger demographic. But it remains a venture into uncharted tolerance for us to accord citizen 15-year-old the same reflexive respect.

But does this mean teens are comfortable with adults in "their" space? Here we have to rely on the always unreliable anecdote and its connection to survey findings. On the one hand, *Monitoring the Future* (Bachman, Johnston, and O'Malley, 2011) finds, over its 35-year history, that fewer teens are spending or feel the need to spend more time with adults 30 and older. It's not that teens hold negative stereotypes about grown-ups the same way as grown-ups hold about the young; when asked, as in Public Agenda polls, large majorities of youths seem to see adults as individuals, most good, some bad. Is, then, the fact that modern teens spend more time around peers and less with adults the result of a natural separation, a reactive one, or an artifact introduced by segregative policies?

What Would "YA Space" Mean?

What, then, might libraries look like if more survey-indicated youth values were incorporated, and would these values necessarily be incompatible with age integration? As noted, age and race are conflated, so that simplistic bigotry against youth is often framed in the same terminologies and remedies as those based on race. However, it still remains hard to reconcile patrons who like quiet and order with those who favor noisier, more-butts-to-a-chair library usage. Thus, one could imagine libraries more practically organized around styles of usage—contemplative versus collaborative, for example—rather than age alone.

Or, it may turn out that libraries will continue to find YA spaces the most efficient service mode because general differences between teen and young adult patrons compared to older adults remain the most important organizing factor. An excellent ethnography by Herb Childress (2000) contains a systematic critique by young people of the human ecology of their small town. Childress found young people favored gathering areas that promoted centripetal values—that is, ones whose design features:

- created a centralizing public focus;
- afforded easy views of comings and goings;
- were not internally divided or separated from other areas by barriers, hard angles, wide corridors, or broad open areas;
- created a sense of density, comfort, and motion with people present at all hours;
- contained both a "centerpiece" to concentrate users for unifying functions and multiple points to "stop and lean" to facilitate mingling;
- included natural elements (presumably plants, or even access to outdoor flora) that were clearly distinct from man-made areas; and
- incorporated diverse uses within easily walkable distances and accessibility to wide varieties of users.

It's hard to imagine a design that looks less like a typical suburban community, where sprawl, decentralization, strip malls, heavily trafficked roadways dividing districts, sparsely populated areas, car dependency, restrictive covenants, privatized rather than public gathering points, and zoned single-use functions predominate, than the one its teenagers wanted. With a stretch of imagination, one can correlate the public spaces teenagers advocate with their political attitudes favoring diverse nodes within larger community, tolerance, and shared public investment (see Bachman, Johnston, and O'Malley, 2011).

Harnessing Synergy

Are these values libraries can build on? In suggesting the leadership of libraries into inaugurating young people as citizens, I argue for three basic premises.

First, I believe from empirical evidence that the global demographics, attitudes, behaviors, skills, and "vision" (if so pompous a generality can be used) of America's young people today generally constitute a far more promising foundation for building the emerging multicultural society than the fearful, tribal anachronisms of the old. These general views and wide varieties of thought exist among all ages. Today's situation did not apply in static, traditional cultures in which the accumulated wisdom of the old was crucial to the survival and continuity of cultures. But in today's rapidly changing and diversifying societies, the recency and flexibility of youth provide a leadership edge.

As young people got more diverse, their attitudes and conduct improved, even as the best traditional sciences would have predicted deterioration. Synergy—in this case, the evolution of a population in directions more beneficial than would be predicted from the sum of the characteristics and trends of its subpopulations—is a uniquely dynamic development. As American kids got darker, they got better, against all odds. Why? Understanding this youthful synergy would yield a leg up in contemplating and realizing the library of the future.

Second, libraries as inherently progressive institutions—that is, as democratizing through the promotion of universal information—are better placed than others to host this generational synergy. This may strike many in the field as dubious or even risible, but consider the alternatives: it's not likely that schools, municipalities, businesses, churches, or government will lead the way to a more age-egalitarian framework, since most at the moment thrive on the fears of an aging society. Universities and university communities are probably the only other, also uncertain, sites of progressive innovation. Even if these institutions did reverse current trends by investing more heavily in younger and future generations, it's likely that it would come with continued age apartheid on the unspoken grounds that darker-skinned teenagers and white elders are not a good mix—along with an unspoken "duh!"

Yet, because youth have decisive potential to facilitate the transition to a more global, variegated culture, I would contend that maintaining age separation is a devastating mistake. Generational integration is not just desirable, but also vital. If you think I'm idealistic, listen to Mead's (1970: 73, 75) exuberance: "We can change into a prefigurative [youth defined] culture, consciously, delightedly, and industriously rearing unknown children for an unknown world" in which "the young, free to act on their own initiative, can lead their elders in the direction of...a viable future."

Third, given the invasion of teens into adult realms of information, popular culture, and cybersocializing to the point that many of these are becoming youth dominated—and evidence of some oldsters taking a shine to certain aspects of youth cultures—the potential of information-disseminating institutions such as libraries to naturalize interactions between old, middle, and young is an easier task than it would be, say, in the church or the Supreme Court. Young people do not have to be forced into the adult world; they are already there. All that is necessary is to stop trying to force them out of it.

To that end, I would suggest some initial steps for those interested in generational integration, divided into "nonnegative" and "positive." In the nonnegative category, libraries' programming and publicity should consciously treat youth the same as adult groups. An after-school reading program for middle-schoolers should not be advertised as a way to "get kids off the streets" or "prevent after-school crime" any more than a senior citizens' function should be advertised as a way to keep a leash on granny. Demands by the police and schools for library collaboration in arresting youths for curfews and truancy, or abrogating teens' Internet communications privacy for various law enforcement schemes such as criminalizing "sexting," should be strenuously resisted. Censorware and restrictive policies should be scaled back so that youths' access to library materials is afforded the same freedom that adults enjoy. Negative generalizations about young people, which often occur after the occasional media-inflamed incident, should be regarded with the same disdain as ones stigmatizing race or gender.

In the positive arena, teens' leadership roles should be expanded past advisory panels and toward active administration, as some libraries now seem to be doing. But the implications of affirming young people as true citizens in library culture challenge traditional assumptions held over from the cellulose-repository era. Teens in general (repeating the caveat that "general" does not mean "universal" or "exclusive") favor a more wide-open, collaborative, technologically fluid, communal, centered, yet busy (in the sense that multiple uses are available in one space) environment. This vision clashes radically with the notion of libraries as enthroning contemplative, individual quiet and order where the inner mind feeds in one's own one-butt chair.

Teen apartheid may be a necessary phase given today's attitudes, but it is not the ideal as a permanent vision. The gossamer of American adulthood—a developmental artifact currently being reified and canonized as the glorious endpoint of human development (indeed, all of evolution) by more sensational "teen brain" and "psychological stage" disciples even as empirical evidence finds it barely distinguishable in practice—does not benefit from continued fortification against the adolescent "invasion." As a graphic example, laws in 43 states allow adults all the way up to geezerhood to have sex legally with 16- and 17-year-olds (presumably those needing lots of money or eye exams); it makes no sense to ban high-schoolers from perusing their own choice of "unnannied" websites.

Still, new technologies and youth-created institutions continue to be depicted as threats even if provable damage remains rare, while traditional institutions such as the family and church remain "Teflonned" from their sins. The Crimes against Children Research Center's (Wolak, Finkelhor, and Mitchell, 2007) nationwide survey of police agencies found only 25 documented cases of rape, physical violence, abduction, or other harm to youths inflicted by people they met online in 2005, a year in which child maltreatment authorities substantiated more than a quarter-million cases of physical and sexual violence against youths within families, nearly all inflicted by parents. More than 5,000 sexual abuses of children by church personnel have been admitted by the Catholic Church alone in recent decades (see Males, 2010b). Yet, check incessant evening news and "expert" warnings about the "dangers of the Internet" to young people, combined with only occasional mentions of traditional institutions as representing dangers many magnitudes worse.

So, I readily acknowledge the difficulties. Libraries are subject to outside political forces demanding censorware and age segregation, and even a handful of save-our-children vigilantes can wreak years of administrative misery. These segregative forces armed with the power to defund libraries along with other publicly shared institutions are likely to strengthen as age demographics continue to diverge. In contrast, libraries' provision of YA spaces—that is, expending funds and real estate on young people—already seems insurrectional in a larger America increasingly bent on banishing youth from public and on dismantling teens' private territories, both physical and virtual, seen as promoting unregulated peer interactions (see Bernier, 2011; Bernier, Chelton, Jenkins, and Pierce, 2005).

Conclusion

Libraries, another microcosm of larger society's failure to reconcile the tribal elders with emerging, multicultural youth, are positioned to lead the way to redefine youth as full-fledged citizens. Should they accept the challenge, their ally is the biggest counterforce to age and generational apartheid: the rising pressure by teens seeking to move into adult society (or, more correctly, to exercise the privileges of adults to choose their society as individuals). The progress in dismantling segregation based on race as minorities gained political power has intensified, not weakened, the pressure to segregate by age, since adolescents as a "temporary minority" are unlikely to accumulate the political power necessary to prevent discrimination. In that light, one particularly stunning manifestation is the surge in the percentage of high school seniors of both sexes telling the annual *Monitoring the Future* (Bachman, Johnston, and O'Malley, 2011) survey they want to assume leadership positions in their communities, up from around one in five in 1975 to nearly half today.

Teenage leadership motivations—another precocity now being treated as a dire threat to the developmental order and demanding of suppression by isolation of youth and by application of special restrictions—are also another force countering today's tribal clamor seeking to thwart generational synergy. Though seldom formulated this way, tribal imperatives seek to head off the dangerous intersection of precocious youth with those geezer gatekeepers who haven't gotten the memo and might see merit in youthful initiative. (President Barack Obama was once seen in that light; no longer.) Adults who accord adolescents adult privileges are particularly condemned for endangering young people by facilitating their premature entry into a dangerous grown-up world—like pedophiles do!—though the real, unspoken fear is that adolescents are succeeding there all too well.

Libraries, along with dozens of other major institutions and thousands of minor ones, consistently fail to respond to historical moments such as these. That is understandable, since interpretations of the ongoing history of the present, to borrow a position from social philosopher Michel Foucault, are inevitably trapped within limited perceptions of alternatives dictated from the past. So long as the stroll to the future represented a leisurely plodding up a gentle trail that diverged only gradually and predictably from generation to generation, then the flaws of past-dictated alternatives would be obscured by their comforting familiarity. For a relevant example, one small step from the original Carnegie Library blueprint of bifurcated adult and children's wings has been to pencil in a logical trifurcation, space for the teen/young adult. Libraries effectively endorsed the larger psychological construct that while an adult from ages 20 to 120 is an adult and a child under age 12 or so is a child, a teenager is something yonder.

I suggest that libraries consciously lead in a different direction justified by the advantages the institution enjoys compared to others in society. First, libraries have more experience than most with teen advisory panels that actually advise (and in some libraries, actively influence resource allocation), a necessary but insufficient step toward generational integration. By providing references and connective technologies needed by low-income youth in particular, libraries are in a position to be both relevant to a wide variety of young people and to expand their institutional power.

Second, libraries fulfill an information dispersion function, an inherently democratizing force. Libraries have (mostly) opposed popular censorship demagoguery such as Congress's Communications Decency Act; censorious ideology is a special case of age-based apartheid. It does not simply involve compartmentalizing adolescents and deterring them from accessing the full range of "adult" information, it also more subtly prevents adolescents from subverting adult library culture with more collaborative, diverse, centripetal styles ("2+ butts to a chair") amplified by their keener technological savvy. The most subversive threat is not the stereotypical "rebellious teen" against whom grown-ups have marshaled statutes, security, and dismissive "science," but the undeniable manifestation of the reality that youth, indeed, might well make better citizens in a dynamic new era to which grown-ups are refusing to adapt.

References

Bachman, J. G., L. D. Johnston, and P. M. O'Malley. 2011. *Monitoring the Future: Questionnaire Responses from the Nation's High School Seniors, 2010.* University of Michigan Institute for Social Research, Ann Arbor, MI. http://www.monitoringthefuture.org/datavolumes/2010/2010dv.pdf.

Bernier, Anthony. 2011. "Representations of Youth in Local Media: Implications for Library Service." *Library and Information Science Research* 33: 158–167.

Bernier, Anthony, M. K. Chelton, C. A. Jenkins., and J. B. Pierce. 2005. "Two Hundred Years of Young Adult Library Services: A Chronology." *Voice of Youth Advocates* 28, no. 2: 106–111.

Childress, Herb. 2000. *Landscapes of Betrayal, Landscapes of Joy: Curtisville in the Lives of Its Teenagers.* New York: State University of New York Press.

FBI (Federal Bureau of Investigation). 2011. *Uniform Crime Reports.* http://www.fbi.gov/about-us/cjis/ucr/ucr/.

Hine, Thomas. 1999. *The Rise and Fall of the American Teenager.* New York: Avon Books.

KCBS. 2007. "Blocking Second-Hand Porn in San Jose." Radio broadcast, October 20.

Kelly, T. 2007. "Lock the Library! Rowdy Students Are Taking Over." *New York Times,* January 2, B2.

Kett, Joseph. 1977. *Rites of Passage: Adolescence in America, 1790 to the Present.* New York: Basic Books.

Males, Mike. 2006. "Youth Policy and Institutional Change." In *Beyond Resistance! Youth Activism and Community Change,* edited by S. Ginwright, P. Noguera, and J. Cammarota, 301–318. New York: Routledge.

———. 2010a. "Is Jumping off the Roof Always a Bad Idea? A Rejoinder on Risk Taking and the Adolescent Brain." *Journal of Adolescent Research* 25, no. 1: 48–63.

———. 2010b. *Teenage Sex and Pregnancy: Modern Myths, Unsexy Realities.* New York: Praeger.

Males, Mike, and Dan Macallair. 1998. *The Impact of Juvenile Curfew Laws in California.* San Francisco: Center on Juvenile and Criminal Justice. http://www.cjcj.org/files/the_impact.pdf.

Mead, Margaret. 1970. *Culture and Commitment: A Study of the Generation Gap.* Garden City, NY: Natural History Press/Doubleday.

Sercombe, Howard. 2010. "The gift and the Trap: Working the 'Teen Brain' into Our Concept of Youth." *Journal of Adolescent Research* 25, no. 1: 31–47.

US Bureau of the Census. 2011. *2010 Census Data.* Accessed July 5, 2011. http://2010.census.gov/2010census/data/.

Wilson, William Julius. 1997. *When Work Disappears: The World of the New Urban Poor.* New York: Vintage.

Wolak, Janis, David Finkelhor, and Kimberly Mitchell. 2007. *Trends in Arrests of "Online Predators."* Crimes Against Children Research Center, University of New Hampshire, Durham, NH. http://www.unh.edu/ccrc/pdf/CV194.pdf.

YouthFacts.org. 2010. "Elder Meltdown Threatens America." Updated September 20. http://www.youthfacts.org/elders.php.

———. 2011. "All Part I (Index) Felony Arrests." http://www.youthfacts.org/indexarr.htm.

8

Imagining Today's Young Adults in LIS

Moving Forward with Critical Youth Studies

Paulette Rothbauer

The psychological "storm and stress" model of adolescence advanced by G. Stanley Hall and others continues to underpin the conceptions of teen library users and teen readers. This chapter questions the ways in which this model has become essentialized in library and information science discourses concerned with public library services to young adults, and offers alternative frameworks for conceptualizing young adults. Moreover, this chapter investigates the possibilities offered by critical youth studies to disrupt and complicate ideas about a universal experience of adolescence and how these might work to transform young adult services.

Asked to consider the question "How should library and information science imagine today's young adults?," I knew in an instant that I wanted to explore our taken-for-granted understanding of those people we call young adults, youth, adolescents, and teenagers as simply belonging to a bracketed age classification, usually between 12 and 19 years of age. In this chapter, I explore a body of work that is sometimes called "critical youth studies" and consider what it offers to the conceptual project that underpins this collection of chapters on transforming young adult (YA) librarianship. Before I go any further, however, it is necessary to be clear about what this chapter *is not*. It is not a critique of YA librarianship or YA librarians, nor is it a critique of advocacy for young adults and YA library services. I am a strong supporter of the efforts of organizations like the Young Adult Library Services Association (YALSA) and Canadian Libraries Are Serving Youth (CLASY) that are composed of groups of individuals who are keenly committed to improving library services to teenagers and young adults in North America, and by so doing, enhancing the lives of teenagers and young adults. However, I intend to examine closely the logic of the discourses we use to explain and justify what it is we do in libraries with youth and why we think we should be doing it (or doing more). Further, I want to explore whether and how such work might be informed by critical youth studies perspectives. The ideas in this chapter are tentative, exploratory, and offered respectfully as part of the ongoing conversation among researchers, library school students, library workers, library users, and others concerned with youth services librarianship.

Consequences of Dominant Stereotypes of Youth

When we examine more closely the general representations of teenagers and young adults in contemporary North American society, we can begin to see the ways in which dominant stereotypes of teenagers also become entrenched in library discourses. Many others have warned of the dangers of reducing young adults to stereotypes (see, for example, Chelton, 2001; Gorman and Suellentrop, 2004: 25–26; Jones and Shoemaker, 2001), but I want to go one step further here. One of the major assumptions underpinning this chapter is that there is no naturally occurring entity in the world called a "young adult," but rather there are competing and changing discourses on what constitutes young adulthood. While many stereotypes exist, some of the most dominant and enduring characterizations of teenagers are described by Nancy Lesko (2001: 4–5) in her book *Act Your Age!* on the cultural construction of adolescence. Each is described in turn.

Adolescents "Come of Age" into Adulthood

The idea that adolescence is a transition from childhood to adulthood is one of the most enduring conceptualizations. It is usually further conceived of as a series of discrete and unidirectional stages or steps with physical, cognitive, and emotional milestones where adulthood is judged to be the more rational and reliable state (Raby, 2007: 40–41). Developmental milestones suggest that on the one hand all youth, regardless of their own situations in the world, progress toward adulthood in the same ways, and on the other hand that if a particular young person, or groups of young people, get stopped or even worse move backwards, that there is something wrong, deficient, inadequate, immature, incomplete, and so on. Critical youth scholars contest such claims for an "essential" stage of human development when they argue that its scientific identification is a recent phenomenon dating only to the early 1900s with the popularization of G. Stanley Hall's so-called discovery of adolescence. Studies like Margaret Mead's anthropological study *Coming of Age in Samoa* are used to argue that adolescence is a product of culture, and as such its meanings vary across cultural contexts (see Côté and Allahar, 2006: 4–5).

Adolescents Are Controlled by Raging Hormones

In the master of library and information science (MLIS) class that I teach on youth, information, and library services, like many other instructors I often begin the term with a discussion of stereotypes—those held by teens about adults and those held by adults about teens. The conceptualization of young adults as people buffeted about by raging hormones in a "storm and stress" framework is often one of the first models of adolescence to be voiced. In this formulation, young adults are seen to be subject to impulses that are uncontrollable, potentially dangerous, and certainly distasteful. Consequent to this idea of youth is the biological inevitability of adolescence—that if we just wait long enough, it will soon be over, but in the meantime young people need to be monitored and controlled by adults.

Adolescents Are Peer Oriented

That adolescents are strongly influenced or pressured by their peers seems like an essential truth about teenagers and young adults, perhaps even more so in the present era of socially mediated communication and entertainment. As Lesko tells us, the subtle consequences of this idea are to take away the individual's ability to determine or judge for himself or herself, to discount his or her full autonomy, and to assume the conformity of youth as young people are socialized to peer norms.

Adolescence Is Signified by Age

For many of us, adults and young people alike, biological and chronological age (i.e., 13 to 19 years of age) or generational age (i.e., millennials, generation Y) have become main entry points for thinking about young adults. Age-graded education is now the norm in most schools in North America, as are age-graded library collections and services in public libraries. Age intersects with all other conceptualizations of young adulthood and operates as a powerful way to eliminate diversity and differences among cohorts of youth. In other words, the statement that "Jane is 15 years old" signifies a great deal to those who read it without any need for further elaboration.

Lesko helps us to understand why we need to pay attention to these dominant characterizations. It is worth citing her at length:

These four confident characterizations of adolescence operate within and across numerous fields, including education, law, medicine, psychology, and social work, as well as in popular culture, such as movies, television, and literature. They declare the nature of youth and they incite us to find instances of their truth in new encounters. In theoretical terms these confident characterizations tell us what adolescents will be like, help us interpret our personal experiences of being teenaged in their light, and inform future observations by telling us what is important and enduring in adolescent lives. We believe that youths are under peer pressure, we understand our own experiences in these terms, and we see new situations in these terms. Thus these characterizations move both into our pasts and into our futures, helping us to shape individual subjective experiences but also objective knowledges. (Lesko, 2001: 4–5)

These characteristics of youth are so prevalent and so taken for granted that we no longer tend to question their validity or see them as stereotypes. There is, however, a growing body of theoretical and empirical research that helps us to interrogate such stereotyping of youth. Along with Lesko, several scholars call into question the idea that adolescence is a transitional period between childhood and adulthood that can be solely explained by biological factors, the raging hormones thesis chief among them (see Jones, 2009; Best, 2007; Côté and Allahar, 2006). Some point to evidence that shows how economic forces dictated the need for youth labor and then later activated a need for new markets that took account of increased earning power of young adults. At the same time, schooling became compulsory for longer periods of time, which kept young people in school, at home and out of the labor force and by extension deferred the possibility of being granted an adult status in society. The basic counterargument to developmental discourses on youth is that over time social demographics and economic trends have as much explanatory power for the frustrations experienced during the coming-of-age period. For example, critical youth scholars James Côté and Anton Allahar (2006) explain the nature of adolescence in the late twentieth century and early twenty-first century as being the result of the decimation of the youth labor markets where meaningful work is replaced by low-paying, temporary service jobs (e.g., so-called McJobs), the rise in credentialism leading to prolonged postsecondary education (despite the depressed outlook for attainment of meaningful professional jobs), and the related extended dependency on parents and caregivers. All of these factors lead to a deferral of so-called adulthood and its associated characterizations (e.g., a rewarding job, marriage, child rearing, mortgages, and so on) and result in prolonged young adulthood well beyond the teenage years upwards even to 30 years of age and older. The persistence of the age bracketing of youth, along with the concept of youth as immature adults even as they approach their thirties, has certain consequences for our interaction with teenagers and young adults. Defining youth by age—one of the most "epidemic" (Lesko, 2001: 4) definitions in library and information science (LIS)—carries the tendency to erase differences among youth related to class, gender, ethnicity, and other social variables. It follows that such erasure leads to the conceptualization of youth as a homogeneous demographic group, allowing us to think of teenagers and young adults in universal or essentialist terms.

Biology-based explanations for youthhood carry similar universalizing consequences. As discussed earlier, despite continual challenges to his ideas (see Griffin, 1993), Hall is often cited as "discovering" adolescence as a unique stage in human development. Hall is recognized as an early proponent of the "storm and stress" model of adolescence that defines it as a period of rebellion, conflict, and discord with authorities. Adolescent turmoil then is seen to be responsible for the perceived social phenomenon of misbehaving youth (see Côté and Allahar, 2006: 16–17). More recently, neuropsychology and brain mapping efforts have been used to explain youth behavior. Evidence garnered from brain mapping efforts is used to argue that the adolescent brain is different from adult brains, resulting in impulsive behavior, lack of foresight, and the inability to exercise both sound judgment and rational decision making among teenagers and young adults (see Côté and Allahar, 2006: 17–18).

One consequence of biology-based explanations of adolescence can be the pathologization of youth by which negative stereotypes come to represent universal truths of human development that posit youth *are by their very nature* imperfect, inadequate, or abnormal. Another consequence is an undue focus on the individual, which some say leads to a kind of victim blaming where young people are themselves seen to be the cause of their marginalization, disenfranchisement, or disengagement. This in turn results in a drive to "fix" the teenager rather than attend to underlying social, economic, and cultural factors (Côté and Allahar, 2006: 31). A third consequence of this line of thinking is the notion that because young adults are incapable of good judgment and are ruled by their emotions and thus dictated by hormone levels, adult guidance is required and further, autonomy is put off until the transition to adulthood is achieved. These "consequences" are also visible in LIS discourse and practice: we need only look to debates related to age-appropriate collections and programming and policies on Internet use and other teen conduct in libraries.

When we design services based on the logic of biology-based theories of adolescence, we may unintentionally propagate some of the damaging trajectories of such logics. Dominant ideologies regarding the roles of education and employment in young adulthood support the victim-blaming thesis as well. Academic achievement among youth is uniformly lauded as desirable, as is the attainment of post-secondary schooling in colleges and universities. Indeed, libraries have always been positioned as partners in school readiness training and lifelong learning initiatives. Participation in schooling is one of the milestone markers of young adulthood, and there is a clear stepping-stone model for success in life that is based on a certain progression through the ranks: elementary, then secondary school, then college or university, increasingly postgraduate degrees, and then ongoing upgrading of credentials or continuing education. Such educational attainment is seen to further one's chances in life for a fulfilling, rewarding, and suitably compensated career.

However, trends in educational and workplace opportunities can be seen to undermine the promise of education for contemporary cohorts of young adults. In fact, some go so far as to say that without a careful scrutiny of realistic education and job opportunities, we do little more than offer false promises of the future to youth by encouraging them to pile credential upon credential, and school debt upon school debt (Côté and Allahar, 2006). There are further potentially damaging consequences of the mainstream psychologized discourses on adolescence. In particular, the tendency to represent individual young people and certain groups of youth as "deviant" or "deficient" or otherwise inadequate can lead to certain moral panics about the same groups of youth. In her book *Representations of Youth*, Christine Griffin (1993) provides an insightful examination of the moral panics or "constructed crises" over young people, such as teenage sexuality (e.g., teen pregnancy, homosexuality) and youth leisure and unemployment (e.g., hooliganism, delinquency). We also have certain youth crises within LIS discourse. For example, Anthony Bernier (2011) illustrates that the overwhelmingly dominant media representation of youth as deviant, criminal, and dangerous has critical implications for service and policy responses related to youth in libraries. Other panics about youth in libraries, some of the most enduring, concern the "reluctant" library nonuser; the resistant, mostly male, reader; and the unruly, disruptive in-house library users. In her work, Mary K. Chelton (2001) has shown the damaging consequences of our reliance on stereotypes of youth in the provision of customer service to them in libraries, most notably in the construction of teens as problem patrons.

The universalizing logic of developmental discourses on youth and the stereotyping related to moral panics about certain groups of youth can have serious consequences on how we conceive of young adults in LIS. Before I turn to a discussion of alternative ways to consider youthhood, it is important to reiterate that processes of human development are not being questioned here. It would be foolish to argue that young adults do not experience physical, emotional, mental, and social changes related to maturation, but these processes on their own cannot offer robust explanations for young adult behavior, nor therefore should they be used uncritically in our service initiatives, research projects, training objectives, or indeed in how we envision youth in LIS.

Alternative Frameworks for Thinking about Young Adults

Scholars and theorists working in the general area of critical youth studies are concerned with actively improving the condition of young people's lives, while at the same time acknowledging youth agency, autonomy, and abilities. Critical youth studies resist the essentializing discourses that posit young adulthood as a stable and universal category of human development that holds steady across time as well as cultural and social contexts. There are two intersecting methodologies for understanding the experiences of adolescence or young adulthood in this framework: political economy and cultural studies.

Critical youth studies is a perspective informed by political economy. Scholars and researchers working in this tradition are critically concerned with the unequal distribution of power and like cultural theorists, with the marginalized status and institutionalized powerlessness of young adults in contemporary society. Educational systems, the media, and other social institutions work to both control and indoctrinate young people into willing participants in their systematic oppression (Tyyskä, 2009: 10). Further, political economists are motivated to uncover the "false consciousness" of youth in society that works to permit and enable young people to undermine their own interests and their own social power. They call for critical consciousness raising by educating young people to be aware of their systematic oppression within the currents of power that affect their lives: the economy and various youth markets, employment and labor, media, and education infrastructures. The goal of this consciousness raising is to reverse both young people's economic and political disenfranchisement and to support meaningful youth participation in civil society. By taking a macro approach, political economy perspectives on youth bring to light deep structural inequities in society.

In cultural studies of youth, the diversity of human experience cannot be erased. Culture is front and center in any analysis of youth experience, and theorizing reflects the particularities of race and ethnicity, gender, class, sexuality, and other cultural and social variables. Furthermore, the agency and autonomy of youth are privileged. Young adults are viewed as competent, thoughtful, rational, and capable. The very idea of *youth* is seen to be an embodied space constituted of contested and dynamic meanings and constructed through social relations of power. In other words, the concept of youth is not a naturally occurring category of humanness—its meaning has been and is continually negotiated. We observe this contestation even when we look at some common ways to describe youth: Does young adulthood begin with puberty? With gainful employment? With marriage? With the establishment of an independent household?

The cultural studies perspective takes serious account of young people's own perspectives on their lives and often privileges their accounts and voices over adult and expert interpretations. One of the overarching goals of many cultural studies of youth is to give voice to those young people who are marginalized from mainstream popular and scholarly discourses and in that way to disrupt universalizing, essentialist, and deterministic understandings of youth.

These two well-established frameworks for understanding youth can compete, resulting in tensions in projects that seek to conceptualize young adulthood. The cultural studies perspective is critiqued for its individualizing analysis, while political economy is often seen as overly deterministic. Nancy Lesko (2001) proposes alternative conceptions in her attempts to privilege youth as "always active, social beings" and at the same time to allow for collective social practices. Lesko recommends thinking about conceptions of growth and change based on contingency and recursive sense making. She also asks us to reject *a priori* frameworks based on development that is rejected for its legacy of racism, sexism, and classism and its inability to account for contexts, or on socialization that is rejected despite its attempt to account for group and social processes for

More Reading on Critical Youth Studies Perspectives

There are many readable books that have been published in recent years that explore ways to imagine young adults that do not rely on developmental discourses. Each work offers a critique of biology-based explanations of youth behavior in contemporary society as well as alternative ways of representing and thinking about young people.

- *Representing Youth: Methodological Issues in Critical Youth Studies,* edited by Amy L. Best (New York: New York University Press, 2007).
- *Critical Youth Studies: A Canadian Focus,* by James E. Côté and Anton L. Allahar (Toronto, ON: Pearson Prentice Hall, 2006).
- *Representations of Youth: The Study of Youth and Adolescence in Britain and America,* by Christine Griffin (Cambridge, UK: Polity Press, 1993).
- *Youth,* by Gill Jones (Cambridge, UK: Polity Press, 2009).
- *Act Your Age! A Cultural Construction of Adolescence,* by Nancy Lesko (New York: Routledge, 2001).

its unidirectionality and its basic assumption on the passivity of youth (Lesko, 2001: 194–195). Lesko (2001: 197) also encourages us to think of youth (and everyone) as "holding seemingly opposing identities *simultaneously*"—by for example, allowing young adults to be both "old" and "young" at the same time. Lesko further claims that if the concept of adolescence emerged to help "identify and create a vision of the modern citizen who would be equipped for the challenges of the new social, economic, and world arrangements" (Popkewitz, 1998, cited in Lesko, 2001: 197), new conceptions of adolescence should emerge alongside the "articulation and popularization of different problems" (Lesko, 2001: 198). This articulation may in turn change how we conceive of youth needs in changing social, economic, educational, and cultural conditions affecting youth experience. Finally, Lesko (2001: 199) calls for advocacy that "undermines the monolithic view of adolescents as supposedly all the same and as fundamentally different from adults."

Toward a Critical Youth Studies Framework for LIS

There is a strand in LIS research on YA librarianship and YA library services that dovetails with some of the major dimensions of a critical youth studies framework. Perhaps one of the ways in which critical youth studies differs most from developmental models of adolescence is in its explicit political motivation to increase the social and at times economic power of young adults as they participate in the currents of society. While it is not possible to provide an exhaustive review, it is instructive and illuminating to revisit some of the historical studies of young adults and libraries to see that we have had, from time to time, cogent articulations of more politicized conceptualizations of youth and youth services within LIS. These studies take a different methodological approach to the conceptualization of youth and youth services that rely solely on developmental frameworks for adolescence.

In LIS, there is a well-known genealogy associated with the emergence of public library services for young people, but as Christine Jenkins (2000: 107) wrote in her review of youth services librarianship, the histories of a distinct set of library services to teenagers and young adults in North America make up a scant field of scholarship; a decade or so later, this would still seem to hold true. However, LIS scholars have provided templates for thinking about teenagers and young adults in libraries that depart from developmental theories of adolescence to take account of the social factors affecting both how adult librarians think about youth but also how services are conceived of and designed to meet their needs. In their respective studies, Jenkins (2000) and Jane Anne Hannigan (1996) provide feminist analyses of youth services librarianship. Jenkins analyzed the work—the mission—of the female librarians who built strong foundations within the profession for a child-centered philosophy of service. A few years earlier, Hannigan also situated the emergence of YA librarianship in the United States within a feminist analysis of the work of several prominent female librarians, from Mabel Williams in the early 1900s through to Mary K. Chelton and her ongoing advocacy for young adults and YA services in libraries. Jenkins is concerned with the emergence of both children's and YA librarianship, while Hannigan focused primarily on YA services and teen advocacy. By examining the roles played by prominent female librarians in the development of YA library services in the United States, both Jenkins and Hannigan provide insights in how to conceptualize collective action across individual accounts. Young adults are situated in their work as subjects within conceptual frameworks that respect their diversity, autonomy, and ability to participate in the design and development of library spaces, collections, programming, and services.

In the 1970s, Miriam Braverman (1979) examined the larger contexts for youth services librarianship. In her landmark study, she compared the development and provision of YA library services in five prominent public libraries and chronicled what she called the cultural and social cycles of YA librarianship in the United States from the 1920s through the 1970s. Braverman made a distinction between the cultural work of librarians she saw as oriented to books, collections, and reading promotion and the social work of librarians who responded with programming and services that addressed the daily lived experiences of teenagers in the community. Further, she claimed that it was a "flawed humanism" that led to a professional "retreat" to books and reading rather than a continued commitment to the ongoing development of socially responsible and socially conscious programming designed to provide information for youth to learn about issues that affected them personally in their lives. Braverman's work is an important history of the emergence of YA services and is notable for its attention to social and cultural factors.

In a similar vein, Lukenbill (2006) examines the emergence of youth librarianship in the United States and looks at how it intersected with various social reform movements through the late 1800s through the twentieth century. Lukenbill reminds us that from the earliest reform movements, the educative function of various social institutions, including the library, was seen to:

> ...address problems of immigrant assimilation, crime, vice, pauperism and juvenile delinquency. Above all, this particular arm of the reform movement stressed the importance of the eradication of the urban slum where most of the working class lived, and the Americanisation of immigrants. These movements emphasized the idea that, through education, every individual could be "uplifted" from the limits of their social roots and environments.... (Lukenbill, 2006: 202)

Lukenbill nicely demonstrates how certain ideas about young adults as "youth at risk" fueled library reform and development. Lukenbill ends with a call for youth librarianship that is conscious of its politics. Following Braverman, Kathleen Craver (1988) looked at how library programming to teens and young adults and collections work continued through the 1960s. Both Braverman and Craver noted that at different times librarians in the United States were effective outreach workers bringing an awareness of library services and collections to communities of young people who might not have opportunities to visit libraries on their own. However, the division between books, collections, and reading on one side, and programming and outreach services on the other, has become entrenched in our understanding of YA librarianship today.

We see the division inscribed in LIS curricula that offer separate courses on YA materials and YA library services, and in job descriptions that feature collections work and outreach and programming as distinctly different positions. This division is sometimes colloquially described as the difference between people who love to work with books and people who love to work with teens. There are important consequences for this divide between books and services. It is a somewhat arbitrary split that artificially pits books and reading against other kinds of engagement with other types of library materials and library services. It also continually reinscribes age-based divisions by following age-based schooling categories for outreach and age-based reading levels for texts. Further, when we consider the ways in which YA materials and services are separated from those developed for children and adults, we begin to see how age-based conceptions of human experience are deeply entrenched in libraries. The idea that youth are different from others, especially adults, becomes a strong rationale for developing specialized collections, designing specialized services and spaces, and fighting for specialized staff.

By the 1970s, the pioneering work of several youth advocates created a stable and enduring foundation for our current understanding of what it means to provide committed service to teenagers in libraries—an understanding, moreover, that has been inscribed into national guidelines for service to teens. Margaret Edwards's (2002) book *The Fair Garden and the Swarm of Beasts* represents one of the first book-length articulations of codified library practice regarding teen services. In 1969, Edwards famously adopted the construction of teenagers as "the beasts" in the "fair garden" of the library for her book, exhorting her colleagues, based on her observations of 30 years of working with young people in libraries, to recognize as she writes in her closing sentence: "It is time to let them in" (2002: 89). *The Fair Garden and the Swarm of Beasts* and other works like it continue (and should continue) to inspire cohorts of library students and YA librarians. There is immeasurable value in their calls to duty that challenge librarians to be creative, sensitive, politically savvy, and tireless in their efforts to carve out dedicated space and resources for young adults, and to be ever vigilant in protecting and promoting their rights to free and unfettered access to information. The histories of youth services in public libraries have consistently shown that the (mostly) female library leaders disrupted developmental discourses inherited to some degree from protectionist philosophies of service for much younger children based on the need to limit access and to create age-appropriate collections and programs.

So, what does this brief review of some landmark studies tell us? As youth services librarians and LIS scholars, our work fits within the paradigm of critical youth studies. Our heavy reliance on theories of human development is, perhaps, unwarranted. Furthermore, there can be real benefits to expanding our understanding of what it means to be a young adult by adopting some of the positions found within a critical youth studies framework.

Conclusion: How Should LIS Envision Youth?

The first answer to this question is to seriously consider a critical youth studies framework and its several claims about young adulthood, including the following:

- As a concept, adolescence is socially constructed and is not a stable, universal, naturally occurring phase of human life. It is always changing, and its meanings must be continually negotiated.
- What it means to be a young adult is contingent on many factors, including race and ethnicity, gender, sexuality, geographic location, and class; therefore, these variables must be addressed in our work.

- Any understanding of young adults must allow for their participation in meaning-making exercises; their voices and perspectives are as important as any adult-observed interpretations of their experience.
- Individual perspectives are critically important to our understanding, but we must also find ways to take account of the influences of collective action.
- Young adults, like adults, are both in a position of "becoming" and of "being," and one does not trump the other.
- Youth participation is of paramount importance in a critical youth studies framework. It is both a method of understanding youth and a goal for our interactions with youth.

All of these claims work to disrupt the biology-based theories of adolescence that rely on definitions of youth derived from age categories. Biological age or chronological age is seen to be a kind of straw horse figure in imagining what is possible in a reconceptualization of young adults. In other words, the numbers of years that a person has been alive can really only ever tell us how many years a person has been alive. In particular when it comes to young adults, we should not rely too much on what age can tell us about them. Whereas the claims listed above allow us to give full play to the already existing as well as developing abilities and interests of young adults, I would challenge readers to consider each point in the context of a specific teen library program or service, or for researchers in the context of your research problem. How do these ideas change to ways in which you think of teens and your work with teens?

The second answer to the overarching question is again to take our cue from critical youth studies by moving between micro and macro perspectives on the issues that concern us in YA librarianship as we recognize that young adulthood is a social and cultural construction that relies on particular and changing ideologies. When we acknowledge that there are competing ideologies (e.g., the difference between liberationist and protectionist stances on adolescence), we can respond to or harness the power of particular sets of discourses and use them to serve the library's interests. On the face of things this may seem cynical, but I would argue that it puts discourses in their proper place: they can be disrupted and challenged, and further, there is no need to "throw the baby out with the bathwater!" For example, when making proposals to conservative library boards about the establishment of special youth programs, collections, or spaces, it can be in our interest to use ideas from developmental discourses to make our pitches. There are still many good reasons for this kind of segregation in services and collections, as in many communities it may signal, for the first time, that youth are being seriously considered as members of a library deserving of services for that reason alone. But at the same time we should work to disrupt such discourses from making a stranglehold on our own conceptualizations of our patron group.

This line of thinking, of course, gives rise to an immediate tension: on the one hand, I am calling for us to jettison age-based and biology-based understandings of youth, but on the other hand, I am saying use the discourses to support the establishment of specialized collections and services for youth. This effort points to the necessity, I think, at this particular juncture in time, to allow competing conceptualizations to coexist, recognizing the role each plays in terms of its influence and effects on our practices and research. If critical youth studies tell us anything, it is the necessity of constantly interrogating the ways in which we define young people. In the early decades of the twenty-first century, there is mounting evidence to suggest that we need to extend services to account for prolonged dependency on parents, and give credence to the concept of the emerging adult, without creating an insoluble age boundary. Honoring this tension helps us to honor the complexity of our work practices as well. For example, in a developmental framework, the promotion of YA literature can be seen as little more than prescription or developmental aid for that discrete phase of human life called adolescence. A framework that sees adolescence as socially constructed, its meanings unstable, contextual, and constantly negotiated, supports the concept that YA literature carries symbolic, cultural, and social freight for its young adult (and older adult) readers at the same time that these same readers contribute to the possible meanings of YA literature—what it is, how it is read, why it is valued, and how it changes.

A critical youth studies approach holds much promise for the study of young adults and their information, library, and reading practices within LIS. The slate of research questions that could be informed by this rubric is quite literally completely open. Interesting work could be done right away by considering how existing research findings related to information-seeking behavior, reading practices, and library use can be reinterpreted by dispensing with developmental frameworks for analysis and discussions of implications of the research—to be replaced instead by the axioms of critical youth studies. For example, rather than construct young people as novice, student, or otherwise inadequate information seekers, we could reframe them as users who are defined by their already existing position in the world as young adults who are seeking information in ways that are wholly appropriate to that position. The point is, we need to understand that reframed position by looking at more than just developmental milestones. Critical youth studies insistence on the negotiated meaning of young adulthood demands consideration of class, gender, race and ethnicity, sexuality, and geography, and we need more research in LIS (and all its cognate areas) that matches this demand. Youth participation has long been valued in youth services librarianship (Tixier Herald and Monnier, 2007), and it is one of the areas of librarianship that corresponds most closely to some of the ideas from critical youth studies. We can do more work to allow young adult voices and perspectives in meaning-making exercises within LIS to inform practice and research. Such perspectives support our efforts to involve youth meaningfully in the governance of libraries: youth membership in library boards, teen run programs, meaningful and respectful use of teen labor in paid and volunteer positions, and youth participation at the level of state and provincial, national, and international library associations. Furthermore, this framework calls for our ceaseless advocacy for full participation of youth in society, as a critical youth studies framework encourages us to renew our, decidedly nonneutral, commitment to the idea of libraries as participating members of civil society and as agents in the creation of a just society for all people, young adults among them.

References

Bernier, Anthony. 2011. "Representations of Youth in Local Media: Implications for Library Service. *Library and Information Science Research* 33: 158–167.

Best, Amy L., ed. 2007. *Representing Youth: Methodological Issues in Critical Youth Studies*. New York: New York University Press.

Braverman, Miriam. 1979. *Youth, Society and the Public Library*. Chicago: American Library Association.

Burek Pierce, Jennifer. 2006. "The Borderland Age and Borderline Books: The Early Practice of Reader's Advisory for Youth." *Young Adult Library Services* 5, no. 1: 42–47.

Chelton, Mary K. 2001. "Young Adults as Problems: How the Social Construction of a Marginalized User Category Occurs." *Journal of Education for Library and Information Science* 42, no. 1: 4–11.

Côté, James E., and Anton L. Allahar. 2006. *Critical Youth Studies: A Canadian Focus.* Toronto, ON: Pearson Prentice Hall.

Craver, Kathleen W. 1988. "Social Trends in American Young Adult Library Service, 1960–1969." *Libraries and Culture* 23, no. 1: 18–38.

Edwards, Margaret. 2002. *The Fair Garden and the Swarm of Beasts: The Library and the Young Adult.* Centennial ed. Chicago: American Library Association.

Gorman, Michele, and Tricia Suellentrop. 2004. *Connecting Young Adults and Libraries: A How-To-Do-It Manual.* 4th ed. New York: Neal-Schuman.

Griffin, Christine. 1993. *Representations of Youth: The Study of Youth and Adolescence in Britain and America.* Cambridge, UK: Polity Press.

Hannigan, Jane Anne. 1996. "A Feminist Analysis of the Voices for Advocacy in Young Adult Services." *Library Trends* 44, no. 4: 851–874.

Jenkins, Christine. 2000. "The History of Youth Services Librarianship: A Review of the Research Literature." *Libraries and Culture* 35, no. 1: 103–140.

Jones, Gill. 2009. *Youth.* Cambridge, UK: Polity Press.

Jones, Patrick, and Joel Shoemaker. 2001. *Do It Right: Best Practices for Serving Young Adults in School and Public Libraries.* New York: Neal-Schuman.

Lesko, Nancy. 2001. *Act Your Age! A Cultural Construction of Adolescence.* New York: Routledge.

Lukenbill, W. Bernard. 2006. "Helping Youth at Risk: An Overview of Reformist Movements in American Public Library Services to Youth." *New Review of Children's Literature and Librarianship* 12, no. 2: 197–213.

Raby, Rebecca. 2007. "Across a Great Gulf? Conducting Research with Adolescents." In *Representing Youth: Methodological Issues in Critical Youth Studies,* edited by Amy L. Best, 39–59. New York: New York University Press.

Tixier Herald, Diana, and Diane P. Monnier. 2007. "The Beasts Have Arrived." *Voice of Youth Advocates* 30, no. 2: 116–119.

Tyyskä, Vappu. 2009. *Youth and Society: The Long and Winding Road.* Toronto: Canadian Scholars' Press.

9

Intellectual Freedom or Protection?

Conflicting Young Adults' Rights in Libraries

Cherie Givens

In order to effectively advocate for minors' intellectual freedom in libraries, librarians must be cognizant of the legal limitations and protections
placed on them. This chapter provides a discussion and overview of some
of the professional and associational positions on intellectual freedom,
including the American Library Association's Library Bill of Rights. In
addition, the legal foundation for minors' intellectual freedom under the
First Amendment to the US Constitution will be explored. The particular
focus is on a minor's right to receive information, the limitations imposed
on young adults through such laws as the Children's Internet Protection
Act, and issues of privacy and confidentiality for minors. (Author's note:
This article is for informational purposes only and does not constitute a
legal opinion. Readers should consult an attorney for legal advice regarding their unique situations.)

Young adults do not shed their legal rights simply by entering the library.
Special laws have been passed to protect minors in library settings. Not
everyone agrees that these laws are in the best interest of minors or that
laws that apply to minors should apply equally to children and young
adults. Sometimes, the laws applicable to libraries appear to conflict with

intellectual freedom policies and positions. How then is one to support intellectual freedom while remaining mindful of these laws?

Understanding the legal landscape can assist in making informed choices that help librarians to support the intellectual freedom of minors, particularly young adults, to the fullest extent possible under the law. It is important for librarians to have a basic understanding of the laws that impact the profession and the rights of library users in order to avoid information malpractice and to understand the options available when a parent, law enforcement officer, or other interested party seeks information about a library user. Understanding the applicable laws and how they impact professional policies and actions is necessary to maintain professional standards and understand the limitations placed on young adults' ability to obtain information.

The First Amendment rights of minors in public and school libraries will be explored. Particular focus will be paid to the right to receive information, the limitations imposed on young adults, and issues of privacy and confidentiality. This discussion is intended to serve as an introduction to some of the information policy and ethical issues library and information science (LIS) professionals need to be aware of that affect services to young adults in school and public libraries. In doing our best to advocate for intellectual freedom and considering how we should imagine today's young adults, we must be cognizant of the legal limitations and protections placed on them and of areas of disagreement and uncertainty concerning minors' rights in libraries.

Professional and Associational Positions on Intellectual Freedom

What rights do young adults have in libraries? The American Library Association's (ALA, 1939b) Library Bill of Rights (LBOR) offers us some guidance. Libraries are places of information and should be places where intellectual curiosity is encouraged and nourished. The LBOR advises that resources should be made available for "the interest, information, and enlightenment" of everyone in a library's community. This would include young adults. The LBOR supports having material available representing "all points of view" for current and historical topics and advocates libraries challenging censorship attempts in the fulfillment of these duties. Most importantly, the LBOR provides that a "person's right to use a library should not be denied or abridged because of origin, age, background, or views."

Based on the LBOR it would appear that the rights of young adults are equal to those of adults. There is an affirmative duty to treat young adults equally and to challenge censorship, which is often aimed at the materials created for or of interest to minors, including young adults. Taken on its own the LBOR stands for the ideals of librarianship. It supports what should be a key mission for all librarians: the desire to make the library a place of uninhibited inquiry where all points of view are represented, not simply the popular or best known views. The vision proposed in the LBOR is one of freedom of inquiry and equality of service and resources for all users, including young adults.

While the LBOR is an important document for North American library professionals, of equal importance to library professionals should be the guidance provided in the Code of Ethics (COE) of the American Library Association (ALA, 1939a). The COE guides the profession, expressing the values and ethical responsibilities of librarians. The COE can also shed light on how we should think about young adults in their status as members of library communities to whom we have a professional obligation. According to the COE, "We have a special obligation to ensure the free flow of information and ideas to present and future generations." The COE reinforces the vision of equal access and service but uncouples it from the library forum, expanding it to the profession of librarianship, which may not be strictly tied to libraries. Librarians who are members of the American Library Association (ALA) are presumed to support this ethical stance.

The eight statements forming the body of the COE serve as a "framework," giving general guidance for ethical conduct. These statements are applicable to the conduct of librarians serving users of all ages. The COE advocates for intellectual freedom and advises librarians to resist censorship of library resources. This resistance may apply beyond the individual censor or censoring school board, and could be seen to apply to governmental actions that may be viewed as forms of censorship as well. We need only look to the actions of the ALA in challenging the constitutionality of the Children's Internet Protection Act (CIPA) to see that it has acted when it viewed the government action of passing a law requiring Internet filtering in libraries to be a form of censorship. The ALA, in advocating an anticensorship position when addressing materials for young adults, helps to define the professional vision of young adults as those deserving of uncensored inquiry and the opportunity to receive information.

The COE addresses areas of concern such as protecting privacy and confidentiality for library users of all ages. In addition to the duties to advocate for intellectual freedom and protect library users' rights to privacy and confidentiality, the COE addresses an important aspect of professionalism that has challenged some in the library and information science field when addressing the needs of minors: the need to "distinguish between our personal convictions and professional duties." The COE advises librarians not to allow our personal convictions to "interfere" with our professional duties. We are challenged, just as professionals in other fields such as law and medicine, to be guided by professional ethics in meeting the needs of our users. The COE offers us a vision of young adults as those deserving of equal service and protection of their intellectual freedom. When we choose to censor as members of the library profession, we choose the personal over the professional. In law or medicine such actions have consequences, and those who would breach ethical duties can lose their right to practice. Should similar restrictions be applied to librarians? It is an interesting question to ponder. Perhaps if these types of restrictions were applied to LIS, the vision of equal access and service for young adults would be more widely followed.

The Freedom to Read Statement (FRS), a joint statement by the American Library Association and the American Association of Book Publishers (1953), is another important document that provides guidance in addressing the challenges to service and professional duties owed to young adults in libraries. This statement, which has been endorsed by several professional organizations, including the National Council of Teachers of English, advises that our freedom to read is "continuously under attack...[by] private groups and public authorities" who seek to censor reading materials in schools.

According to the FRS, fear that stems from outside attempts to censor materials may lead to "an even larger voluntary curtailment of expression by those who seek to avoid controversy or unwelcome scrutiny by government officials." The truth of this statement is bolstered by several studies of librarians censoring materials for various reasons, including the pressure felt by outside forces (Fiske, 1962; Buscha, 1972; McDonald, 1993). Our professional history shows that librarians have moved from the role of censors to supporters of intellectual freedom. It is not surprising then to discover that some among us may still harbor a desire to censor materials or to give in to the pressures to censor being exerted by external forces.

McDonald (1993: 3) explains that at the time of librarianship's professional beginnings in 1876, under the national political climate, librarians "endorsed themselves as moral censors." Scholars such as Geller (1984: 79) have examined our professional history and found that the role of censor was a common one for our predecessors. It was during the early 1900s that librarians took on the role of censoring. The ALA's position opposing censorship did not emerge until the late 1930s with the Library's Bill of Rights, the precursor to the current LBOR (Krug and Morgan, 2010). Though we currently have a robust intellectual freedom presence, there remain forces seeking to censor access to information from others, especially young adults. As librarians, we are called upon professionally to resist censorship attempts in all forms, even the internal voice that may prod us to go with the majority view or to support personal views that are not in keeping with professional policies. The vision of LIS services to youth at the professional association level is one that resists internal and external efforts to censor materials and services.

The LBOR, the COE, and the FRS are the "three basic codes for the library and information science profession" that provide ethical guidance (Carson, 2007: 235). These codes do not cover all situations but provide a strong foundation that embodies our professional ethics and publicly presents them. They help to define the essence of the profession of librarian. Those looking for more in-depth guidance from the ALA concerning interpretations of the LBOR, the COE, or the FRS should consult the *Intellectual Freedom Manual* (OIF, 2010), which contains interpretations and the historical backgrounds of these policies as well as essays on intellectual freedom.

The ALA has become and remains a strong advocate of intellectual freedom. Such advocacy is needed in today's complex and often contentious library legal landscape. In recent years we have seen the introduction of several laws that directly impact the rights of library users, particularly the rights of minors. These include CIPA, the USA Patriot Act, and various state harmful-to-minors laws. The US Supreme Court has also been the battleground for several struggles to clarify the First Amendment rights of minors. The limitations of these laws and the Supreme Court's ruling on minors' First Amendment rights must be considered as we determine how LIS should view young adults and provide them with the most effective service within the boundaries of the law.

The Legal Foundation for Minors' Intellectual Freedom

The principles of intellectual freedom espoused in the ALA's LBOR and COE have their origins in the US Constitution's First Amendment:

> *Congress shall make no law respecting an establishment of religion, or prohibiting the free exercise thereof; or abridging the freedom of speech, or of the press; or the right of the people peaceably to assemble, and to petition the government for a redress of grievances.*

The US Supreme Court has recognized that minors have First Amendment rights, but those rights are not identical to those of adults. In *Tinker v. Des Moines Independent Community School District*, 393 U.S. 503 (1969), the Supreme Court affirmed that students "do not shed their constitutional rights to freedom of speech or expression at the schoolhouse gate" (506). In *Tinker*, student protestors of the Vietnam War were suspended for wearing black armbands of protest. The Supreme Court found that the wearing of the armbands "was entirely divorced from actually or potentially disruptive conduct...and as such was closely akin to 'pure speech' which is entitled to comprehensive protection under the First Amendment" (505–506). The language of the Court's opinion shows a clear protection of the "pure speech" of young adults in a public school setting.

The First Amendment provides for freedom of speech, but does it provide for the corollary right to receive information? The Supreme Court has intimated on a number of occasions that the First Amendment's guarantees of freedom of speech and freedom of the press imply a corollary right to receive information. The right of minors to receive information in a public school library setting was first considered by the Court in *Board of Education v. Pico*, 457 U.S. 855 (1982). In this case, the board of education rejected recommendations of an appointed committee of parents and staff, ordering that books the board deemed objectionable be removed from the high school and junior high school libraries. Students challenged the decision of the board in federal district court and lost. The decision was reversed on appeal. The case then went to the Supreme Court, which upheld the court of appeal's ruling. The Supreme Court, in a plurality opinion, stated:

> We have held that in a variety of contexts "the Constitution protects the right to receive information and ideas." ... This right is an inherent corollary of the rights of free speech and press that are explicitly guaranteed by the Constitution.... The right to receive ideas follows ineluctably from the sender's First Amendment right to send them.... More importantly, the right to receive ideas is a necessary predicate to the recipient's meaningful exercise of his own rights of speech, press, and political freedom. (Pico, 457 U.S. at 867)

The Supreme Court's opinion in *Pico* is an important one when considering how the LIS profession should envision young adults. In *Pico*, the US Supreme Court stated plainly that minors have the First Amendment right to receive information and ideas. The Court considers this necessary to the "meaningful exercise" of First Amendment rights. Young adults should be viewed as active participants in society with rights to information that should only be restricted in limited circumstances as determined by law.

Pico involved high school and junior high school students. The Court affirmed the right of minors to receive information. The importance of this right should not be overlooked. Young adults are just a step away from being adults. Sheltering them from unpopular ideas that they have a right to receive and may be exposed to as adults simply leaves them unprepared. Teaching information literacy and critical thinking skills can prepare young adults to competently interpret and respond to new, different, and sometimes disturbing ideas.

While the First Amendment rights of minors have been affirmed by the US Supreme Court, it has also placed some limits on these rights in a public school environment. The Court in *Pico* cited *Tinker*, explaining that the First Amendment rights of students "must be construed 'in light of the special characteristics of the school environment'" (*Pico*, 457 U.S. at 868, quoting *Tinker*, 393 U.S. at 506). These characteristics allow materials to be restricted if the materials are "educationally unsuitable" or "pervasively vulgar" (*Pico*, 457 U.S. at 890). The school's judgment must be "based objectively on the fact that the information is 'educationally unsuitable'" (Chmara, 2010b: 352). Other courts have followed *Pico's* guidance that examining the motivation behind the action is important in book removal cases.

Although school boards enjoy broad discretion concerning questions of school curriculum, provided their actions are reasonably related to legitimate pedagogical concerns, the removal of books from public school libraries implicates protected First Amendment rights. While a public school library environment presents some limitations on the First Amendment rights of minors, the US Supreme Court's rulings make it clear that these limitations are few and must be based objectively on fact. They present a few caveats that temper the professional vision of service and intellectual freedom espoused by the ALA in a public school library environment.

Laws to Protect Minors from the Harmful and the Obscene

Material may be restricted from minors if it is obscene, harmful to minors, or child pornography. The determination of whether material fits any of these categories is determined by state or local law (Chmara, 2010a: 18). Obscene speech is not protected by the First Amendment. Under *Ginsberg v. New York*, 390 U.S. 629 (1968), "states may completely bar minors from receiving material deemed obscene for them but not for adults" (Chmara, 2010b: 352). In *Ginsberg*, a magazine seller was convicted under a state law of selling two "girlie" magazines to a 16-year-old. Courts have acknowledged limits to the *Ginsberg* case, holding, "States may not simply ban minors' exposure to a full category of speech, such as nudity, when only a subset of that category can plausibly be deemed obscene for them...

[and] states must determine *Ginsberg* 'obscenity' by reference to the entire population of minors—including the oldest minors" (Chmara, 2010b: 352).

"States generally pattern their laws on the *Miller* decision... [but] may define 'obscenity' more liberally" (see Minow and Lipinski, 2003: 134). In *Miller v. California*, 413 U.S. 15 (1973), the US Supreme Court developed a three-factor test to determine if a work is obscene:

a. Whether the "average person, applying contemporary community standards" would find that the work, taken as a whole, appeals to the prurient interest,

b. Whether the work depicts or describes, in a patently offensive way, sexual conduct specifically defined by the applicable state law, and

c. Whether the work, taken as a whole, lacks serious literary, artistic, political, or scientific value. (*Miller*, 413 U.S. at 15)

In 2001, efforts to restrict the access of minors to materials that are obscene, harmful to minors, or child pornography took a leap forward when the CIPA became law. This federal law requires libraries and schools that accept discounted services under the federal Schools and Libraries Program of the Universal Service Fund/E-rate Program or direct federal funding through the Elementary and Secondary Education Act (ESEA) to certify that they have installed "technology protection measures" on all computers that are used to access the Internet. Under CIPA, minors are considered individuals of less than 17 years of age.

CIPA was challenged and in 2002 held unconstitutional by a federal district court. This holding was reversed by the US Supreme Court in June 2003 in *U.S. v. American Library Association*, 539 U.S. 194 (2003). The Supreme Court ruled that this act does not violate First Amendment rights. The justices have provided reasons for finding this act constitutional. These include Justice Kennedy's conclusion that adults can still have unfettered access to the Internet because "a librarian will unblock filtered material or disable the Internet software filter without further delay" upon the request of an adult patron (*American Library Association*, 539 U.S. at 214). The justices, citing *Rust v. Sullivan*, 500 U.S. 173, 194 (1991), also concluded:

The Government is not denying a benefit to anyone, but is instead simply insisting that public funds be spent for the purpose for which they are authorized: helping public librarians fulfill their traditional role of obtaining material of requisite and appropriate quality for educational and informational purposes.

The justices go on to state that "because public libraries have traditionally excluded pornographic material from their other collections, Congress could reasonably impose a parallel limitation on its Internet assistance programs" *(American Library Association,* 539 U.S. at 211).

Libraries have the option to refuse federal funding and therefore not be subject to the requirements of CIPA, but even if libraries choose this option they may still be subject to state laws, known as harmful to minors laws, that require Internet filtering in publicly funded schools or libraries. According to the National Conference of State Legislatures, as of February 2012, 26 states have passed these types of Internet filtering laws "to prevent minors from gaining access to sexually explicit, obscene, or harmful materials" (NCSL, 2012).

Are Legal Protections for Minors Too Generalized?

These types of protective measures frequently fail to distinguish young adults from children, attaching the same standards to both, but the information needs of a 16-year-old are not the same as those of a 6- or 9-year-old. If society treats young adults like children, then we risk the possibility that they will emerge as adults without the skills and experience to prepare them for the adult world and the sometimes harmful or obscene information in it. Exposure to material that makes us uncomfortable in our youth may act to provide us with greater resilience when handling stresses in adulthood.

According to Lyons, Parker, and Schatzberg (2010: 402), "early intermittent exposure to stress...enhances arousal regulation and resilience." If the premise of the protective measures is to prevent harm to minors, perhaps we as a society need to reevaluate whether some limited exposure or "inoculating" is actually harmful. Heins (2007: 259) advocates for "more thoughtful and finely calibrated judgments" about legal protections. She cites the Supreme Court in *Planned Parenthood of Missouri v. Danforth*, 428 U.S. 52, 74 (1976), explaining that "constitutional rights 'do not mature and come into being magically only when one attains the state defined age of majority.'"

Just as the obscenity standards are rooted in community norms, our ideas about what materials are harmful to minors stem from American culture. "Standards are relative, culturally driven, and often employed rhetorically for political ends that may have little to do with any objective showing of harm to youth" (Heins, 2007: 200). The differences are readily identifiable when we compare how differently cultures address sex education. "The United States…was the only country in the industrialized world to have, at the turn of the 21st century, legislated 'abstinence unless married' as official policy" (Heins, 2007: 153).

According to an Advocates for Youth (Alford and Hauser, 2011) study of adolescent sexual health in Europe and the United States, comparing statistics from 2002–2009, the incidents of adolescent pregnancy, birth, abortion, and HIV in the United States far exceed those of France, Germany, and the Netherlands. In a more limited comparison between the United States and the Netherlands, it would appear that the United States also experiences more incidents of adolescents contracting sexually transmitted diseases, or STDs. A major difference between the United States and those countries is that adolescents in France, Germany, and the Netherlands have better access to sex education information.

The *Newsletter for Intellectual Freedom* has documented the active and continuing censorship efforts of sex education materials for children and young adults since the 1970s. Levine (2002: xxi) makes a powerful argument that the sexual politics of fear in the United States is what is harmful to minors. The practice of emphasizing abstinence is not shared by Western European countries where youth are taught sex education with the assumption that during their teen years they will initiate "sex play short of intercourse" and that "sexual expression is a healthy and happy start to growing up" (Levine, 2002: xxxii).

The emphasis on abstinence-only education in the United States poses unique problems for youth seeking information about sex. For many, the library serves as one of the only avenues for obtaining sex education materials. As Cornog and Perper (1996: 4) point out, parents may provide incorrect information and "sex education in schools is...bound up with bureaucratic concerns and agendas.... [C]urricula may be mandated that do not tell a full story about sex." This is why there is a need for sex education information to be made readily available in libraries.

The LIS profession needs to examine how we treat minors, especially young adults, seeking information. Young adults are subject to the will of bureaucratic concerns and agendas but in need of and entitled to intellectual freedom. LIS professionals must fight to protect the freedom of young adults to receive information to the best of our abilities within the boundaries of the law. Librarians should examine how harmful-to-minors laws and filtering practices affect the search processes and receipt of information needed by minors.

Schools Have a Duty to Protect

In addition to understanding the laws applicable to library and information resource settings, the school librarian must be familiar with the laws that apply to educational institutions. Both state and federal laws are applicable in school library settings. In K–12 schools, librarians assume some *in loco parentis* responsibilities. "In loco parentis is a legal doctrine describing a relationship similar to that of a parent and child. It refers to an individual who assumes parental status and responsibilities for another individual, usually a young person, without formally adopting that person" (Lehman and Phelps, 2005: 352). This concept of legal responsibility for minors by school administrators, which stems from English common law, has shaped the responsibilities of public school teachers and has implications for the school library, which is necessarily a component of the school. Carson (2007: 237) elaborates on these responsibilities:

> *Schools have a legal duty to protect their students in a different way from public or academic libraries.... There is a special duty to report potentially dangerous behavior to the school guidance counselor or principal. Educators have a legal duty to report*

students who may have been abused, appear suicidal, or in any way appear to be at risk.

These responsibilities can potentially change the dynamics of the professional relationship between a school librarian and students seeking information in the library. It presents a vision of young adults as a group requiring protection in all areas of the school, including the library. The role of school administrators as guardians has gained greater attention in recent years with the increased concern about school violence. School librarians must work to strike a balance when creating an environment that welcomes users and encourages information seeking while maintaining a mindfulness of the unique responsibilities school librarians undertake as part of the work environment.

Legal Support for the Protection of Privacy for Young Adults

Privacy issues in libraries come in many forms. It may be an informal request from a parent or law enforcement officer for information concerning a minor user's reading choices, or it might be a more official request such as a subpoena, search warrant, or request under the Patriot Act. Decisions about how to address these matters and what rights to privacy users have in a given situation depends on who is asking and what laws govern the situation. It is important to be aware of the laws and policies that impact user privacy in libraries.

Intrusions on privacy may have a chilling effect on users if they believe information such as their reading habits, Internet browsing history, or listing of the resources they use while in the library can be made public. This is the reason that librarians work to protect users' rights, and the ALA has developed policies to address privacy in different contexts. Individual library policies should address these matters as well in order to maximize user privacy. Case law from lower federal courts, state courts, and "analogous First Amendment cases decided by the Supreme Court strongly supports the position that a qualified privilege exists" for patron use records (Chmara, 2009: 16).

Every state provides some measure of protection for library circulation records through statutes, with the exception of Hawaii and Kentucky, which both rely on attorney general opinions. The extent to which they protect these records varies by state. The following states explicitly allow parents access to the records of their minor children: Alabama, Alaska, Louisiana, South Dakota, Utah, West Virginia, Wisconsin, and Wyoming. Colorado allows access if the parent has the minor's account number. In New Mexico, school library records of minors are accessible to their parents, and Florida allows the disclosing of minors' circulation records to parents for the collection of fines (Chmara, 2009).

Allowing parents to access the records of their minor children, particularly the records of young adults, may have a chilling effect on information inquiry. Some controversial materials may only be read in the library, safe from parental inspection and comment. Librarians working with young adults in states where their records are accessible to parents will need to give particular thought as to how best to assist them. These library users are on the cusp of adulthood, but with limitations imposed on their rights to privacy checking out materials on certain controversial, embarrassing, or disapproved-of subjects may become unlikely. Young adults from states that allow parents to access the library records of their minor children represent a unique subset of young adults generally, and they deserve special consideration to meet their intellectual needs while maintaining as much privacy and confidentiality as possible.

In addition to state laws that may impinge on privacy, librarians need to be aware of federal laws that can do the same. The Patriot Act was signed into law on October 26, 2001, following the terrorist attacks on American soil on September 11. This act expands law enforcement's powers of surveillance and investigation. Under the powers of the Patriot Act, federal law enforcement officers can request information or demand it by means of a National Security Letter that contains a nondisclosure order (Chmara, 2009). Library users' Internet transaction records, loan history, and search history are covered by the Patriot Act.

The Patriot Act was renewed at the end of May 2011 for another four years by President Obama. It applies to people of all ages. As the powers granted through this act can impinge on young adults' privacy and confidentiality, it is important for library professionals to be familiar with the act and how it impacts patrons and library services.

Conclusion

Young adults are a crucial segment of the society. Their information needs are different from the needs of children with whom they are often grouped for purposes of protection under the law. As individuals who will shortly become adults, they arguably have more in common with adults in terms of information needs and desires, but do not share the same level of First Amendment rights. As minors they have fewer avenues to obtain information and may lack the financial power and opportunities to obtain needed information outside of school and public libraries.

Young adults need the support of professionals knowledgeable of the laws that affect libraries and the First Amendment rights of minors, as well as of the positions espoused by LIS professional associations. Librarians must be guided by the ethical codes of our profession and take seriously our professional duties to fight censorship and to support intellectual freedom by providing young adults with library environments that encourage uninhibited information inquiry.

As LIS professionals, we must see young adults as vital members of our society who need to be prepared to understand and evaluate information, even if that information is unpopular or controversial. We must temper our vision of young adults in light of both the laws that are designed to protect minors and the rulings of the US Supreme Court that specifically address and endorse minors' First Amendment rights. When thinking about how the LIS profession should view young adults, we can look to the success of other countries that provide their young adults with sex education information and have correspondingly lower numbers of teen pregnancies and STDs than the United States. A closer examination is needed of the decisions made to restrict information without respect to the maturity level of the information seekers.

Society has not always considered young adults to be in need of the types of legal and moral protections currently applied to information access in school and public libraries. Are young adults being infantilized in an effort to protect them and thus hinder their transition to adulthood? What does it cost those who are kept from information? Can society afford to continue on such a path? These are questions LIS professionals must consider as we move forward in creating a comprehensive vision of young adults' rights, freedoms, and services.

References

ALA (American Library Association). 1939a. "Code of Ethics of the American Library Association." Last amended January 22, 2008. http://www.ala.org/ala/issuesadvocacy/proethics/codeofethics/codeethics.cfm.

———. 1939b. "Library Bill of Rights." Last amended January 23, 1996. http://www.ala.org/ala/issuesadvocacy/intfreedom/librarybill/index.cfm.

Alford, Sue, and Deb Hauser. 2011. *Adolescent Sexual Health in Europe and the US.* Advocates for Youth. Revised March 2011. http://www.advocatesforyouth.org/publications/419?task=view/.

American Library Association and Association of American Publishers. 1953. "The Freedom to Read Statement." Last amended June 30, 2004. http://www.ala.org/ala/aboutala/offices/oif/statementspols/ftrstatement/freedomreadstatement.cfm.

Buscha, Charles H. 1972. *Freedom versus Suppression and Censorship.* Littleton, CO: Libraries Unlimited.

Carson, Bryan M. 2007. *The Law of Libraries and Archives.* Lanham, MD: Scarecrow Press.

Chmara, Theresa. 2009. *Privacy and Confidentiality Issues: A Guide for Libraries and Their Lawyers.* Chicago: American Library Association.

———. 2010a. "Minor's First Amendment Rights: CIPA and Schools." *Knowledge Quest* 39, no. 1: 16–21.

———. 2010b. "Minors' First Amendment Rights to Access Information." In *Intellectual Freedom Manual*, compiled by the Office of Intellectual Freedom, 351–360. 8th ed. Chicago: ALA Editions.

Cornog, Martha, and Timothy Perper. 1996. *For Sex Education, See Librarian: A Guide to Issues and Resources.* Westport, CT: Greenwood Press.

Fiske, Marjorie. 1962. *Book Selection and Censorship: A Study of School and Public Libraries in California.* Berkeley, CA: University of California Press.

Geller, Evelyn. 1984. *Forbidden Books in American Public Libraries, 1876–1939: A Study in Cultural Change.* Westport, CT: Greenwood Press.

Heins, Marjorie. 2007. *Not in Front of the Children: "Indecency," Censorship, and the Innocence of Youth.* New Brunswick, NJ: Rutgers University Press.

Krug, Judith F., and Candace D. Morgan. 2010. "ALA and Intellectual Freedom: A Historical Overview." In *Intellectual Freedom Manual*, compiled by the Office of Intellectual Freedom, 12–36. 8th ed. Chicago: ALA Editions.

Lehman, Jeffrey, and Shirelle Phelps, eds. 2005. *West's Encyclopedia of American Law*. Farmington Hills, MI: Thompson Gale. PDF e-book.

Levine, Judith. 2002. *Harmful to Minors: The Perils of Protecting Children from Sex*. Minneapolis: University of Minnesota Press.

Lyons, David, Karen Parker, and Alan Schatzberg. 2010. "Animal Models of Early Life Stress: Implications for Understanding Resilience." *Developmental Psychobiology* 52, no. 5: 402–410.

McDonald, Frances Beck. 1993. *Censorship and Intellectual Freedom: A Survey of School Librarians' Attitudes and Moral Reasoning*. Metuchen, NJ: Scarecrow Press.

Minow, Mary, and Tomas A. Lipinski. 2003. *The Librarian's Legal Answer Book*. Chicago: American Library Association.

Morgan, Candace D. 2010. "Challenges and Issues Today." In *Intellectual Freedom Manual*, compiled by the Office of Intellectual Freedom, 37–46. 8th ed. Chicago: ALA Editions.

National Endowment for the Arts. 2007. *To Read or Not to Read: A Question of National Consequence*. Research Report #47. http://www.nea.gov/research/ToRead.pdf.

NCSL (National Conference of State Legislatures). 2012. "Children and the Internet: Laws Relating to Filtering, Blocking and Usage Policies in Schools and Libraries." Last update February 13. http://www.ncsl.org/IssuesResearch/Telecom municationsInformationTechnology/StateInternetFilteringLaws/tabid/13491/Default.aspx.

OIF (Office of Intellectual Freedom), comp. 2010. *Intellectual Freedom Manual*. 8th ed. Chicago: ALA Editions.

Conclusion

Historical Contexts and Consequences of the LIS Youth Consensus

Anthony Bernier

At the Crossroads: From Conflict to the Praxis of Citizenship

As referred to in the preface of this collection, the library information and science (LIS) broad and lingering avoidance with social theory continues to indulge the century-long deficit assumptions inherent in what I call today's youth development industrial complex (YDIC). More specifically, the LIS youth consensus has consequently largely failed to reflect on or develop its own normative vision of youth. It has relied almost entirely on other disciplines to define its young adult (YA) target audience and consequently left unexplored more relevant theoretical and strategic contexts in which to advance its own professional contributions. This is LIS's blind spot with reference to YA services.

Reliance on dated and borrowed approaches leaves LIS in general and YA service in particular with seemingly obvious, naturalized, assumed, and unreflexive visions of youth as a needy and marginalized population, one nearly entirely confined within a false youth/adult binary opposition—a marginalization rooted largely in a focus on difference and conflict (Dimitriadis, 2008). LIS discourse thus continues to concentrate chiefly on an inadequate model of youth in the life of the library, while deflecting the potential role the library might otherwise play in the life of today's actual youth (Wiegand, 2003). We continue deferring to others LIS's more urgent responsibility for developing its own vision of youth.

Thus, as true three decades ago as it is today, if libraries take YA service data seriously at all, they continue to do so almost entirely rooted in institutionally defined and age-segregated output measures: How many young adults came to a YA program? How many attended the Teen Advisory Group?[1]

Negative consequences for LIS spring from these legacy assumptions and practices. One negative consequence yields a conceptually banal approach to service assessment and evaluation, one that encourages and reproduces success bias: *success* occurs simply because something happened. The same holds true for best practices. Mere accomplishment does not qualify as a model. Simply counting heads or circulation statistics (though useful to some degree) is not a persuasive value proposition during the present neoconservative onslaught on the very notion of public service itself.[2]

A second consequence for LIS's legacy practice is revealed in the continuing cliché about library school being "too theoretical." This sentiment reveals how LIS remains allergic to social theory when it should be directly engaged (Leckie, Given, and Buschman, 2010). In order to benefit from and keep pace with insights and interventions advancing in many other disciplines and fields, even those in general youth studies, researchers and the YA practitioners who influence them must strive to better incorporate the theoretical/conceptual into daily practice and action. Theory calls this linkage *praxis*, or the process by which theory, ideas, or skill is enacted into daily practice.

This conclusion of *Transforming Young Adult Services* asks the question: How can theory combine with practice to produce a rich praxis—alternatives to LIS's otherwise derived and dated youth consensus—necessarily transforming our vision of young adults and thus YA services? After contextualizing a turn toward critical social theory, we will investigate and problematize several distinct "paths" toward which LIS might begin to debate its own specific vision of young adult library users to inform a transformative YA service praxis.

At least one answer to this question emerging most explicitly from the last section of this collection lies in exploring the notion of YA-as-citizen. Thus, before considering a variety of specific implications or paths about this notion for LIS praxis, this conclusion first probes the critical social theory landscape and the notion of citizenship in general. The first path toward developing a transformational LIS vision of YAs, as emerges explicitly in the last section of this collection in Chapters 7, 8, and 9, is to more creatively explore the notion of citizenship. How might this notion of YA-as-citizen impact various aspects of the library's applied service profile? How might it transform collection management to better serve YAs? How might an LIS-specific YA-as-citizen vision impact library space design? How would YAs-as-citizens impact intergenerational library services? When LIS critically engages important theoretical interventions and applies them to creating its own vision of YA-as-citizen in our daily postmodern world, powerful possibilities of praxis emerge.

In Defense of Theory

All professions require critical self-reflection, theory, and grounding in conceptual foundations. And yet one of the enduring clichés about library school is that it is too theoretical. Indeed, there is abundant evidence that LIS's refusal of theory is deeply ingrained in our professional culture. In 1933, for instance, Lee Pierce Buttler, dean of the University of Chicago library school, noted, "Unlike his colleagues in other fields of social activity the librarian is strangely uninterested in the theoretical aspects of his profession" (Buttler, 1933: xi–xii). More recently, LIS scholar John Budd (2003) has observed: "Within library and information work there is a fairly long-standing antipathy toward "theory.""[3] And there is also ample evidence that youth serving fields in general share this aversion.[4]

Nevertheless, conceptual foundations exist, recognized and valued or not, in the background of LIS work. They exist as assumptions about what we perceive as "true" and "false," as assessments about what we value and what we do not. But we ought not confuse these assumptions with timeless and universal truths. Thus, the conceptual engagement as presented in these chapters urges us to debate and qualify what is enduring from what is fleeting as well as highlight the difference between mere glad tidings and testimonials versus demonstrable and defensible practice.

Why does LIS need critical theory? LIS needs critical theory because the nature of our professional obligations to society, to libraries, and most particularly to our young people, requires that we not shirk our responsibilities to constantly engage our research and practice critically. Our obligation to this vigilance goes far beyond the books we may review, rank, and recommend, to how we envision our users as well as our institutional interventions.

There is, necessarily, a higher degree of ambiguity in assessing and applying theory to our work. With theory the same phenomena or data can plausibly be described or explained in very different ways and inform different interpretations, understandings, and meanings. But also, at base, theory permits professionals to interpret data and relationships to make higher quality, more creative, and more confident decisions.

We advance the field when alternative paradigms or theoretical models are examined, learned, scrutinized, debated, and modified. In contrast, technicians or paraprofessionals simply and repetitively apply uncontested methods fitting preconceived circumstances. Without theory we are only trained employees. Without theory true and viable professional volition cannot exist.

The best way the field has discovered to even begin a conversation about this widely shared and observed ambivalence with theory is to pursue praxis. Praxis represents the actionable intersection of theory, education, and practice. Praxis denies common assumptions about theory and practice existing in simplistic opposition to one another. Simply put, the pedagogical goal of praxis is to understand and explicitly teach the relationship between professional activity and theory so that practice does not function as mere unrelated sequences of isolated elements, procedures, methods, or techniques. Or, as John Budd (2003: 20) has put it, "Praxis refers to action that carries social and ethical implications and is not reducible to technical performance of tasks."

But praxis also provides LIS an opportunity to apply a conceptual framework in the design of a new project, new interpretation of data, and the critical engagement of legacy practices such as relying on other disciplines to define library users. Thus, this is not the study of theory for theory's sake. Praxis furnishes the profession with legitimizing criteria by which to assess practice beyond pedestrian or paraprofessional interventions. Instituting praxis distinguishes LIS as intellectual and professional labor. And without theory, we compromise our claims to the "science" in library and information science.

From Positivism to Postmodernism: Toward an LIS/YA Praxis

Modernist analysis projects absolutist confidence in its universal truth claims, rooted in positivist notions of "objective" and universal knowledge. Postmodernism, on the other hand, finds a more complex, contingent, situated, and diverse world. Where G. Stanley Hall and Emmett L. Holt, for instance, claimed to have discovered the "crisis" and "turmoil" at the root of all youth for all time, cultures, and places, postmodernism's inquiry enjoins those claims with concerns over, among other things, universal applicability.

More specifically, positivism focuses its concerns broadly on the nature of experience. In the case of YA services, positivism manifests its concerns largely in "behavior." Thus, and because LIS and YA librarianship has reclined in the shadow largely of developmental psychology, it should come as no surprise that the questions driving its research agenda would concentrate on such topics as information behaviors, search behaviors, reading behaviors, antisocial behaviors, and the "needs" of YAs (YALSA, 2012a; Walter, 2003).

The institutional vision of the YA patron emerging from such concerns necessarily by definition produces a view of youth as other, deficient, different, and needy. This conventional approach asks youth to fit into the life of the existing institution. What YA needs, for instance, can library resources address? What library skill sets and capacities match the needs of YAs? LIS responses have therefore orbited around and continue to focus nearly exclusively on answers connected to institutional resources (mainly books), access (to collections and sometimes to participation), and skills (mainly bibliographic and curricular in nature) (Bernier, 2007).

Postmodernism advances an entirely different set of concerns. Postmodern inquiry is rooted in questions of dynamic meanings and power relations rather than concerns for experience or behavior (Deodato, 2006; Foucault, 1972, 1977, 1978). Dramatically new questions emerge from this trajectory and offer a transformative vision of young people and thus a new and LIS-specific service praxis. What meanings of library resources and uses do YAs know, define, and create? How do they create these meanings, and why? What can libraries do or do better to help them pursue these meanings? Further, what power relations connect or disconnect YAs, information, and libraries? These are vastly different questions than ones LIS has been asking in trying to fit YAs into the life of the library. These are vastly different concerns than have preoccupied LIS practice and research.

When LIS becomes self-reflexive about the ways in which it has derived its vision of separateness, difference, and inadequacy of youth from other disciplines, driven largely by nineteenth-century adultist ideals and models—either sentimentally as timeless innocents or condescendingly as depraved agents of threat—we can better contrast these long-standing views about the library's larger role in society against the cultural meanings defined by the young people libraries serve. LIS could begin such self-reflection by reimagining youth not as deficient blank slates on which to inscribe bibliographic skills but as already fully entitled citizens in the democratic culture libraries putatively seek and help define.

Framed this way, new questions emerge through praxis: How can today's youth better experience meanings of democratic culture in their libraries? How can YAs contribute their own meanings to democratic culture? How and under what circumstances do different YA experiences derive variant meanings of democratic culture? And what are the best ways for LIS to study or facilitate responses to these questions?

These are not remotely the questions posed by LIS's deficit legacy view of youth, which are rooted either in the youth-at-risk approach or its kissing cousin youth development (see for example, Ahn, 2011; Julien, 1998; Callison, 1997; Howe, 1997; Neuman, 1995). But these new questions do begin to point the way to a different institutional imagination of young people.

So, how do we proceed in reimagining young adults through praxis? How can LIS, better informed by critical social theory, offer alternatives to the deficit-based youth consensus of its past? What can praxis deliver for a more relevant and LIS-specific vision of young people in diverse and contemporary circumstances? Without the benefit of broader LIS research engagement, such as that inaugurated in this collection, any innovation through this century-old master narrative consensus can provoke only speculation for future debate. Postmodern interventions can, however, certainly help us recognize and better cultivate a more measured confidence than LIS has historically adopted.

Critical social theory can help LIS more clearly recognize how its past is tethered to a focus on oppositions and differences between young people and idealized notions of adulthood. But critical theory can also, in combination with insights and energies gained from practice, help generate and identify a new categorical praxis in serving young people and thus light new paths toward discovering institutional relationships with them. These concerns carry the potential of impacting our work with youth not on a piecemeal basis but systematically across our entire institutional footprint.

A Praxis of Broad Citizenship

As suggestively unfurled in the chapters of *Transforming Young Adult Services*, one promising new vision of youth emerging from these essays considers YAs as fully entitled citizens: a citizenship of praxis. This notion in particular offers LIS the opportunity to build on the notion of citizenship that it has used for other patron groups in the past. But what exactly is a citizenship of praxis?

There are, of course, many definitions and meanings of *citizenship*. The term certainly and immediately begs a raft of questions about applying such a word to youth. But it is precisely because it is a complex term— one rooted in the present as well as the past, capable of being sculpted for particular purposes, and informed by postmodern inquiry about meaning and power, as well as still intimately and deeply connected to a familiar LIS institutional mission within a democratic culture—that it offers LIS such opportunities for transforming YA services.

The approach percolating from this collection does not endorse qualifying the notion with terms like *youth citizenship* or *junior citizenship*.[5] Contemporary democratic culture does not qualify this notion with diminutive labels. We do not, for instance, use the term *female citizenship* or *elder citizenship*. But this does not mean that all those considered citizens enjoy every right, responsibility, or privilege at all times. Society imposes many qualifications on citizens for many reasons. But the notion of citizenship itself is not compromised in this process. Thus we should consider the expression YAs-as-citizens and not the term *youth citizenship*.

Another argument in favor of reimagining and applying this notion to a new LIS vision of youth is that the term *citizen* has recently gained tremendous currency in the broader fields of youth studies.[6] It should be noted here that there is a good deal of debate about its application and definition. But this very fact offers LIS a rare opportunity to not simply join in and contribute to these broader conversations in a way that has eluded it in the past, but also to reinforce the validity of its own definitions.

Still, there are some uncontested features of the term that might help LIS begin to envision YAs-as-citizens. One view regards citizenship connected to more static notions of political practice. Here we would more closely associate it with the utilitarian exercise of a rather zero-sum legal or political process and/or associate it with political identity bestowed through the administration of state or governmental authority. We might refer to this form as "thin" or *narrow citizenship*. In this model a person is either a citizen or not, either entitled to vote or not.

In order to evolve an LIS-specific vision of YAs-as-citizens, however, we are perhaps better served in avoiding this all-or-nothing static construct by employing more creativity. Part of that creativity would recognize that the state does not hold a monopoly on the idea of citizenship. Civil society, too, including civic institutions like libraries and the people who interact with them, is also capable of asserting sufficient cultural power to define its own forms or features of citizenship.

Thus, a more creative view of citizenship might include dynamic and multidimensional features such as practices of participation defined and exercised at the local level and under specific circumstances. This notion of citizenship recognizes anyone who: participates in or contributes to making community, culture, or society; takes part in the practice of organized memory as is conducted in the library; appears in the presence of others, by assuming a degree of responsibility for one's actions, and negotiates the rights and obligations of a shared resource.[7]

This broader vision is predicated on connecting somehow with strangers in the way we aspiringly build on the trust of strangers in a democracy. Participation here might include not simply joining those prescribed and approved endeavors emanating from the YDIC, for instance, forever preparing for the future, but rather on pursuing current interests in contributing to the present public sphere through any number of wide-ranging civic engagements. This evocative notion resides more within a broad and active civil society and not exclusively in the narrow or "political" realms. We might call this "thick" or *broad citizenship.*

Broad citizenship, unlike the narrow version, does not question *whether* youth should have power in civil society. It does not delay granting power or status until some arbitrarily defined date or age by suddenly throwing the power switch to full-on: one day you can't drive, drink, or vote, the next day you can. Nor does it perpetuate the nagging contradiction inherent in LIS professionals granting "empowerment" to youth. Youth requiring that power be bestowed upon them (particularly by unrelated government employees) implicitly recognize, or construct, the receivers of such beneficence by definition as powerless. Adults feeling the need to empower youth inherently recognize how little they have and indeed become invested in perpetuating that dynamic (Eliasoph, 2011).

Instead, realization of a broad citizenship asks *how* citizen power is defined, negotiated, earned, navigated, exercised, manifested, expanded, and advanced. Broad citizenship already assumes and envisions local participation of youth in a way that neither narrow citizenship nor the YDIC can: claustrophobic, static, and universally delimited fields of action and agency based merely on demographic (age-segregated) and highly circumscribed criteria.

If LIS envisioned youth within this broad citizenship construct, it may become easier to conceive of youth as not only already possessing but contributing to and producing culture and less defined by marginalization (Rubin, 2004). Envisioned this way, citizenship refocuses the prevailing conceptualization of youth as "other" by concentrating more on the *commonalities* youth share with the adult community so that not every aspect of youth experience is viewed as different, alien, or only negatively when compared to putatively high-functioning adults. Envisioned this way, youth are not relegated to a condition of ever and always *becoming*, but they can be also recognized and valued for their *present* circumstances, concerns, interests, and contributions in the here and now.

Informed by core postmodernist concerns with meaning and power, the notion of YA-as-citizen as capable is a transformative YA service praxis for LIS and libraries. The next four subsections explore in more detail some key aspects of the contemporary YA service profile. Each respectively addresses the question about how, with the notion of a YA-as-citizen praxis, LIS can transform prevailing YA services. The first examines the fundamental practice of collection development and management. The second addresses library YA spaces. The third explores incorporation of YA services across intergenerational library service. And the last subsection moves analysis beyond the physical walls of library buildings. Together these topics and questions demonstrate a capacity to launch rich discussions and debates about transforming YA services from a dated and moribund model toward an approach capable of reinvigorating LIS with rich research and relevant practice.

"Sweet Frauds," Collection Management, and Meanings of YA Literacies

How would LIS concern for collection management be impacted by a YA-as-citizen vision? Rather than continuing to privilege books, curricular experience, and a construction of youth as mere preadult and subpar information consumers, an LIS approach to collections that envision YAs-as-citizens might more easily recognize the multiplicity of ways in which they manifest literacy enactments themselves. Well beyond the commercially published books or materials delivered digitally through commercial databases and websites libraries could also begin to incorporate the myriad of cultural forms youth increasingly produce themselves to express and document their own meanings *as* youth. This is a sentiment echoed in Richard Rubin's (2004: 33) observation of LIS history: "Our current concept of information provision has been historically conditioned by a traditional preoccupation with the collection rather than people."

A collection management process and ethic informed by a vision of YAs-as-citizens would, of course, require that LIS reposition itself with respect to the historically anointed and disproportionate energy currently devoted to book selection, book awards, and book lists—at the expense of all the other ways youth enact literacy themselves. Of course, it should be expected that the interests invested in legacy and unreflective practice would take issue with this vision, notably fiction publishers, publishing agents, writers, curriculum advocates, and ALA selection committees, among others. While it should go without saying that conventional publications have their place in libraries, given LIS's reliance on the youth-as-deficit paradigm, though, it has traditionally privileged these materials over the literacy enactments and meanings of young people. (Note that the term *paradigm* is used to mean dominance of a totalizing and grand scheme of thought about which no alternative is apparent or recognized.)

Some immediate questions present themselves. What are the meanings of the cultural forms youth produce themselves? How do they produce cultural meanings through literacies? What is produced? (See Chapter 1 for evidence that the adaptation to personal information devices is beginning to be taken seriously.) Where do they produce them and how do they use them? Other than the literacies they produce themselves, what other forms do they value? In what ways is youth culture manifested in the various meanings and enactments of literacy? Perhaps LIS would do well to consider YAs as harbingers of things to come, prefiguring future library usage, and as resources for libraries to learn about the future of their own value rather than as a way to determine the future of youth. Further, how can libraries best document, collect, organize, store, preserve, curate, exhibit, promote, and serve as an access conduit for the literacy acts produced and valued by YAs-as-citizens? And finally, what positions have LIS taken on these literacy acts and artifacts in the past? What have the impacts on service to YAs been as a consequence? (See Chapter 5.)

In terms of collection management, an LIS vision of YAs-as-citizens would eschew more of the traditional pedantic YDIC practices concentrating on the differences between youth and adults and build more on *similarities*, even those inherent in traditional LIS core values. LIS could create diagnostics, for instance, more similar to how libraries cultivate, build, and evaluate adult collections.

Adults create cultural meaning in their use of libraries. Libraries document, collect, organize, store, preserve, curate, and make accessible this cultural record.[8] Libraries accomplish this by taking the processes of adult culture meaning making and products of these practices seriously. And libraries do all this because they understand that it is in the concerned and professional collection, organization, preservation, and curation of the products of adult culture that they uphold their mission to make the human record accessible in a democratic society (McCook, 2004).

What would an LIS vision of YAs-as-citizens contribute to collection practices and management? What are the literacy enactments and activities that capture YA attention? What can their own preferred domains of meaning creation (e.g., friendship, self-expression, play and fun, passion, the building of social capital, and community) teach LIS about information seeking and the library's role in these areas? In shifting from a deficit vision of the information user to one grounded in a contemporary definition of culturally productive citizenship, institutional attention necessarily shifts to taking social worlds, self-directed experience, independence, interdependence, and peer experience seriously rather than continuing to marginalize, ignore, or prohibit it.

Among the many possibilities of literacy enactments meaningful for youth, libraries could begin taking seriously the more conventional formats of cultural production emerging in the past quarter century, such as the new youth journalism promoting "youth voices" (e.g., Youth Communication in New York and Pacific News Service's youth journalism arm, Youth Communications Team, in San Francisco).

But there are many other forms of youth literacies: YA zine culture; student newspapers and yearbooks (current as well as historical, in paper as well as digital formats); youth sports culture; prom culture; social organizations; public performance (poetry, music, art, dance programs and drama playbills, rap and hip-hop culture, and coming-of-age rituals from the diversity of racial and ethnic experiences); and many other cultural forms that constitute and document YA daily and lived meanings in the here and now. Often these manifestations of YA literacies will be assembled from what young people find at hand or bend to their own will from their insurgent communities, bootlegged technologies, pirate media, and rebel utopias. To my knowledge, no library in the country systematically values even conventionally printed student newspapers, let alone zines and other forms of what I call the "fugitive" literacies of young adults. As librarians, we need to revalue the relationships of the facts contained in our holdings and compare them to the experiences they can help youth create for themselves.

Author Tobias Wolff (1996: 162) captures the adult world's quick dismissal of youth meanings as "a series of sweet frauds" in a passage from his short story "Smorgasbord":

We're supposed to smile at the passions of the young, and at what we recall of our own passions, as if they were no more than a series of sweet frauds we'd fooled ourselves with and then wised up to. Not only the passions of boys and girls for each other but the others, too—passion for justice, for doing right, for turning the world around. All these come in their time under our wintry smiles. Yet there was nothing foolish about what we felt.

This approach to the literacy enactments, documents, and meanings of YAs-as-citizens would more specifically also take social behavior more seriously. It would include reconsidering and reorienting library service philosophy, ethics, practice, space, and the other dimensions of service by designing them with YA social norms as a legitimate dimension of the process, not something tacked-on, inconvenient, or peripheral. In both peer-driven and individual interest-driven activity, the cultural forms of youth expression would be valued as a legitimate contribution to the cultural production of the community, just as the products of adult culture are valued.

In the immediacy and breadth of these literacy enactments, new expectations, practices, and visions of the role of the library in the life of today's youth would dramatically lower traditional barriers previously assumed impenetrable by assumptions rooted in a vision of merely tolerated and marginalized youth. By cultivating and facilitating new interests, in tinkering and "messing around" with new forms of media (i.e., a broader view of collections and materials), youth acquisition of technical and media literacy skills would number among their *present* cultural expressions as well as hold potential value for the future. And their growing expectations for immediate feedback from and with others they select would be viewed institutionally as a respected outcome, not the exotic or unrealistic white noise of youth. It is in these new collection management roles, geared more to the current daily life of culturally productive citizens and information creators than institutional visions of itself, that LIS professionals could build new and exciting relationships with young people.

Why have libraries found applying such core values that have been forever vaunted and trumpeted for adult users and culture so difficult to apply to its younger users? The answer is simple: We cannot expect an institution so dedicated to a vision of its young users as inherently other, less-than, and needy, compared only to a mythical self-actualized future adult, to recognize the value of its young users' own cultural meanings. If we are to learn anything from a postmodern intervention into LIS practice and research with respect to YA services, it is that this incapacity has been a consequence of a field subscribing uncritically to a disciplinary approach that makes this higher practice conceptually and institutionally impossible. However, informed by an aspirational YA-as-citizen vision, LIS would ask new questions and drive collection development, management, and curation through different assumptions. LIS would accomplish this by taking the processes of youth meaning making no less seriously than it has for adults. LIS would accomplish this by taking the products of these practices seriously.

All of these LIS concerns about collections emerge as the product of a vision of YAs-as-citizens rooted in praxis. They represent a new path, a new diagnostic criterion, for executing a vision of young people that avoids their assumed universal deficiency. Such praxis would support an LIS discipline dedicated to thriving within the rich cultural legacy, values, and institutional resources libraries already possess, and thus contribute to making more of the human record accessible.

Citizenship and YA Space

What difference would an LIS-specific YA-as-citizen vision produce for library space design? In pursuing a praxis for YA service, the opportunities for libraries are nowhere more material and visible than in how they inscribe their public spaces. Because libraries continue to devote more space and design consideration to restrooms than YAs, they inherit a long legacy of denying young people public space equity and have produced little research on the connections between YAs and space (see Harden and Huggins, 2004; Chelton, 2001, 2002; Glick, 2000; Bernier, 1998).

It is also true, of course, that libraries ideally serve the entire public within one facility or built environment. However, once inside it is clear that library space becomes immediately segregated (more commonly bifurcated as either adult or children) by age demographic. Public library history is, it should also be remembered, replete with examples of defining, redefining, and overcoming spatial prohibition, access, and segregation based on demographic categories such as sex, race, language, and social class. Today, even after over a decade of robust conversation and innovation, libraries continue largely to understudy, undertheorize, and relegate YA spaces to repurposed and remainder spaces (Bernier, 2009a, 2010; Cranz, 2006; Lee, 2009; Pusey, 2008), including the nation's signature YA library spaces (e.g., Los Angeles Public Library, Phoenix Public Library, Chicago Public Library, and New York Public Library).

Beyond better addressing an adequate and equitable share of a library's public space through designing equitable YA-specific spaces, there is another way in which library space can better incorporate a vision of YAs-as-citizens. Libraries, contrary to succumbing to prevailing spatial competition between young people and adults (a competition it should be noted that is rarely if ever won by youth), could well stand as an institutional role model, a bulwark against reducing the seemingly inexorable segregation and erasure of youth from public space. As historian Steven Mintz (2004: 383) observed, "More than ever before, children are segregated in a separate world of youth." (See also Abbott-Chapman, 2009; Owens, 2002; Aitken, 2001; Childress, 2000; Sibley, 1995; White, 1990.)

In imagining youth with an entitled right to the library and on equitable footing with other library user groups, LIS would necessarily serve as a more democratic foil to a broader and growing age-based "Jim Crow junior" public policy (see Lefebvre, 1991, 1996)—through actually *expanding* the public sphere for young people into the broader true "third space" of the entire community rather than following prevailing trends to find ever more effective ways in which to marginalize, discourage, or prohibit YAs. Envisioning young people as citizens, however, opens up a vast and rich physical terrain in which the broader community might see the library as an exemplar to be copied, not a dumping ground or self-satisfied "safe" island on the land.[9]

As space manifests power, the marginalized role libraries institutionally assign to youth is clearly understood. Young people realize how little power they have in libraries. This perhaps explains why they have told us for decades how libraries number among the least desirable places to inhabit and even described them as "aristocratic, authoritarian, unfriendly, and unresponsive" (Rubin, 2004: 46). (See also Cook, Parker, and Pettijohn, 2005; DeWitt Wallace–Readers Digest Fund, 1999; Benton Foundation, 1996.)

Libraries institute meaning and power in the design of YA spaces in one way when they view youth as at-risk and focus on surveillance, slightly another way when they view them through a youth development focus on skills (as in "homework centers"), and an entirely different way again when they envision them as citizens with a focus on production and consumption of cultural meanings. And without a grounding in research, LIS frequently fails to acknowledge the differences and confuses these positions. Note the common conflation of curricular goals with the YDIC agenda evident in this recent articulation of a grant awarded to build a new YA library space: "This competition was announced in answer to President Obama's 'Educate to Innovate' campaign, a nationwide effort to bring American students to the forefront in science and math, to provide the workers of tomorrow with the skills they need today" (IMLS, 2011). The same confusion maintains for many components of the LIS YA service profile. At-risk is one approach. YDIC represents a different paradigm. And YA-as-citizen represents a third. The first two are rooted in hegemonic nineteenth-century deficit assumptions. The third is not.

Here postmodern concerns about meaning and power can help LIS generate an entirely new agenda of YA spatial praxis. How would library space defined with a vision of YAs-as-citizens transform spatial design values, processes, criteria, practice, and research? What process would be required of LIS to incorporate YAs-as-citizens into library design? And because even the most progressive library institutions limit youth involvement in the library design process to "the YA space," how might LIS extend sharing the democratic civic experience of the entire library space planning process with YAs-as-citizens?

Aided by praxis it is easier to understand how YA service truths would percolate up from the local and situated, under particular circumstances, in specific places, and at specific times. This is a principal difference to the grand truths about all youth, such as those issuing from the YDIC: a new YA service praxis does not simply flow down wholly conceived from on high.

Spatial equity through envisioning YA-as-citizens establishes libraries as a tangible democratic entitlement to a fully public resource, just the way LIS changed for white middle-class women in the late nineteenth century and for African-Americans and Latinos after the middle of the twentieth century. Until that time arrives, however, libraries for increasing numbers of youth will remain irrelevant and avoidable—merely adult "temples of youth improvement" and hostages to the YDIC (Childress, 2000: 248).

Young Adults as Intergenerational Agents

YAs now have at their disposal many ways in which to communicate, create, and distribute information, thus increasingly circumventing adult and institutional scrutiny. To do this, and perhaps adjusting to the continuing segregation of YAs from physical public space, they can now often dictate more of the terms of that separation. Where does this leave the library in the life of young people? What difference would a YA service praxis offer in the relationship between YAs and libraries?

Despite the seeming inexorable growing separation of YAs from the public realm, the library can still serve a critically important role as a space of intergenerational mediation by curating, collecting, exhibiting cultural production in a public space that few other civic institutions can or are willing to provide. Thus, in addition to a new LIS trajectory on collection management, another promising path toward a praxis of youth-as-entitled-citizens might better explore and exploit the library's meaning as a nearly unique intergenerational public resource within contemporary civil society. And in Chapter 6 Wendy Lesko certainly begins to beg many intergenerational questions for attentive LIS professionals (see also Soep and Chavez, 2010).

Confined all day to *de facto* age-segregated educational facilities and then increasingly remanded to additional age-based after-school programming as well, as promulgated by the YDIC and what I have termed *after-school apartheid,* today's youth are sequestered away from the community's mainstream to a degree unimaginable even a few decades ago. In expanding the late-nineteenth-century view of youth-as-other, we have not only removed them from the dangers of the industrial workplace but also increasingly erased them from public life altogether (Miranda, 2003; Aitken, 2001; Borden, 2001; Childress, 2000; Sibley, 1995; White, 1990).

Ideally, libraries already offer YAs-as-citizens the potential to preserve and even extend access to civic life on equal footing with other members of the community, that is to say with other citizens. On the other hand, in practice, until LIS more critically engages its philosophical approaches, it will continue to reproduce age-based segregation along with other institutions.

Envisioning youth as entitled citizens would require rethinking the narrow roles to which we have thus far confined them: criminal intruders on our quiet and orderly world at worst, marginalized library users in most cases, and hand-picked volunteers for the Teen Advisory Group or children's room at best. While libraries continue to serve all generations, they have done so largely within the confines of age-based service silos.

Beyond the most obvious manifestations of age-based collections, programming philosophy appears even more age-segregated. Here, justified either by the implementation of a strict youth development catechism of skill enhancements for the future or the more lax and ill-defined YA "interest" criteria (with developmental "assets" and measures lurking just off-stage), YA programming is rarely considered outside the bounds of age-segregation (Gorman and Suellentrop, 2009; Alessio, 2008; Brehm-Heeger, 2008; Alessio and Patton, 2007).

Teen Advisory Groups and summer reading programs (the nearly ritualized *sine qua non* of YA librarianship) are by definition age-limited, as are gaming nights and nearly all manner of age group programming experiences. As with the literacy enactments and cultural productions of YAs, intergenerational models of programming are rarely written about, experimented with, demonstrated, promoted, evaluated, or studied.[10]

What difference would an LIS-specific YA-as-citizen vision produce for intergenerational library programming praxis? Answering this question lies chiefly in outcomes of future debates. But on first blush, a view of YAs-as-citizens might include youth representation and visibility at all library public events, not simply as audience members but as hosts, guest introducers, or content contributors to some portion of the events themselves. YAs would routinely serve as members of library boards, commissions, and Friends groups. YAs would attend, along with adult community members, annual legislative days so elected officials and policymakers hear directly from young people. YAs might contribute to the content and assembly of library annual reports. They would appear at city council and subcommittee meetings at times other than simply to testify against resource cutbacks. YAs would appear as panelists at local, regional, and national conferences as library users, not simply to perform as age-defined "exemplars." Again, answers to the question of how to imagine YAs-as-citizens comprehensively in a praxis of institutional age-integrated operations are not the same as when we engaged in relegating them decade after decade to a skill-deficient silo.

An LIS Praxis of YA Services Beyond the Walls

Discovering how a vision of YAs-as-citizen can transform LIS practice inside of library buildings into potentially flourishing new relationships does not nearly exhaust the possibilities. Library buildings clearly represent, of course, the largest institutional environment in which LIS professionals serve young people. But LIS professionals also possess skills particularly valuable to institutions and service environments that either directly or indirectly serve YAs beyond and outside of libraries as well. These skills range broadly across a variety of capacities, commitments, principles, and proficiencies. These competencies include advanced education preparation, training, and records management skills, for instance. LIS professionals understand the nature of applying research and delivering professional presentations, and they increasingly understand how best to exploit an expanding toolkit of communication technologies, among other skills.

All of these skills and competencies can be used in serving and connecting young people with information both directly and indirectly in institutions beyond the library. In one instance, LIS skills can be applied to leading a strategic planning process to build a library for a nonprofit law firm representing a county agency's foster youth. In fact, I supervised one graduate LIS student in doing this very thing, and the law firm is currently considering hiring a professional librarian as a consequence. An educational advocacy office that fights to ensure that special education youth receive the services to which they are entitled can benefit from a LIS professional capable of developing information and records processing protocols. The editor of a journal or the director of a professional association supporting youth work would also benefit from the capacities contained in LIS training and experience. And a nongovernmental organization dedicated to international development through building youth libraries in urban Zambia benefited from personnel with LIS skills capable of building relationships with local educational, governmental, and other civic organizations (both virtual and in physical places) (see Lubuto Library Project at http://www.lubuto.org/).

None of these scenarios can thrive by perpetuating a less-than-adult view of youth that separates them into a hierarchy of marginalized social importance or by impugning them as necessarily oppositional to normative (or idealized) adulthood. Stated differently, it is difficult to maintain a near religious fervor for the hegemony of the YDIC when serving urban youth in Zambia or foster youth in the United States. Not all youth are served by the same assumptions.

But a praxis infused with critical social theory, combined with professional excellence, can make strong, positive, and valuable contributions to these efforts because they work more consciously with daily local circumstances, within the context of a particular time and place, and with actual youth. Working in what might otherwise be considered "alternative" environments affords such perspective-expanding opportunities to help sharpen critical distance on LIS's historic and fatigued youth consensus, while at the same time demonstrating professional capacities and competencies in wide-ranging venues.

Conclusions and New Directions Toward Praxis

While LIS has maintained a "tunnel vision" legacy with respect to critical social theory, particularly regarding the practice of YA librarianship, the same is not true for other youth studies disciplines. There is a gathering new discourse in this scholarship, informed by more theoretical sophistication, that can meaningfully contribute to a rich and informed debate about an LIS-specific vision of young people.

The concept quickly gaining purchase among academic youth scholars and allies calls for nothing less than "the end of adolescence" (Dimitriadis, 2008; Epstein, 2007; Savin-Williams, 2006; Graham, 2004). This notion advances that contemporary culture has infantilized young people, based not on their capacities but on an arbitrary and superficial age-based demographic profile, and finds them fundamentally incompetent. By altering LIS's current proscriptive and reductionist view of young people to incorporate more complexity and diversity into that view, by recognizing their respective and demonstrated capacities, and in granting them rights and responsibilities based on those capacities, youth would flourish, these advocates claim, at much higher levels of accomplishment.

From our own library history, we can witness young peoples' volition and how they have called each other forward into civic participation. Historian Patterson Toby Graham, for instance, documents one such call when between 1961 and 1963 in cities throughout racially segregated Alabama young adults (adolescents) led, staged, and ultimately succeeded in desegregating libraries through "read-ins" (Graham, 2002). In addition to today's Occupy movement or the movement against the previous Bush administration's earlier immigration reform efforts, youth pressing for social justice in the early 1960s (founders of Students for a Democratic Society) insisted that their landmark founding document begin with the word *we* (Hayden, 2012).

These examples illustrate ways of envisioning young people as both autonomous and as agents interdependent on each other, on adults, and on the institutions impacting their lives. While there is no denying that adults played important roles in these events, neither can it be denied that it was youth, individually and collectively, igniting the fires of broad and active citizenship, sometimes at the risk of their lives. While there are many such stories in the history of youth, the YDIC does not know a vocabulary for these ways of being civic through advancing social justice.[11] Such a competency-based youth vision, however, closely mirrors the YA-as-citizen concept percolating in the essays collected in *Transforming Young Adult Services*.

As LIS better recognizes youth capacities to act as citizens within the library's larger civic context, focused on what they share with adults more than ever and only emphasizing the differences, it may well become easier to grant YAs commensurate rights, privileges, and involvements. Certainly one possible consequence is that youth might be taken seriously for their cultural impacts and contributions more on their own terms rather than be institutionally marginalized as deficient and needy preadults.

The question and debate before LIS now is this: How can praxis (the combination of critical theory and reflective practice) help reimagine YAs-as-citizens? The notion of citizen aligns, it bears repeating, much more closely with LIS's broader historical, institutional, and ethical aspirations in promoting intellectual freedom and information access. It adheres to the aspirations of LIS instructors and students in preparing new professionals to contribute to the well-being of community through information service. And it will likely enhance the daily practice of current professionals by revaluing their own daily interventions. Appropriately applying this concept, however, would require critical engagement and reconciliation with LIS's legacy of systematic and institutional marginalization of youth.

Systematically applying the broad definition of YAs-as-citizens would require considering them as subjects in their own rights, in their present moment, as opposed to objects in which to pour unexamined, dated assumptions and future-oriented adultist agendas. Methodologically, this requires developing an LIS research agenda *with* young people rather than conducting research simply *on* them and how their needs are or are not met on institutional terms.[12] It means asking questions about power relations and user meanings. This is the difference between youth in the life of the library versus the library in the life of youth.

Answers to these questions about defining the features and contours of an LIS YA-as-citizen vision remains a key challenge before the profession generally and YA librarianship in particular. And while this vision may not yield "neat and clean" directives for advancing these professional concerns, it does promise hope for building better relationships with young people than trafficking in our century-old economy of deficits.

Imagining new paths toward meaning with youth, viewed first as fully entitled citizens, also immediately begs questions about power relations between young people and the libraries ostensibly financed to serve them. And thus, whatever debate ensues would necessarily involve more discussion of the nexus of youth, culture, and libraries as institutional actors rather than our prevailing prescriptive focus on what we think youth need. How do youth, viewed as entitled citizens, interpret, create, negotiate, and navigate their own volition and the institutional meanings contained in libraries? What are the competing and cooperative circuits and levels of power YAs engage and encounter in libraries? How are those institutional circuits manifested and negotiated? How do libraries respond to, study, and deploy their institutional power with youth when viewed not as interlopers or needy less-than adults?

Engaging these questions might well result in reducing LIS's legacy preoccupations and perhaps emphasizing more of the meanings youth reach

Contrasting Visions of Young Adults in Library Practice

The following table begins to feather out some of the more obvious contrasting aspects between YA services grounded on the dated and borrowed vision of youth from the YDIC instead of an emerging LIS vision of YAs-as-citizens. It is important to realize how even in this sampling different visions of YAs produce different praxes in nearly every aspect of the professionally defined YA service profile. It also should go without saying that not every aspect or service idea generated with a youth development perspective is "wrong" or useless. A reflective and critical professional practice would determine these distinctions. But without a self-aware praxis to recognize the differences, the challenge to do so becomes that much more difficult.

	Youth Development	YAs-as-Citizens
Collections	• Privilege conventionally published materials (particularly proscriptive and curricular literature and fiction)	✓ Emphasis on youth-produced literacy enactments documenting contemporary experience ✓ Youth creative forms highlighted
Space	• Houses collection • Homework/tutor space • Computer or learning lab • Matching tables and task chairs • Necessarily separated as far as possible from children's space • Competition with adult spaces/purposes	✓ Privileges social experience, community building, sharing ✓ Wide variety of seating options, configurations, policies ✓ Better understanding of how in some communities parents rely on older youth to care take for younger children, thereby suggesting distinctive (but not necessarily distant) spaces ✓ Reduced competition with adult spaces/purposes

(continued on next page)

(continued from previous page)

	Youth Development	YAs-as-Citizens
Atmosphere	• Academic, curricular • Rule-centric behavior	✓ Conviviality of a school hall-way between classes ✓ Socially enforced behavior
Participation	• Largely individualistic • TAG helps with YA collection development • Reproduced bureaucratic culture • Volunteers help with summer reading program	✓ Group/peer-centered ✓ TAG integrated into all public library operations (not just YA activity) ✓ Socially determined and en-forced organizational culture ✓ Volunteers exposed to tasks throughout the entire institu-tion (including administra-tion)
Programming	• Youth development and skill enrichment programs determined and produced by library (rarely evaluated) • General library programming contains no youth compo-nent	✓ Program content determined and delivered by youth (con-stantly evaluated) ✓ All library programs contain youth component
Staffing	• Job descriptions designed by legacy administrative practice	✓ Job descriptions of staff periodically reviewed by youth panel (*Note*: differs from formal staff evaluation from youth)

for every day. It could mean less library-determined proscriptive program-ming content, collection management prerogatives, and perpetual focus on teen behavior, and more youth-centric initiatives in creating, collect-ing, exhibiting, preserving, curating, and promoting their own literacy enactments. It could mean less youth avoidance of libraries and more expectations of welcome, exploration, discovery, acceptance, affinity, community, and the flourishing of civic identity (see YALSA, 2012b).

The debate over how an LIS-specific YA-as-citizen comes about offers opportunities for the entire profession. It is a particularly important question, of course, for LIS students at the beginning of their careers. But it is as essential a debate for experienced researchers and practitioners grounded in decades of uncritical youth consensus and the YDIC paradigm.

A healthy debate toward defining an LIS-specific vision of YAs affords many positive outcomes. Critical youth studies scholar Greg Dimitriadis (2008: 17) is correct: "No one has felt the brunt of neoliberalism, the withering of the public sphere, or the rise of rampant worldwide capitalist logics more than young people." But this new debate offers an opportunity to create a flexible and dynamic new LIS-specific vision of youth for our institution and thus move it beyond our historic reliance on other disciplines.

A fitful debate over a new YA service praxis also potentially contributes something meaningful to emerging interdisciplinary conversations and inquiry in the broader field of youth studies. Yes, LIS indeed needs concepts that fit the work we need to do. But we are not going to arrive at these concepts by being confined to or complicit with the agendas of therapists, counselors, or "soft cops."

Finally, an LIS-specific vision of YAs offers a transformative opportunity to leave a more positive, contemporary, and exciting institutional legacy for future LIS professionals to inherit than one forever grounded in century-old assumptions of deficits and preadult candidacy. A YA-as-citizen vision positions the library in the here-and-now of daily youth meanings and power.

LIS's tunnel vision and blind spots remain the lingering consequence of the ways in which it has adopted, integrated, reproduced, and institutionalized a nineteenth-century vision of YAs. On the other hand, by incorporating the answers through a turn toward postmodern concerns about the power and meanings citizens make themselves, an LIS YA services praxis stands to gain new positions in the actual lived experience of today's youth. The authors contributing to this collection have attempted to launch and propel the discussion into the future of our professional interventions, and they welcome the coming debate.

Notes

1. This undervaluing of YA service data inhibits the conduct of professional program evaluation as much as it inhibits more generalizable YA services research. Even when libraries do collect basic output measures there is seldom evidence that the data is incorporated back into program evaluation, revision, or reform (see Bernier, 2009b).

2. Success bias and unsubstantiated best practice claims persist, however, despite our colleague Eliza Dresang's urgings to systematically evaluate by measuring outcomes—things that actually change as a consequence of service interventions—not simply what we report doing. Granted, we have done a good job of incorporating technology into YA service discourse. But technology offers a delivery system, not a service vision (see Dresang, Gross, and Hold, 2006). And no matter how powerful and plentiful individual accounts are, the plural of "anecdote" is not "scientific data" and analysis.

3. The long-standing antipathy toward critical social theory is echoed throughout youth studies (see Belton, 2010).

4. "In many fields of academic research, the actual experiences of youth are not always considered important sites for developing theory and methodology and are seen as secondary in importance to the actions and imaginations of adults" (Maira and Soep, 2005: xv).

5. For an excellent historical treatment of this "junior" form of citizenship emanating in the Progressive Era's city improvement movement (complete with assumptions about "distracting" youth from presumed negative predispositions to urban ills, "preparing" them for adult life, as well as easily recognizable avoidance of the distinctions in social and material conditions), see Light (2012).

6. It may be instructive to note here that while the United States numbered among only 3 countries out of 193 that was not a signatory to the United Nations Convention on the Rights of Children (ratified in 1989), the growing discourse on a vision of youth as citizens specifically stipulates that young people should "participate fully in family, cultural and social life." From among many sources demonstrating recent interest in this discourse, see Kennelly (2011); Sherrod, Torney-Purta, and Flanagan (2010); and Buckingham (2008).

7. The public realm in general has drawn the attention of many critical social theorists in the late twentieth and early twenty-first centuries. One such example is Hannah Arendt: "For Arendt the public sphere comprises two distinct but interrelated dimensions. The first is the space of appearance, a space of political freedom and equality which comes into being whenever citizens act in concert through the medium of speech and persuasion. The second is the common world, a shared and public world of human artifacts, institutions and settings which separates us from nature and which provides a relatively permanent and

durable context for our activities. Both dimensions are essential to the practice of citizenship, the former providing the spaces where it can flourish, the latter providing the stable background from which public spaces of action and deliberation can arise. For Arendt the reactivation of citizenship in the modern world depends upon both the recovery of a common, shared world and the creation of numerous spaces of appearance in which individuals can disclose their identities and establish relations of reciprocity and solidarity" (d'Entrèves, 1994: 15).

8. Libraries collect nearly every type, mode, technique, method, style, and format of how adults capture, create, and represent their experiences in the world. Libraries do nearly none of this for the cultural artifacts YAs produce: the systematic collection of youth-produced literacies (archives of zines or scrapbooks); youth journalism (school newspapers, for instance); records of youth sports and cultural performance; and repositories of youth social or voluntary organizations. This does not include the papers and documents of even famous adults created during their youth and certainly excludes collections created by ordinary young people of their own contemporary documents. For a more thorough treatment of what libraries commonly refer to as "ephemera," what I have termed YA "fugitive" literacies, see Bernier (2007).

9. Previous references to the library as a "third space" for youth too narrowly perpetuate a false "safe haven" cliché that libraries as an actual public place cannot deliver. For reference to the "safe place" cliché, see Kendal (2003). For scholarly treatments of the "third space" metaphor, see Soja (1996).

10. The obvious exceptions are the involvement of youth in the children's reading program and the teen volunteers who help elders learn how to navigate computer technology. However, it should be pointed out that these exemplify only youth involved with preconceived programming processes. And in both of these instances, YA meaning and experience is subsumed under the needs of the other groups and institutional prerogatives. This must be distinguished from more truly reciprocal intergenerational program content, development, models, and execution.

11. There is an entire and growing critical youth studies historiography documenting the strong civic roles youth collectively have assumed throughout the twentieth century. LIS would do well to begin incorporating some of its wisdom into praxis. See, from among many recent examples, Blackwell (2011), Forman-Brunell and Paris (2011), Soep and Chavez (2010), Jorae (2009), and Alvarez (2008).

12. Chin (2007) cites a number of examples of research that is child-centered, where young people control the work and research. One example of this methodological approach is youth participatory action research (PAR) as it is implemented at the Institute for Community Research (ICR). "The ICR's philosophy is that youth are citizens too and that they are capable of research" (see also Kellett, 2010; Caputo, 1995).

References

Abbott-Chapman, J. 2009. "'Adolescents' Favorite Places: Redefining the Boundaries between Private and Public Space." *Space and Culture* 62, no. 4: 419–434.

Ahn, J. 2011. "The Effect of Social Network Sites on Adolescents' Social and Academic Development: Current Theories and Controversies." *Journal of the American Society for Information Science and Technology* 62, no. 8: 1435–1445.

Aitken, S. C. 2001. *Geographies of Young People: The Morally Contested Spaces of Identity.* New York: Routledge.

Alessio, A. 2008. *Excellence in Library Service to Young Adults.* 5th ed. Chicago: American Library Association.

Alessio, A. J., and K. A. Patton. 2007. *A Year of Programs for Teens.* Chicago: American Library Association.

Alvarez, L. 2008. *The Power of the Zoot: Youth Culture and Resistance during World War II.* Berkeley, CA: University of California Press.

Belton, B. 2010. *Radical Youth Work.* Lyme Regis, Dorset, England: Russell House Publishing.

Benton Foundation. 1996. *Buildings, Books, and Bytes.* Washington, DC: Benton Foundation.

Bernier, A. 1998. "On My Mind: Young Adult Spaces." *American Libraries* 29, no. 9: 52.

———. 2007. "Not Broken by Someone Else's Schedule: On Joy and Young Adult Information-Seeking." In *Youth Information-Seeking Behavior: Theories, Models, and Issues,* edited by M. K. Chelton and C. Cool, xiii–xxvii. Lanham, MD: Scarecrow Press.

———. 2009a. "'A Space for Myself to Go': Early Patterns in Small YA Spaces." *Public Libraries* 48, no. 5: 33–47.

———. 2009b. "Young Adult Volunteering in Public Libraries: Managerial Implications." *Library Administration and Management* 23, no. 3: 95–112.

———. 2010. "Spacing Out with Young Adults: Translating YA Space Concepts Back into Practice." In *The Information Needs and Behaviors of Urban Teens: Research and Practice,* edited by D. E. Agosto and S. Hughes-Hassell, 113–126. Chicago: ALA Editions.

Blackwell, M. 2011. ¡*Chicana Power! Contested Histories of Feminism in the Chicano Movement.* Austin, TX: University of Texas Press.

Borden, I. 2001. *Skateboarding, Space and the City.* Oxford, England: Berg.

Brehm-Heeger, P. 2008. *Serving Urban Teens.* Westport, CT: Libraries Unlimited.

Buckingham, D., ed. 2008. *Youth, Identity, and Digital Media.* Cambridge, MA: MIT Press.

Budd, J. M. 2003. "The Library, Praxis, and Symbolic Power." *Library Quarterly* 73, no. 1: 19–32.

Burnett, L., and A. Spelman. 2011. "Creative Citizenship: Building Connection, Knowledge, Belonging and Leadership in Young People." *Aplis* 24, no. 1: 23–31.

Buttler, P. 1933. *An Introduction to Library Science.* Chicago: University of Chicago.

Callison, D. 1997. "Evolution of Methods to Measure Student Information Use." *Library and Information Science Research* 19, no. 4: 347–357.

Caputo, V. 1995. "Anthropology's Silent 'Others': A Consideration of Some Conceptual and Methodological Issues for the Study of Youth and Children Cultures." In *Youth Cultures: A Cross-Cultural Perspective,* edited by V. Amit-Talai and H. Wulff. London: Routledge.

Chelton, M. K. 2001. "Young Adults as Problems: How the Social Construction of a Marginalized User Category Occurs." *Journal of Education for Library and Information Science* 42, no. 1: 4–11.

———. 2002. "The 'Problem Patron' Public Libraries Created." *The Reference Librarian* 36, no. 75/76: 23–32.

Childress, H. 2000. *Landscapes of Betrayal, Landscapes of Joy: Curtisville in the Lives of Its Teenagers.* Albany, NY: State University of New York.

Chin, E. 2007. "Power-Puff Ethnography/Guerrilla Research: Children as Native Anthropologists." In *Representing Youth: Methodological Issues in Critical Youth Studies,* edited by A. L. Best, 269–283. New York: New York University Press.

Cook, S. J., R. S. Parker, and C. E. Pettijohn. 2005. "The Public Library: An Early Teen's Perspective." *Public Libraries* 44: 157–161.

Cranz, G. 2006. "Body Conscious Design in a 'Teen Space': Post Occupancy Evaluation of an Innovative Public Library." *Public Libraries* 45, no. 6: 48–56.

d'Entrèves, M. P. 1994. *The Political Philosophy of Hannah Arendt.* New York: Routledge.

Deodato, J. 2006. "Becoming Responsible Mediators: The Application of Postmodern Perspectives to Archival Arrangement and Description." *Progressive Librarian* 27 (Summer): 52–63.

DeWitt Wallace–Readers Digest Fund. 1999. *Public Libraries as Partners in Youth Development.* New York: The Wallace Foundation.

Dimitriadis, G. 2008. *Studying Urban Youth Culture.* New York: Peter Lang.

Dresang, E. T., M. Gross, and L. E. Hold. 2006. *Dynamic Youth Services through Outcome-Based Planning and Evaluation.* Chicago: American Library Association.

Eliasoph, N. 2011. *Making Volunteers: Civic Life after Welfare's End.* Princeton, NJ: Princeton University Press.

Epstein, R. 2007. *The Case Against Adolescence: Rediscovering the Adult in Every Teen.* Sanger, CA: Quill Driver.

Forman-Brunell, M., and L. Paris, eds. 2011. *The Girls' History and Culture Reader: The Twentieth Century.* Urbana, IL: University of Illinois Press.

Foucault, M. 1972. *The Archaeology of Knowledge and the Discourse on Language.* New York: Pantheon.

———. 1977. *Power/Knowledge: Selected Interviews and Other Writings, 1972–1977.* New York: Pantheon.

———. 1978. *An Introduction.* Vol. 1 of *The History of Sexuality.* New York: Random House.

Glick, A. 2000. "The Trouble with Teens." *School Library Journal* 46, no. 10: 18–19.

Gorman, M., and T. Suellentrop. 2009. *Connecting Young Adults and Libraries: A How-To-Do-It Manual.* 4th ed. New York: Neal-Schuman.

Graham, P. 2004. *The End of Adolescence.* Oxford, England: Oxford University Press.

Graham, P. T. 2002. *A Right to Read: Segregation and Civil Rights in Alabama's Public Libraries, 1900–1965.* Tuscaloosa, AL: University of Alabama Press.

Harden, S. B., and M. Huggins. 2004. "Here Comes Trouble: A Surefire Approach That Works with Unruly Teens." *School Library Journal* 50, no. 7: 32–26.

Hayden, T. 2012. "Participatory Democracy: From Port Huron to Occupy Wall Street." *The Nation* 294, no. 16: 11–23.

Howe, E. 1997. "Using Student Surveys to Build and Evaluate an Information Skills Program." *School Libraries Worldwide* 3, no. 2: 68–77.

IMLS (Institute for Museum and Library Services). 2011. "National Competition Selects 12 Libraries and Museums to Build Innovative Learning Labs for Teens." Accessed March 19, 2012. http://www.imls.gov/national_competition _selects_12_libraries_and_museums_to_build_innovative_learning_labs_for _teens.aspx.

Jorae, W. R. 2009. *The Children of Chinatown: Growing Up Chinese American in San Francisco, 1850–1920.* Chapel Hill, NC: University of North Carolina Press.

Julien, H. 1998. "Adolescent Career Decision Making and the Potential Role of the Public Library." *Public Libraries* 37, no. 6: 376–381.

Kellett, M. 2010. *Rethinking Children and Research: Attitudes in Contemporary Society.* London: Continuum International Publishing.

Kendal, K. 2003. "YA Spaces of Your Dreams: Teen Central: Safe, Structured, and Teen-Friendly." *Voice of Youth Advocates* 26, no. 5: 380–381.

Kennelly, J. 2011. *Citizen Youth: Culture, Activism, and Agency in a Neoliberal Era.* New York: St. Martin's.

Leckie, G. J., L. M. Given, and J. E. Buschman, eds. 2010. *Critical Theory for Library and Information Science: Exploring the Social from Across the Disciplines.* Santa Barbara, CA: Libraries Unlimited.

Lee, S. A. 2009. "Teen Space: Designed for Whom?" Unpublished doctoral dissertation, University of California, Los Angeles.

Lefebvre, H. 1991. *The Production of Space.* Translated by D. Nicholson-Smith. Oxford, England: Blackwell.

———. 1996. "The Right to the City." In *Writing on Cities,* edited and translated by E. Kofman and E. Lebas, 63–181. Oxford, England: Blackwell.

Light, J. S. 2012. "Building Virtual Cities, 1895–1945." *Journal of Urban History* 38, no. 2: 336–371.

Maira, S., and E. Soep, eds. 2005. *Introduction in Youthscapes: The Popular, the National, the Global.* Philadelphia: University of Pennsylvania.

McCook, K. 2004. *Introduction to Public Librarianship.* New York: Neal-Schuman.

Mintz, S. 2004. *Huck's Raft: A History of American Childhood.* Cambridge, MA: Harvard University Press.

Miranda, M. 2003. *Homegirls in the Public Sphere.* Austin, TX: University of Texas Press.

Neuman, D. 1995. "High School Students Use of Databases: Results of a National Delphi Study." *Journal of the American Society for Information Science* 46, no. 4: 284–298.

Owens, P. E. 2002. "No Teens Allowed: The Exclusion of Adolescence from Public Space." *Landscape Journal* 21, no. 1–2: 156–163.

Pusey, A. E. 2008. "Public Library Teen Space Design: An Evaluation of Theory in Practice." Unpublished master's thesis, University of North Carolina at Chapel Hill, North Carolina.

Rubin, R. E. 2004. *Foundations of Library and Information Science.* 2nd ed. New York: Neal-Schuman.

Savin-Williams, R. C. 2006. *The New Gay Teenager.* Cambridge, MA: Harvard University Press.

Sherrod, L. R., J. Torney-Purta, and C. A. Flanagan, eds. 2010. *Handbook of Research on Civic Engagement in Youth.* Hoboken, NJ: John Wiley and Sons.

Sibley, D. 1995. *Geographies of Exclusion: Society and Difference in the West.* London: Routledge.

Soep, E., and V. Chavez. 2010. *Drop That Knowledge: Youth Radio Stories.* Berkeley, CA: University of California Press.

Soja, E. W. 1996. *Thirdspace: Journeys to Los Angeles and Other Real-and-Imagined Places.* Cambridge, MA: Blackwell.

Walter, V. A. 2003. "Public Library Services to Children and Teens: A Research Agenda." *Library Trends* 51, no. 4: 571–589.

White, R. 1990. *No Space of Their Own: Young People and Social Control in Australia.* New York: Cambridge University Press.

Wiegand, W. A. 2003. "To Reposition a Research Agenda: What American Studies Can Teach the LIS Community About the Library in the Life of the User." *Library Quarterly* 73, no. 4: 369–382.

Wolff, T. 1996. *The Night in Question.* New York: Knopf.

YALSA (Young Adult Library Services Association). 2012a. "Managing the Swarm: Teen Behavior in the Library and Strategies for Success." Webinar. Accessed April 2010. http://www.ala.org/yalsa/managing-swarm-teen-behavior-library-and-strategies-success?utm_source=YALSA+Members&utm_campaign=1eb17a1e7d-YALSA_March_2012_E_News3_9_2012&utm_medium=email/.

———. 2012b. "YALSA National Research Agenda." Accessed March 26. http://www.ala.org/yalsa/guidelines/research/researchagenda/.

ABOUT THE EDITOR AND CONTRIBUTORS

Anthony Bernier, PhD, is associate professor at California's San Jose State University School of Library and Information Science. As a critical youth studies scholar his primary field of research explores the administration of library services with young people. He served as a professional librarian for nearly 15 years as a Young Adult Specialist Librarian and administrator, during which time he designed nationally recognized youth outreach and programming models, including the first purpose-built library space for teenaged youth: the Los Angeles Public Library acclaimed TeenS'cape. In 2010 he received a National Leadership Grant from the Institute of Museum and Library Services to advance research on public library spaces designed for young people. He is former chair of several national professional and academic associations and currently serves on two editorial boards. In 2011 he was appointed to a four-year term on the American Library Association's Committee on Accreditation. Dr. Bernier's doctoral dissertation at the University of California examined changing notions of public space in twentieth-century America.

Denise E. Agosto, PhD, is associate professor in the College of Information Science and Technology at Drexel University. Her research and teaching interests include youth social media practices, children's and teens' digital information practices, and public library services. She has published over 100 articles, book chapters, and other scholarly publications in these areas, and she has completed several related funded research projects. Dr. Agosto is the winner of numerous research and teaching awards, including the 2011 ALISE Award for Teaching Excellence in the Field of Library and Information Science Education, the 2007 Christian R. and Mary F. Lindback Distinguished Teaching Award, and the Drexel University 2007 Outstanding Contribution to Online Learning Award. She is currently serving as PI on an IMLS-funded research grant titled "Libraries and the Social Web: Developing the Next Generation of Youth Information Services."

John M. Budd, PhD, is professor in the School of Information Science and Learning Technologies at the University of Missouri. He has also taught at Louisiana State University and the University of Arizona. His PhD is from the University of North Carolina at Chapel Hill. Dr. Budd is the author of more than 100 publications.

Michael Cart, former director of the Beverly Hills (CA) Public Library, is the author or editor of 21 books. He is a columnist and reviewer for the American Library Association's *Booklist* magazine and a past president of both the Young Adult Library Services Association (YALSA) and the National Council of Teachers of English's Assembly on Literature for Adolescents (ALAN). Mr. Cart is the recipient of the 2000 Grolier Award, and in 2008 became the first recipient of the YALSA/Greenwood Publishing Group Service to Young Adults Achievement Award. Before his relocation to the Midwest, he taught young adult literature at UCLA.

Lucia Cedeira Serantes is a PhD candidate at the Faculty of Information and Media Studies, University of Western Ontario, Canada. Her primary research lies at the intersection of young adult library users and readers, reading, and public libraries, with an emphasis on reading practices related to comics. In 2011 her doctoral project was awarded the John A. Lent Scholarship in Comics Studies by the International Comics Arts Forum. She previously worked as a young adult librarian and researcher for the International Center for Children's and Young Adults' Books (Salamanca, Spain).

Karen Coats, PhD, is professor of English at Illinois State University, where she teaches children's and young adult literature. She publishes widely on how children's and young adult literature showcases, examines, and helps form identity in youth culture. Her most recent book is the coedited *Handbook of Research on Children's and Young Adult Literature* (with Shelby A. Wolf, Patricia Enciso, and Christine A. Jenkins). She is also a staff reviewer for the *Bulletin of the Center for Children's Books.*

Cherie Givens, PhD, JD, is an LIS lecturer, information privacy specialist, and attorney-at-law. She holds a doctorate in Library, Archival, and Information Studies from the University of British Columbia and a JD from Louisiana State University. Dr. Givens's particular interests are in privacy law, the First Amendment, and intellectual freedom. She has written and presented on issues related to social policy, intellectual freedom, and the First Amendment. Dr. Givens has taught courses on the law of libraries and archives, research methods, and information and society. Her dissertation explores the phenomenon of censorship prior to publication of the works of children's and young adult authors and illustrators, with particular focus on the lived experiences of Canadian children's and young adult authors. She has held positions in academic, legal, public, and special libraries.

Kafi D. Kumasi, PhD, is an assistant professor of Library and Information Science at Wayne State University. She teaches in the areas of School Library Media Studies, Urban Librarianship, Multicultural Education, and Research Methods. Her research interests revolve around issues of literacy, equity, and diversity, particularly in urban environments spanning K–12 and graduate-level educational contexts. She has authored several publications, including an award-winning journal article titled, "Are We There Yet? Results of a Gap Analysis to Measure LIS Students' Prior Knowledge and Actual Learning of Cultural Competence Concepts" (*Journal of Education for Library and Information Science*, October 2011), and a popular book chapter, "Critical Race Theory and Education: Mapping a Legacy of Scholarship and Activism," appearing originally in *Beyond Critique: Critical Social Theories and Education*, edited by B. A. U. Levinson (Boulder, CO: Paradigm, 2011).

Wendy Schaetzel Lesko is president of the Youth Activism Project, a national nonpartisan clearinghouse that encourages those not yet of voting age to be agents for change. In 1998, she coauthored and self-published *Youth! The 26% Solution* with 19-year-old Emanuel Tsourounis. Lesko has written training manuals designed for adults on effective multigenerational advocacy, including *Youth as Equal Partners* for United Way of

America. In 2004 she launched School Girls Unite with a group of seventh graders in the United States and a sister organization in Mali. In 2009 these American and African teens wrote the bilingual action guide titled *Girls Gone Activist! How to Change the World through Education*, and in 2011, they led the successful campaign to mobilize US support to establish the United Nations International Day of the Girl. Her forthcoming publication is *Saving Starfish and Seeking Sea Change*.

Mike Males, PhD, is senior researcher for the Center on Juvenile and Criminal Justice, San Francisco; former sociology instructor at the University of California, Santa Cruz; author of five books and numerous journal and periodical articles on youth issues; and a consultant to the San Jose State University Library and Information Science research team on young adult library spaces.

Paulette Rothbauer, PhD, is associate professor of Information and Media Studies at the University of Western Ontario, where she primarily teaches in the Library and Information Science graduate program. For several years she has been researching the out-of-school reading practices of youth marginalized from mainstream print culture due to social, cultural, geographical, and personal barriers of access to both printed and digital texts. She has published findings from these studies in recent issues of *The Library Quarterly* and *Journal of Research on Libraries and Young Adults*. Dr. Rothbauer is coauthor of the popular professional book *Reading Matters: What the Research Reveals about Reading, Libraries and Community*. She is currently working on two major research projects, one concerned with the construction of youth readers as agents and audience in Canadian young adult literature contexts, and the other an investigation of adult reception of works of young adult literature.

INDEX

Fictional characters are indexed under first name.
Letter *t* denotes a table. Letter *n* denotes an endnote.

A

Absolutely True Diary of a Part-Time Indian,
    The (Alexie), 64
abstinence-only education, 199
academia and faculty of color, 110
Act Your Age! (N. Lesko), 172, 180
acting out, 72
activism among youth, xx–xxi, 20, 24n11,
    227. *See also* School Girls Unite;
    Youth Activism Project
adolescence
    Carlsen's stages of, 81
    definitions of, 3, 81
    emergence as category, 55–59, 79–80, 175
    "end of," 226
    expansion of, xix, 81–82, 175, 186
    second decade of, 82–83
    terms applied to, 42–43
    as threat, 13, 212
Adolescence: Its Psychology (Hall), 55–56
adolescent medicine, 82
adolescent race, 4, 5
adult authority, 4–5, 6–7
Adult Books for Young People, 85
adult-centered perspective, 33–35, 49
adultescents, 78–79, 81–84
Adventure Girls, 59
Adventures of Huckleberry Finn (Twain), 59
Advocates for Youth, 199
affective/emotional register, 71
after-school apartheid, 223
age as category, xvi, xviii, 2, 23n1, 183, 185
age stereotype, 174, 175
age-based apartheid
    after school, 223
    argument against, 157
    censorship and, 168

libraries' role in challenging, 163–164, 166
    as temporary solution, 156, 165
    YA programming and, 224
    youth spaces and policies and, 161
Agosto, Denise E., xviii, 44
ALA. *See* American Library Association
    (ALA)
Alex Award, 86
alienation of the old, 153, 157, 158
Allahar, Anton, 175–177, 180
alternative environments for serving youth,
    225–226
Alvarez, Julia, 88
Amazon, 96
American Library Association (ALA)
    Code of Ethics, 191–192, 193
    Freedom to Read Statement, 192–193
    intellectual freedom and, 193–194
    Library Bill of Rights, 189, 190–191, 193
    lists of books for teens by, 85
    privacy protection and, 201
Ameritocracy myth, 110
amygdala, 69
Anderson, M. T., 65, 88
Andi Alpers (fictional character), 61
anime, 125, 126
Arendt, Hannah, 232–233n7
Arnett, Jeffrey Jensen, 79
Aronson, Marc, 42–43
association, ix
atmosphere in library for YAs, 230t
Augustine, St., 60

B

Babbitt, Natalie, 56–59
Bachman, J. G., 161, 163, 166–167

Barnes and Noble, 89, 96
Bauer, Megan, 126
Baxter, Kent, 12–13
BBYA (Best Books for Young Adults), 85–86
Beam, Cris, 65
Beauty Queens (Bray), 64
behavior and positivism, 211
Bell, Derrick, 105–106
Bergin, Melissa, 125–126
Bernier, Anthony, 155–156, 177
Bernstein, Leonard, 58
Best, Amy L., 180
Best Books for Young Adults (BBYA), 85–86
best practice, xiv–xv, 208, 232n2
Between (Warman), 58
Big Lake (TV show), 79
biology-based explanations for youth, 176–
     177, 180, 185, 186. *See also* brain
     development research; developmental
     psychology
Birch, Carol, 93–94
blogs, 95–96, 97–98
Board of Education v. Pico, 195
Board of Young Adult Commissioners, New
     Haven, CT, 143
Bonham, Frank, 62
"Book Beast" (section of *Daily Beast*), 97
Book Report Network, 97
book reviews
     for crossover books, 89–95
     in digital format, 95–98, 99
Book Thief, The (Zuzak), 93
Bookforum (website), 96–97
Booklist, 86, 89–90, 91, 96, 118
Booklistonline.com, 97
Bookreporter.com, 96–97
Books and the Teenage Reader (Carlsen), 81
boomer generation, 57, 157
Borrower, The (Makkai), 92–93
Boy Meets Boy (Levithan), 65–66
Bracher, Mark, 71
Bracher's theory of identity, 71–72
Brady, Margaret, 123
brain development research
     on amygdala, 69
     brain mapping and teen behavior, 176
     on cerebellum, 69, 82
     efficiency *vs.* flexibility, 158
     gray matter overproduction and pruning,
          68–69
     information processing and, 53, 72–73
     practical outcomes of, 69–71

on prefrontal cortex, 68–69, 82
self-fashioning of identity and, 54
See also teen brain
Braverman, Miriam, 18, 182, 183
Bray, Libba, 64
Brenna, Beverly, 64
broad citizenship, 214–215, 227
Brown, Tina, 97
Budd, John, 209, 210
Burns, Ty R., 126
Buschman, John, viii, 2
Bush, George W., 227
Buttler, Lee Pierce, 209

C

Caletti, Deb, 66–67
Canadian Libraries Are Serving Youth
     (CLASY), 172
Carlsen, G. Robert, 80–81, 87
Carson, Bryan M., 200–201
Cart, Michael, xix, 43, 55, 56, 59
Catcher in the Rye, The (Salinger), 87
categories of young adult literatures, 78
Cedeira Serantes, Lucia, xx, xxi
censorship
     age-based apartheid and, 168
     COE and, 191–192
     comics and, 129
     FRS and, 192–193
     LBOR and, 190–191, 193
     professional duties to fight, xxiii, 139, 203
     of young adult material, 160
censorware. *See under* Internet
Center on Juvenile and Criminal Justice, 155
CEO of the brain. *See* prefrontal cortex
cerebellum, 69, 82
chair-sharing, 152–153
Chambers, Aidan, 88, 90–91
Chbosky, Stephen, 87
Chelton, Mary K., 177, 181
Cherry Ames (fictional character), 59
child pornography, 196, 197
child-centered research, 233n12
Children and Libraries, 118
Children's Internet Protection Act (CIPA),
     189, 191–192, 194, 197–198
Childress, Herb, 162
Chin, E., 233n12
Cimarron (Ferber), 85
CIPA (Children's Internet Protection Act),
     189, 191–192, 194, 197–198

critical youth studies (cont.)
  critical social theory and, 226
  cultural studies, 178, 179
  as framework for LIS, 171–172, 181–187
  Lesko's alternative conceptions, 180
  political economy, 178–179
  reading on, 180
  youth consensus of LIS and, 13
  youth development model and, xxii
Critical Youth Studies (Côté and Allahar), 180
crossover books, 86–89, 98–99
CRT. *See* critical race theory (CRT)
CSI (TV show), 128
cultural deficit perspective, 106–107
cultural meanings of youth, 216–220, 222,
    227, 228–231
cultural studies of youth, 178, 179
Culture and Commitment (Mead), 153
Cures for Heartbreak (Rabb), 88
curfews, 143, 155, 161, 164
*Curious Incident of the Dog in the Nighttime,
    The* (Haddon), 87, 89
Cushman, Philip, 64

D

Dahl, Roald, 128
Daily Beast (website), 97
Daily News, 121
Daly, Maureen, 59
D.A.R.E. (Drug Abuse Resistance Education)
    program, 23n4
Day of the Girl, 139
Dear Bully anthology, 67
deficit views of youth
    among contemporary experts, 15–16, 24n9
    biology-based explanations and, 176
    collection management and, 216–217,
        218, 219–220
    Hall's and Holt's, 3–6, 10–11, 15
    LIS youth consensus and, 11, 14, 15–17,
        24n11, 207, 211–212
    moral panics and, 177
    YA spaces and, 222
    See also youth development model; youth-
        at-risk model
democratic culture in libraries, 163, 168,
    212, 213, 222
demographic revolution, 154–155, 158–159
Demos, 84
desegregation of libraries, 227
developmental psychology
    adolescence defined by, 80

LIS reliance on, xxii, 1, 12–13, 15, 17, 211
  youth studies research and, 16–17
dialogism and identity, 54, 62, 63, 67–68,
    72, 73
Dickinson, Gail, 127
digital divide, 19
digital natives discourse, 47
Dimitriadis, Greg, xiii, 231
disability issues, 64
discipline
    defined, vii
    LIS as, viii–ix
    psychology as, vii
discourse about comics, historical, 120–123
discourse analysis of comics articles, 115,
    118–120, 124–130
discourse *vs.* Discourse, 119
diversity
    age as means to eliminate, 174
    promotion of, 106–107
    respect for, 63, 73
    youth comfort with, 158
divide between books and services, 183
dominant personality types of Lasch, 57, 59
Donelson, Kenneth L., 55
Donna Parisi (fictional character), 66
Donna Reed / Harriet Nelson stereotype, 56
Donnelly, Jennifer, 61, 64
Dresang, Eliza, 232n2
Drug Abuse Resistance Education (D.A.R.E.)
    program, 23n4
Durango Street (Bonham), 62

E

eating disorders, 64
economic downturn, 81–82, 95
economic inequalities, 19
Educate to Innovate campaign, 222
education and employment ideologies,
    176–177
Edwards, Margaret Alexander, 24n11, 86,
    183–184
Elementary and Secondary Education Act
    (ESEA), 197
Emerging Adulthood (Arnett), 79
empirical science, 2, 5, 6
empowerment, 215
English as a second language (ESL) students,
    124, 125
ephebiphobia, 159
Epstein, Robert, 82
Erikson, Erik, 23n2, 68, 80, 81

language and identity, 71
Lasch, Christopher, 57, 59
Law and Order (TV show), 128
LBOR (Library Bill of Rights), xxiii, 189, 190–191, 193, 194
leadership motivations of teens, 166–167. *See also* partnering with young adults
Leckie, Gloria, viii, 2
Lesko, Nancy, 172–175, 179–180
Lesko, Wendy Schaetzel, xx–xxi, 223
Levinas, Emmanuel, ix
Levine, Judith, 199
librarians. *See* teen librarians
library and information science (LIS)
    contemporary visions of youth in, xxiii–xxiv, 1–2, 53–55
    critical youth studies framework for, 171–172, 181–187
    deficit views of youth in, 11, 14, 16, 24n11
    as a discipline, viii–ix
    social theory and, 208, 209–210
    youth of color and, 103–104, 106–107, 108–109, 111–112
    See also praxis; teen librarians; youth consensus of LIS
library as place, viii
Library Bill of Rights (LBOR), xxiii, 189, 190–191, 193, 194
Library Journal, 118
Library Literature and Information Science Full Text database, 36
Library Media Connection, 118
LibraryThing, 97
Lichtenstein, Heinz, 71
Life of Pi (Martel), 87
Lipsyte, Robert, 85
LIS. *See* library and information science (LIS)
literacy acts and values of youth, 216–220, 230. *See also* cultural meanings of youth
literacy and youth of color, 108–109
Locke, John, 60–61
Lockhart, E., 64
Lone Cowboy (James), 85
Los Angeles Times, 95
Lubuto Library Project, 225–226
Lukenbill, William, 8, 182–183
Luna (Peters), 65
Lyga, Allyson, 125
Lyons, David, 198

M

Makkai, Rebecca, 92–93
Males, Mike, xxi–xxii, 8–9
manga, 124–125, 125–126
manufacturing and adolescence, 56
Margulis, Elizabeth, 123
Martel, Yann, 87
material conditions, impacts of, 19
Maushart, Susan, 94–95
Maximum Youth Involvement (W. Lesko), 142
McConaughey, Matthew, 79
McDonald, Frances Beck, 193
Mead, Margaret, xxi, 147, 153, 158, 164, 173
mental health issues, 64
Merleau-Ponty, Maurice, ix
Mexican Whiteboy (de la Pena), 64
middle school literature, 78, 86, 98
middle-class orientation of services, 18–19, 20
Miller v. California, 197
Mindblind (Roy), 64
Mind's Eye (Fleischman), 64
Mintz, Steven, 7, 221
mirror neurons, 69
modernism, xxi, xxii–xxiii, 2–6, 11, 211
modernist self, 59, 60–61, 68
Monitoring the Future (Bachman, Johnston, and O'Malley), 161, 163, 166–167
Mooney, Maureen, 124
moral agenda of libraries and librarians, 8, 23n3, 23n5
moral panics, 177–178
Morrison, David, 84
Moskowitz, Elaine, 124
motherhood, 4
MTV demographic, 82
multicultural paradigm, 107
multigenerational teamwork. *See* intergenerational collaboration; partnering with young adults
music, 58–59, 61
Music Was IT (Rubin), 58
MySpace, 97

N

Nancy Drew (fictional character), 59
narcissism and relationships, 65–66
narcissistic parenting, 57–58
narrow citizenship, 214
"National Disgrace, A" (North), 121

National Institute of Mental Health, 82
National Security Letter, 202
neglectful parenting, 57
neoconservatism, 17–18, 19
New York Times, 95, 96
Newsletter for Intellectual Freedom, 199
niche identities, 63–64, 70
Nilsen, Alleen Pace, 55
nineteenth-century visions of youth, 1, 2–6, 7
nonfiction, 94–95
North, Sterling, 120–21, 122
"Notes from the Teenage Underground" (*VOYA* column), 126
Nothing (Friedman), 58, 64

O

Oates, Joyce Carol, 88
Obama, Barack, 167, 202, 222
obscene speech and the First Amendment, 196–98
Occupy movement, xx–xxi, 227
Octavian Nothing (Anderson), 88
O'Malley, P. M., 161, 163, 166–67
organization man myth, 59
othering, 15, 24n9, 108, 111
"Out of Sight, Out of Mind" (Wiegand), 116–17
Outsiders, The (Hinton), 62, 85

P

"Papercutz" (blog), 96
PAR (youth participatory action research), 233n12
parents, 56–58, 79, 202
Parker, Karen, 198
participation of youth. *See* partnering with young adults
partnering with young adults, 137–147
    adult attitude adjustment and, 137–138, 146
    advantages of, xx–xxi, 146–147
    for all library functions, 224–225
    citizenship and, 214–16, 228, 230t
    critical youth studies framework and, 185, 187
    examples of, 138–39
    individual interactions and, 141–143
    internships, 139, 143–44, 145–146
    library as ideal climate for, 139–140, 144–146, 167–168
    programming and, 140–141

teen-centered perspective and, xiv, 34–35, 43–45
    time issues, 143–44
    youth development model and, 9, 13, 230t
    See also activism among youth; intergenerational collaboration; Teen Advisory Groups
PATRIOT Act, 194, 201, 202–203
Paus, Tomas, 158
Pawuk, Michael, 129
Pease, Howard, 59
pedophilia, 159
peer orientation stereotype, 173–174
Perks of Being a Wallflower, The (Chbosky), 87
Perper, Timothy, 200
Peter Pan syndrome, 78
Peters, Julie Ann, 65
phenomenology, x
physicality of teens, 152–153
pillow books, 90–91
Planned Parenthood of Missouri v. Danforth, 199
political economy, 178–179
popular culture, 54, 63, 79, 164, 174
positive youth development, 14
positivism, 2–3, 5–6, 10, 109, 211
post-Darwinian biology, 3
postmodernism
    citizenship and, 213, 215, 231
    LIS applications of, 211–212, 215, 220, 222
    modernism *vs.*, xxii–xxiii
postmodernist self, 59, 61–63, 64, 65, 67–68
power and control concepts of youth, 1, 4–5, 6
power relations between youth and libraries, 228–231
praxis
    critical social theory and, 208, 210, 212, 213, 226
    defined, 208, 210
    YAs as citizens and, 220, 227–228, 231
prefrontal cortex, 68–69, 82
Prep (Sittenfield), 87–88, 92, 93
privacy and confidentiality for minors, 189, 192, 201–203
problem novels, 59, 60
Prose, Francine, 88
protection of minors, laws for, 189–190, 196–198, 203
protectionist philosophies, 13, 161, 184
proto-Freudian psychology, 3
proximal development, 70

psychology as discipline, vii. *See also* developmental psychology
Publishersweekly.com, 97
publishing industry, 88–89, 98
Pulliam, June, 43
Putting Makeup on Dead People (Violi), 58, 66
Putting Makeup on the Fat Boy (Wright), 64

R

R. R. Bowker, 98
Rabb, Margo, 88
race. *See* adolescent race; critical race theory; whiteness
racism, 20, 111
Ragged Dick series (Alger), 13
raging hormones stereotype, 173, 175, 176
Ranma ½, 126
reactionary politics, 158
reader reviews, 96–97
"readers who lack" and comic books, 123, 124, 125, 130, 131
reading and brain development, 69, 70
"Reading for the Innocent" (Wertham), 121
read-ins, 227
Reeves, Anne, 125
reluctant readers, 124, 125, 127, 130, 177
Representations of Youth (Griffin), 177, 180
Representing Youth (Best), 180
Revolution (Donnelly), 61, 64
Ricoeur, Paul, ix
romantic self, 59, 60, 68
Rothbauer, Paulette, xxii
Rover Boys, 59
Rowling, J. K., 87
Roy, Jennifer, 64
Rubin, Richard, 216
Rubin, Susan Goldman, 58
Ruby Oliver books (Lockhart), 64
Rudiger, Hollis Margaret, 129
rugged individualist myth, 57, 59
Rust v. Sullivan, 197–198

S

safe place, library as, 233n9
Salinger, J. D., 887
Salon.com, 97
Salt Lake City Public Library, 145
Saturated Self, The (Gergen), 65
Schatzberg, Alan, 198
Schliesman, Megan, 129

School Girls Unite, xxi, 137, 138–39, 139–140, 144–145
school librarians, legal responsibilities of, 200–201
School Library Journal, 89–90, 96, 118
scorned literature and materials, 115, 116–117
second decade of adolescence, 82–83
secondhand porn, 159
Seduction of the Innocent, The (Wertham), 121
segregation of youth from adults
    demographic revolution and, 154–156
    generational decorum and, 153
    as mistake, 164
    political forces and, 166
    role of libraries in addressing, 221, 223–224
    tribalism and, 151–152, 156, 160
    YA spaces and, 159–162
    See also age-based apartheid
sentimental view of youth, 11, 12, 212
Sercombe, Howard, 158
series books, 115, 116, 131
seven rights of passage of Havighurst, 80–81
Seventeenth Summer (Daly), 59
sex abuse and violence against children, 165–166
sex education, 199–200, 203
sexism, 20
Seyfried, Jonathan, 127–128
Shakespeare, William, 54, 55, 56
$#! My Dad Says* (TV show), 79
Sinatra, Frank, 56, 58–59
Sittenfield, Curtis, 87–88, 92, 93
Six Rules of Maybe (Caletti), 66–67
skills, focus on acquisition of, 10, 13–14, 15–16, 18, 20
Slate.com, 96–97
Sleeping Beauty, 55
"Smorgasbord" (Wolff), 218–19
Snicket, Lemony, 128
Snow White, 55
Snowball, Clare, 125
social class awareness, 18–19
social ethics and libraries, 23n3
social justice movements, xx–xxi, 227
social networking and book reviews, 97
social reform movements, 182–83
social theory, 208. *See also* critical social theory
soft approaches to child-rearing, 4, 7, 8
St. Lifer, Evan, 128
staffing and visions of young adults, 230t
state protection of privacy, 202

state role in youth experience, 19–20
statistical bigotry, 156
stereotyping of youth, xxii, 172–78
Stigma (Goffman), 62
storm and stress conflict mode, 11, 56, 171, 173, 176
storytelling and youth involvement, 145
Strenger, Carlo, 57, 64
Structure of Scientific Revolutions, The (Kuhn), vii
Students for a Democratic Society, 227
Sturm und Drang. *See* storm and stress conflict mode
success bias, 208, 232n2
Sue Barton (fictional character), 59
summer reading programs, 224
sweet frauds, 218–219
synergy in libraries, xxii, 163–165, 167

T

Tashjian, Janet, 64
Tate, William F., 107
Tattooed Man, The (Pease), 59
Tea Party, 154, 158
Teen Advisory Groups
    age-based segregation and, 224
    contrasting visions of young adults and, 230t
    partnering with youth and, xx, 9, 167
    teen-centered approach and, 34
    time issues for, 143
    YA programming and, 140–141
    YA service data and, 208
teen brain, 11, 156–157, 165. *See also* brain development research
teen development, 44–46. *See also* youth development model
teen embodiment, 68–71
teen input into professional writing, 39–40, 40t, 49
Teen Leadership Councils, 9
teen librarians
    as activists, 109
    comics and, 115–117, 121–123
    cultural and social work of, 182, 183
    feminist analysis of, 181–182
    negative teen behavior and, 72
    as part of feedback loop, 63–64
    partnering with youth. *See* partnering with young adults
    privacy of teen patrons and, 202–203
    professional literature for, 35–41, 47–48, 117–118

publishing industry and, 88, 98
role in teen development, 72–73
youth of color and, 106–107, 108, 109, 111–112
teen literature, 78, 86, 98. *See also* young adult literature
teen spaces
    calls to create, 184
    citizenship and, 220–223, 229t
    political forces and, 166
    questioning of, 160–162
    segregative movements and, 151–52, 153, 155–156, 159
    teen vision of, 162–163, 165
teen-centered perspective, 33–50
    vs. adult-centered perspective, 33–35, 49
    library school curricula and, 49–50
    professional literature and, 40–41, 44
    teen development focus and, 44–46
    teen information needs and, 47–48
    teen input and, 39–40, 40t, 49
    teens as individuals and, 46–47
    terminology used for, 41–44
    YALSA and, 50
Teenreads.com, 97
teens/teenagers
    as concept, 80, 81
    as individuals, ix, 46–47
    as subjects rather than objects, x, 17, 34, 44, 228
    See also youth
Tender Morsels (Lanagan), 87
third space, library as, 221, 233n9
This is All (Chambers), 88, 90–91
Thompson, Audrey, 108, 110
Tilley, Carol L., 121, 122
Time, 85
timeout, 83
Tinker v. Des Moines Independent Community School District, 194, 196
Toffler, Alvin, 153
transmodern view of self, 59, 68, 71
tribal identity groupings, 62
tribalism, adult
    Internet and, 155
    libraries' position to challenge, xvi, xxii, 152, 161, 166, 167–168
    as outdated, 163
    segregative movements and, 151–152, 156, 160
    teen leadership and, 167
tritone, 61
Tsourounis, Emanuel, 138

young adult literature
analyses of, 33–34
Cart's categories of, 78, 86, 98
crossover books, 86–89
as a genre, 85
self-fashioning of identities and, 53–55,
64–65, 72–73
Young Adult Services Division (YASD), 43,
81, 85
Young People's Reading Round Table, 85
youth
biology-based explanations for, 176, 180,
185, 186
as citizens. *See* citizenship
of color. *See* critical race theory (CRT)
cultural meanings of, 216–220, 222, 227,
228–231
as damaged or deficient. *See* deficit views
of youth
dominant stereotypes of, 172–178
as individuated beings, 17–18
informational culture of, 159
as intergenerational agents, 223–225
nineteenth-century visions of, 1, 2–6, 7
as participants and partners. *See*
partnering with young adults
public library benefits for, 45
scholarship of history of, 6
segregation from adults. *See* segregation
of youth from adults
sentimental view of, 11, 12
spaces for. *See* teen spaces
as superagents, 11, 12
twentieth-century visions of, 6–10
as works in progress, 16, 21
See also critical youth studies; teens/
teenagers
Youth (G. Jones), 180
Youth Activism Project (YAP), xx, xxi, 137,
138. *See* also School Girls Unite
youth choice awards, 34

youth citizenship, 213, 232n5
youth consensus of LIS
alternative environments and, 226
alternatives to, 212
developmental psychology and, 15–17
examination of, 10–15
failure to address, 21–23, 208
reimagining. *See* citizenship
YDIC and, 15, 17–21, 207, 231
youth development industrial complex
(YDIC). *See* YDIC
youth development model
historical youth discourse and, 13
LIS shift to, 9–10
moving beyond, 212
skepticism of, xxii
YA programming and, 224
YA spaces and, 222
YAs-as-citizens contrasted with, 229–30t
youth journalism, 218
youth literature awards, 34
Youth Marketing Company, 80
youth participatory action research (PAR),
233n12
Youth! The 26% Solution (W. Lesko and
Tsourounis), 138
youth-at-risk model
adoption by libraries, 8–9, 10
D.A.R.E. program and, 23n4
historical youth discourse and, 13
library reform and development and, 183
moving beyond, 212
YA spaces and, 222

Z

Zangwill, Israel, 54
zine culture, 218
zones of proximal development, 70
Zuzak, Markus, 87